COLLEGE READING RESEARCH AND PRACTICE

Articles From
*The Journal
of College Literacy
and Learning*

Eric J. Paulson
University of Cincinnati
Cincinnati, Ohio, USA

Shirley A. Biggs
University of Pittsburgh
Pittsburgh, Pennsylvania, USA

Michaeline E. Laine
University of Cincinnati
Cincinnati, Ohio, USA

Terry L. Bullock
University of Cincinnati
Cincinnati, Ohio, USA

Editors

INTERNATIONAL
Reading Association
800 Barksdale Road, PO Box 8139
Newark, Delaware 19714-8139, USA
www.reading.org

Director of Publications   Joan M. Irwin
Editorial Director, Books and Special Projects   Matthew W. Baker
Production Editor   Shannon Benner
Permissions Editor   Janet S. Parrack
Acquisitions and Communications Coordinator   Corinne M. Mooney
Associate Editor, Books and Special Projects   Sara J. Murphy
Assistant Editor   Charlene M. Nichols
Administrative Assistant   Michele Jester
Senior Editorial Assistant   Tyanna L. Collins
Production Department Manager   Iona Sauscermen
Supervisor, Electronic Publishing   Anette Schütz
Senior Electronic Publishing Specialist   Cheryl J. Strum
Electronic Publishing Specialist   R. Lynn Harrison
Proofreader   Elizabeth C. Hunt

Project Editor   Shannon Benner

Cover   Design, Linda Steere; Image, PhotoDisc

Library of Congress Cataloging-in-Publication Data
College reading research and practice : articles from the journal of college literacy and learning / Eric J. Paulson ... [et al.] (editors).
    p.   cm.
Articles originally published in the Journal of college literacy and learning.
    ISBN 0-87207-001-8
1. Reading (Higher education)   I. Paulson, Eric J.   II. Journal of college literacy and learning.
    LB2395.3 .C65 2003
    428.4'071'1—dc21
                                                                2002152868

Contents

Foreword   vii
Donna E. Alvermann

Introduction   1
*Eric J. Paulson, Michaeline E. Laine, Shirley A. Biggs,
and Terry L. Bullock*

SECTION I

Theoretical Issues   5

A Brief History of College Reading   7
Albert J. Kingston

In Defense of College Developmental
Reading Education   13
Jian Zhang

Metacognitive Awareness and Monitoring
in Adult and College Readers   19
Steve D. Rinehart and Jennifer M. Platt

Reading as Assignment Versus Reading as Art:
Reader-Based Criticism Applied to Freshman
Composition   30
DeWitt Clinton

Reading, Writing, and Reality: A Cultural Coming
to Terms   38
Andrea R. Fishman

SECTION II

Research 55

Students' Conceptions of Learning, Their Motivations, and Their Approaches to Study 58
Marilyn G. Eanet and Kay Camperell

What Research Has to Say About Instruction in Text-Marking Strategies 68
Beverly Bartel

Characteristics of Highly Proficient College Freshman Readers 75
Margaret L. Henrichs

A Qualitative Study of College Developmental Students' Perceptions of the Reading and Writing Relationships in a Co-Taught Paired Reading Course 88
Michaeline E. Laine

Studying Hard for a College Level Geography Course: A Case Study 102
Joseph W. Guenther and Thomas H. Anderson

Text Demands in College Classes: An Investigation 118
Vincent P. Orlando, David C. Caverly, Leslie A. Swetnam, and Rona F. Flippo

Directing Prose Learning With Analogical Study Guides 126
David A. Hayes

EFL Learners: Summarizing Strategies in Academic Settings 133
Ana Maria Morra de de la Pena

Main Idea Clues 149
Michael F. O'Hear and Patrick J. Ashton

Adding In-Class Writing to the College Reading
Curriculum: Problems and Plusses   161
Arden B. Hamer

An Examination of At-Risk College Students' Sexist
Attitudes Toward Reading   170
Maria Valeri-Gold and Nannette E. Commander

College Students' Use of Computer Technologies   177
Alice Scales

SECTION III

Program and Strategy Descriptions   187

The Goals, Administration, and Organization of a College
Developmental Reading Program   190
Mary L. Dillard

Previewing for a New Age   205
Kate O'Dell and Judith Cope Craig

A Cyclical Plan for Using Study Strategies   215
David A. Hayes and Donna E. Alvermann

Effective Studying From Text: Applying Metacognitive
Strategies   223
Ebo Tei and Oran Stewart

Strategies for Considerate and Inconsiderate Text
Instruction   235
Jeanne Shay Schumm, Alexandra G. Leavell, and Diane S. Haager

Promoting Text Engagement Through Reader-Generated
Elaborations   248
Hiller A. Spires

Teaching Annotation Writing to College Students   259
Susan L. Strode

Reader Response in the College Reading Class   271
Cynthia Chamblee

Reflection and Developmental Readers: Facilitating
Metacognition With Learning Logs   280
Laura B. Soldner

Enriching the Developmental Teaching and Learning
Environment With Portfolio Assessment   286
Martha E. Casazza

Afterword   302
Shirley A. Biggs

Author Index   305

Subject Index   313

Foreword

College Reading Research and Practice crosses epistemologies and time. The first edited book of its kind to concentrate solely on college developmental reading, this collection reflects diversity in knowledge of the field and how that knowledge has both changed and yet retained a marked familiarity over the years. Therein lies its appeal and usefulness. For as a compendium of ideas that have been theorized, researched, and put into practice—though not always in that order—it is a milestone in its own right.

Positioned between K–12 and adult education, the college reading field might seem to the outsider to be sealed off, perhaps even a captive within its own borders. In fact, some insiders might perceive it similarly. However, to the editors' collective credit, this volume should put that perception of college reading to rest, and soon. For although focused singularly on developmental reading issues at the college level, the articles themselves report on programs, strategies, studies, and theories that cross easily into secondary and adult education territory.

This border crossing is healthy because it breaks down the imaginary and truncated spaces between leaving high school and entering the so-called adult world. It also challenges the notion that individuals wedged into those spaces are not yet adults whose reading goals, attitudes, strategies, and habits are somehow caught in a time warp that isolates them from the "real world."

The contributors to College Reading Research and Practice are themselves border crossers. Some will be recognized as having experience in researching and teaching at more than one level. Others will be viewed as being primarily interested in secondary, postsecondary, or college reading but criss-crossing subject matter domains. Still others will be hailed as the field's newcomers, long-timers, and yes, even interlopers. What their work shares in common, however, is a commitment to taking readers at whatever point they are in their development as literacy learners and moving them to places both imagined and not yet known.

Donna E. Alvermann
University of Georgia
Athens, Georgia, USA

Introduction

Eric J. Paulson, Michaeline E. Laine,
Shirley A. Biggs, and Terry L. Bullock

A few years ago, one member of our editorial team (Eric) had the privilege of serving on the board of directors of a regional literacy organization. On the day Eric began his term, the director of the program confessed that the branch had a decided lack of what she termed "corporate memory." She explained that the organization accomplishes many worthwhile goals, but as soon as current volunteers or staff move on or lose interest in a finished project, that project becomes forgotten. Eric soon found out that, for all its admirable efforts, reinventing the wheel was a primary activity of this board.

In many ways, the field of college reading also has a lack of corporate memory. What kind of teaching patterns have cycled through our field? What are the research trends in college reading over the last century? In what ways have we affected and been affected by strides in broader educational theory? These questions, quite easily discussed in the context of emergent literacy or beginning reading, are not as easily answered when applied to college reading.

One key to an organization's—and a field's—corporate memory is the periodic compiling and presenting of the "state of the art" of the discipline. In the organization that gave rise to this volume, the College Literacy and Learning Special Interest Group of the International Reading Association, this has not previously been done on a large scale; although the organization has had a peer-reviewed journal for more than 30 years, the editors of this volume had difficulty putting together a complete set of issues of the journal. In fact, it became necessary to tap longstanding members to locate some of the earlier issues.

It became clear that we needed to collect significant articles from this journal and present them to the field—our contribution to corporate memory in the field of college reading. Indeed, that is one of the central goals of *College Reading Research and Practice: Articles From* The Journal of College Literacy and Learning: to make the excellent articles accessible to a wide audience.

Yet, we hardly view this project as a simple exercise in maintaining some kind of educational corporate memory. Instead, we believe this volume can instruct and inform both the new professional and the seasoned veteran. For those new to our field, this collection presents itself as a primer in college reading, and for those who have been involved with college reading throughout their careers, it serves as a survey of important issues.

The articles presented here are all from the pages of *The Journal of College Literacy and Learning*, a peer-reviewed journal whose history, under its former title of *Forum for Reading*, dates back more than 30 years. Out of these decades of production, dozens of issues, and hundreds of articles, we have chosen 27 articles to present here. We based our selection decisions on factors that included usefulness to today's reader, significance of topic, usefulness of pedagogical technique, timelessness of research findings, and balance within the overall volume. In addition, we considered each article's clarity of writing, level of scholarship, originality, and accuracy. Each of us on the editorial team chose articles he or she would have liked to include but could not due to length considerations; yet we are greatly pleased with the collection we have produced.

The articles have been grouped into three broad areas: theory, research, and practice. Although we have consciously chosen this order to indicate our belief that theory grounds research, which provides the basis for practice, we also believe that practice, in turn, informs theory. The nature of the articles we have chosen for inclusion in each of these sections demonstrates our belief in the cyclical and interactive nature of theory, research, and practice—in these articles, research is never far removed from practice, theory is not considered an ivory-tower phenomenon, nor are the techniques in the practice section presented without an implicit or explicit theoretical perspective. Further, within each section, the articles are grouped thematically.

The collection of articles that make up the Theoretical Issues section represents a 16-year span and includes thoughts about the need for college reading programs as well as treatises focused on the nature of the programs and classes themselves. This is the briefest section, but it implicitly and explicitly raises some of our most important questions: What is reading? How is the field of college reading grounded? How do we fit into the larger university culture? How do students and instructors weave their own personal backgrounds and understandings of literacy into the framework of the reading course? What is the relationship of cognition and metacognition in the college reading classroom?

The Research section is noteworthy because of the variety of top-ics addressed. Research that examines the efficacy of various pedagogical approaches is well represented, but the articles here go beyond simply reporting whether the experimental group outperformed the control group. Student attitudes and understandings of texts and learning are explored, as well as an examination of the demands of college-level textbooks and study requirements. The diversity inherent in our field is made evident as well, because the articles focus not just on college de-velopmental readers, but also English-as-a-foreign-language learners, proficient readers, and at-risk students.

We hope the articles in the Program and Strategy Descriptions section may be summed up with one word: *useful*. Most of the articles describe instructional practices that pass the "Monday morning test"—readers of this volume will be able to put them to use immediately. In addition to descriptions of techniques, articles in this section include discussions about administrative matters surrounding college reading programs, as well as assessment issues. What separates the articles in this section from a simple listing of techniques that work is their ground-ing—generally, the authors of these articles provide the *why* it works and *how* it works, in addition to the expected *what to do*. Here, theory and re-search are never far removed from practice.

It is our hope that you, the reader, find *College Reading Research and Practice: Articles From* The Journal of College Literacy and Learning an informative volume that answers some questions about college reading. But we also hope that the articles herein spur the creation of more ques-tions—and that, in a small way, this book can become part of the cycle of research and thinking about college reading that keeps our field mov-ing forward.

SECTION I

Theoretical Issues

Theory provides educators the necessary link to research and, in turn, pedagogy. The theorist provides the ideas, insights, and models that allow researchers the chance to develop research paradigms that can be tested. Once paradigms are tested, the practitioner can develop teaching strategies and materials to be used in the classroom.

When working with the underprepared or developmental student in a college reading class, the primary goal should be to help the student develop the skills to be academically successful. If this occurs, the student can achieve his or her academic and professional goals. The five articles in this section provide insights and perspectives for instructing, designing, and implementing college reading programs.

Although a Marxist interpretation is not generally applied in the field of college reading, it is important to recognize the role of the class struggle for a young man or woman trying to achieve their full potential, including economic independence. If they can develop, refine, and apply the skills necessary to succeed in college, students also stand a much greater chance of upward mobility. Therefore, the pivotal role theory plays in college reading transcends the normal boundaries of the educational hierarchy, thereby making the critical difference for today's student to achieve the "have" status rather than the "have not" label.

The five articles in this section provide theoretical insights and perspectives for instructing, designing, and implementing college reading programs. In Kingston's and Zhang's examinations of college reading, we find that theories of adult reading are as varied as the scholars who contemplate this issue. Both authors make it abundantly clear that having developmental programs in place for college students is a necessity in order to help these students achieve their educational goals and, in turn, their career and other life goals.

The article by Rinehart and Platt discusses the role of metacognition in the reading process. In particular, these authors suggest that reading-deficient adult and college readers need strategy training because they possess the abilities to monitor their mental processes when they read.

This leads to Clinton's article, which questions the traditional manner in which fiction is taught in the classroom, such as text analysis, and makes the case that the reader of a text is an important component of the textual structure.

Finally, Fishman's article brings a fresh perspective about how cultural differences affect the way in which people read the printed word. Her pioneering work in the Amish community helps us reexamine not only how we view the comprehension process, but also how we bring our world perspective to the literacy process.

These articles represent several different viewpoints about our field. We hope and expect that as a reader not only will you examine these different perspectives, but also insert your own ideas, thoughts, and personal educational philosophy into this mix. One final hope is that these articles will challenge the way you think about college reading programs.

A Brief History of College Reading

Albert J. Kingston

Although many educators believe that reading instruction in institutions of higher learning is a recent phenomenon, a survey of the literature reveals that informal experimental programs were conducted as early as the 1920s. In the 1930s and 1940s, an increasing number of reports were published concerning the reading ability of college students and the results of short programs involving class-sized groups (Booker, 1934; Buswell, 1937, 1939; Pressey, 1931; Robinson, 1931; Triggs, 1941). World War II influenced the development of college reading in two ways. First, during the war it was discovered that a surprisingly large number of draftees were functionally illiterate and thus deemed unsuitable for military service. Second, Public Law 16 (designed to provide rehabilitation training for servicemen with service connected disabilities) and Public Law 346 (the so-called G.I. Bill, which provided on-the-job or academic training for honorably discharged veterans) enabled many men and women to enroll in colleges and universities. Many veterans had somewhat inadequate high school backgrounds, and almost all had experienced a lapse of time between leaving high school and enrolling in the college of their choice. As many of the students were deficient in reading ability, institutions proceeded to inaugurate reading improvement or remedial programs. Unfortunately, the programs were highly varied and often of dubious value. At the time, there were few reading experts who were knowledgeable about college or adult reading. There were comparatively few systematic studies of the demands imposed by college reading and the skills required for successful study. Most school systems had language arts specialists rather than reading specialists, and few concentrated on reading at the secondary level (Mursell, 1939).

The university presented an even bleaker picture. Many instructors of English had never completed a course in reading. Typically, they saw their task as teaching composition and helping students to interpret literature. Psychology professors had shown some interest in reading in the 1930s. They had measured the eye movement of readers (Tinker, 1934,

Originally published in Forum for Reading *(1990), volume 21, number 2, pages 11–15*

1947), and experimented with instruments to measure reading more reliably or validly (Davis, 1942, 1946). Professors of education also knew little about how to improve the reading skills of college men and women. Those interested in reading were generally engaged in training primary grade teachers. It is small wonder, then, that college reading programs in the late 1940s and early 1950s were highly varied. Some provided college credit, while others did not. Some were voluntary, while some were compulsory for students deemed to have deficiencies. Some were located in education departments, others in English or psychology departments, while others were set up as separate programs under student personnel services.

As many university administrators thought in terms of "classes" and "credit hours," many reading programs were originally organized as group programs. When pupil personnel services expanded in the 1950s and 1960s, many reading programs became more individualized, and provisions for personal counseling expanded (Kingston, 1959). To this day, however, many college reading programs are still group programs that meet at specified times and days throughout the quarter or semester.

Most of the early programs could best be described as mechanistic. There was widespread use of motion picture films (specially developed to increase speed) and tachistoscopes (projectors with camera lens attachments which flashed an image at various speeds). Both of these aids were thought to provide perceptual training, which would be transferable to reading. At that time, there was considerable discussion of techniques designed for increasing the "span of recognition" (the number of letters or words seen at a single eye fixation). It was widely thought that the number of saccadic eye movements could be decreased by such training and hence reading rate increased. Another widely used device was a type of rate controller, or accelerator, consisting of a shuttered device which could be adjusted so that lines of print were covered at various speeds. This device forced the student to read faster than customary. Almost all college and university reading programs, at that time, listed increased reading rate as one of their major goals.

In addition to the mechanical devices employed, most instructors regularly used some type of manual of exercises, or workbook, designed to provide practice or instruction in various reading skills. As can be imagined, the value of such manuals was variable. Most provided short reading selections, and comprehension was checked with multiple-choice type items. These exercises often were used in conjunction with the mechanical devices. As many reading tests also had a similar format, it was common to see college programs described in the professional literature as successful because students improved their rate and comprehension by various percentages. These were calculated by comparing the time spent reading the selections before and after training. Similarly, the numbers of correct items on the comprehension tests accompanying each selection were compared. The concepts of a single reading rate and a percent of comprehension, of course, is extremely naive. Neither the reading specialist nor the measurement specialist now accepts these concepts as representing valid or reliable indications of reading ability.

Most of the reading programs also claimed to emphasize vocabulary development. Some taught roots, prefixes, and suffixes. Others employed various word lists of unknown origin. Very few directors of programs asked academic faculty for lists of words that students would need to study in the different disciplines. Additionally, many programs incorporated the Survey, Question, Read, Recite, Review (SQ3R) method of study developed by F.P. Robinson (1946) in an effort to improve remembering after studying.

Most directors of college reading programs felt a need for assistance as they became increasingly aware of the shortcomings of their programs. A number of organizations were formed as a source for sharing information. In 1952, the Southwest Reading Conference was organized. It later became the National Reading Conference. The College Reading Association was founded in 1955, and a number of regional groups were also organized during the decade of the 1950s. By the 1960s, the International Reading Association also provided an increasingly popular forum for junior college and four-year college faculty participants. During this period, Purdue University (which had a large college reading program) began publishing the *Journal of Developmental Reading*, which provided a source of information regarding college reading. This journal later was taken over by the International Reading Association and became the *Journal of Reading*. The College Reading Association's *Journal of the Reading Specialist*, which also started during this period, is still in existence. The name was changed to *Reading World* and has more recently been changed to *Reading Research and Instruction*.

Although the number of college reading programs mushroomed during the 1950s, concern about their effectiveness became evident. Many programs relied on pretest and posttest scores and/or student opinions to demonstrate the value of the programs. Those involved in teaching reading became increasingly aware of the naiveté of many of the pedagogical and assessment procedures commonly in use. H. Alan Robinson (1950) expressed the concerns of an increasing number of college reading instructors.

As for remedial texts available during that time, no particular professional acuity is required to penetrate the superficiality of the types of exercises and treatments which characterized most of those volumes. The shallowness and malfunctioning of college reading programs at large is reflected (and at the same time reinforced) by the patent over-concern for a simple increase in reading speed, by the plethora of timed selections for the measurement of speed with no more than a passing regard for a well-rounded index of comprehension, by the relative absence of working materials to develop basic organizational skills, and by the fetish usually made of a "high level of interest," which has produced a spate of materials and workbooks on a level of difficulty utterly impertinent to the task at hand.

By the 1960s, the established reading programs seem to have undergone significant changes. There was less reliance on films and mechanical devices. A number of articles citing the inadequacies of many published standardized reading tests began appearing in the literature. Practitioners became aware that vocabulary development which relied upon memorization of lists of words was not efficient. Above all, there was increasing recognition that reading comprehension was not simply the percentages of correct responses made on multiple choice or other objective type measures. The better programs modified the class format originally inaugurated, and considerably more individualization and personal counseling were undertaken. Reading laboratories which provided broadened practice materials became increasingly common. Students also were given assistance in studying their own textbooks and in preparing for examinations. Most of the established programs no longer stressed rate, vocabulary, and comprehension as before. Rather, the goal became one of developing active readers, who were flexible in reading and varied their methods according to their purpose and the nature of the material. Work-study skills such as note-taking while reading and during lectures, preparing for and taking tests, and similar skills also became part of the typical college reading program. Additionally, the public schools began recognizing the need for secondary school reading specialists. Many underprepared high school graduates were attempting college due to the opportunities afforded by the new junior and community colleges which sprang up throughout the

United States during this period. Secondary school reading specialists served as helpful bridges between the elementary school experts who knew a great deal about reading and methods of teaching it, and the self-taught college reading instructors.

Beginning in the 1970s and continuing into the 1980s, a social consciousness, a competition for students, and an increasing influx of foreign students seemed to emerge, causing many postsecondary institutions to alter their traditional standards of admission and providing an opportunity for enrollment of the so-called nontraditional students. These included older students seeking new skills and knowledge in order to change their careers or who have retired from the workplace and are taking advantage of free or lower tuition costs, women who have raised their families and wish to reenter the job market, or others simply desiring training in the new, emerging fields of study. Many institutions became increasingly aware that such special students may need additional academic help. Today, many reading programs have become inaugural parts of what are commonly known as developmental studies programs. Typically, students enrolled in such programs also can receive help in writing, mathematics, and tutoring in some content areas. In most developmental programs, the college reading instructor plays a key role.

Academicians who argued that students should only learn to read in the primary grades are rarely heard today. Rather, it looks like college reading and study strategies programs are here to stay. Despite past trials and errors, most established programs appear to be on firmer ground. And for institutions seeking to inaugurate or substantiate reading and study strategy programs, there now is an established, published body of knowledge for consultation.

REFERENCES

Booker, I.A. (1934). *The measurements and improvement of silent reading among college freshmen*. Chicago: The University of Chicago Libraries.

Buswell, G.T. (1937). How adults read. *University of Chicago Supplementary Educational Monographs, 45*, 139–146.

Buswell, G.T. (1939). Remedial reading at the college and adult levels: An experimental study. *University of Chicago Supplementary Educational Monographs, 50*.

Davis, F.B. (1942). Two new measures of reading ability. *Journal of Educational Psychology, 33*, 365–372.

Davis, F.B. (1946). The factorial composition of two tests of comprehension in reading. *Journal of Educational Psychology, 37*, 481–486.

Kingston, A.J. (1959). Problems of initiating a new college reading program. In O.S. Causey & W.B. Eller (Eds.), *Eighth yearbook of the National Reading Conference* (pp. 15–24). Fort Worth, TX: Texas Christian University Press.

Mursell, J.B. (1939). The defeat of the schools. *Atlantic Monthly, 163,* 353–361.

Pressey, L.C. (1931). College students and reading. *Journal of Higher Education, 2,* 30–34.

Robinson, F.P. (1931). Can college freshmen in the lowest tenth in reading be aided scholastically? *School and Society, 34,* 843–846.

Robinson, F.P. (1946). *Effective study.* New York: Harper and Brothers.

Robinson, H.A. (1950). A note on the evaluation of college remedial courses. *Journal of Educational Psychology, 41,* 83–98.

Tinker, M.A. (1934). The role of eye movements in diagnostic and remedial reading. *School and Society, 39,* 147–148.

Tinker, M.A. (1947). Time relations for eye movement measures in reading. *Journal of Educational Psychology, 38,* 1–10.

Triggs, F.O. (1941). Current problems in remedial reading for college students. *School and Society, 44,* 376–379.

In Defense of College Developmental Reading Education

Jian Zhang

Developmental programs have served the academic needs of students in institutions of higher education in the United States since 1630 (Stahl & King, 1999). Yet, developmental educators and the work that they do have been under attack for almost as long as the programs have existed. A number of researchers and practitioners interested in developmental education have recently chronicled the history of institutional efforts to assist students who come into higher education underprepared (Boylan & White, 1994; Casazza & Silverman, 1996; Wyatt, 1992). Even though the programs have existed in some form or other since the 1600s, each generation seems to produce critics who loudly proclaim that such programs have no place in higher education.

More recently, programs like the Texas Academic Skills Program (McMillan, 1997) and developmental courses at the City University of New York (Breneman & Haarlow, 1999; Schmidt, 1998) have been under attack and threatened with extinction. Despite the devotion and hard work of developmental educators who see positive results of their efforts, these attacks leave them feeling unappreciated and unsure that they will be able to continue to make a difference for students in higher education. I, like other developmental educators, point to the results of studies like the National Adult Literacy Survey conducted in 1993 that revealed that 47 percent of American adults have very limited literacy skills; further, the majority of American adults do not have the literacy skills necessary to integrate complex information, analyze special conditions, or handle mathematics tasks that require background knowledge (Kirsch et al., 1993). Further, we argue that as a result, individuals with low literacy skills are unable to find decent jobs, and are likely to live in poverty. Data from the National Assessment of Educational Progress indicate that the situation is worsening. Reading proficiency scores for the period between 1971 and 1992 remained stable, but between 1992 and 1994 a decline is evident (Walberg, 1996). And, we also

Originally published in The Journal of College Literacy and Learning *(2000–2001), volume 30, pages 43–49*

worry that there is a significant gap between high school reading proficiency and expected skills for successful workers.

Many developmental educators view their mission as one that serves those who are attempting to change their lives through their efforts to become more educated. These students are often less privileged and viewed as less than gifted. While they can learn, they have not had sustained opportunities to do so. Carriuolo (1994) argues that what developmental students need is to acquire skills that they have not previously learned. The problem is not lack of ability but lack of preparation for college work.

While developmental education has had its detractors over the years, it also has had its supporters. Maxwell (1979) observed that "It seems that every generation, at some point, discovers that students cannot read as well as they would like or as well as professors expect" (p. 269). Wyatt (1992) determined, as a result of her historical study of academic efforts to assist underprepared students, that developmental education was and continues to be a tradition in higher education. For example, she noted that in 1907 more than half the students enrolled at Harvard, Yale, Princeton, and Columbia failed to meet the institutional entrance requirements. As a result, each institution added formal college-level developmental courses to their curricula. Further, Maxwell (1979) also noted that in 1915 approximately 350 colleges reported to the United States Commissioner of Education that they had "preparatory" departments. Over the years, the names of the courses have changed. For example, "Remedial Reading" has changed to "Reading Class" and "Basic Writing" to "Introduction to Expository Writing." Another example is the use of the term "learning center." Sanford University has kept a learning center since 1972 to house developmental programs for its students (Wyatt, 1992).

Currently, college developmental programs can be found all over the United States. Data from the National Center for Education Statistics indicate that approximately 78 percent of all higher education institutions offer developmental courses; these courses are taken by 29 percent of their first-time students (Hebel, 1999).

Because reading problems can reflect general literacy difficulties and problems in mastering most subject area content, developmental reading is the focus of this paper. Students with reading difficulties are much less likely to complete their college studies than those with writing or mathematics problems. For example, Fleischauer (1996) found that students completing the reading and study skills course remained at the university at a significantly higher rate than those with the same reading levels who did not take the developmental course. She also noted that students who completed the reading course earned significantly more credit hours than their counterparts throughout the semesters. Duignan (1993) noted similar results when studying the impact of the university learning center reading program on persistence and achievement. Students with low initial reading skills who participated in learning center reading in Duignan's study persisted and succeeded at almost the same level as those students who started out with higher reading skills. Further, the investigator in a comprehensive study involving students at 116 two-year and four-year colleges across the country concluded that students who passed their developmental courses were about as likely to persist and graduate as their better prepared peers (Carriuolo, 1994). The programs in Carriuolo's carefully randomized study involved 62.5 percent white students. The author's institution experienced similar results. Napoli (1993) concluded from an analysis of data that students who completed the developmental reading courses at the college earned a statistically significantly higher grade point average (GPA) than a group of nondevelopmental reading students when GPA was statistically adjusted for total credits completed for initial reading levels. He argued that "The developmental reading program not only accomplishes its goal of preparing students to meet the demands of content area course work, but in addition elevates performances to a level above those of nondevelopmental students" (p. 11).

On one hand, it can be argued that higher education should be democratized and made available to as many people as possible. On the basis of that argument, a number of institutions of higher education provide service to a variety of nontraditional students, including those who are severely underprepared academically. On the other hand, this position is being challenged. According to some, the undergraduate programs have been diluted and teaching has been distracted because of the admission of some ill-prepared students (Shattuck, 1997). What these challengers may fail to take into account are the changes in the uses of literacy because of globalization and the advancement of technology and the view of who should be educated. Developmental educators continue to argue that the goal of education is no longer reserved for the few who may focus on a narrow area of intellectual studies (e.g., Casazza & Silverman, 1996; Spore, 1997/1998). They believe that it should include a concern for raising the national literacy level, expanding opportunities to learn, and diminishing inequities and poverty. They believe that exclusion in the guise of the pursuit of excellence can only lead to the limitation of the talent pools from which colleges draw, loss of the cultural richness that the heterogeneity of students can provide, and a sacrifice of academic diversity that can lead to teaming that can potentially solve many of the world's problems.

Ideally, developmental education can bridge the gap between what a student learns in high school and what is expected of her or him in college. An important component of developmental education is teaching skills that are needed to learn college content. Because it takes time and money to do this, developmental programs have been attracting unfriendly fire from legislators, administrators, mainstream faculty members, and even the students who benefit from them. The programs continue to be an easy target for those who argue that money can be saved if these programs are cut or pushed back into secondary schools. They also remain targets when mainstream faculty stigmatize teachers and students who are involved in them despite evidence from research that the developmental programs improve student retention and academic success. They provide a stunningly successful solution to a long-standing problem—bridging basic and higher education. As Biggs (1995) argued, it is important that educators and others who make decisions about college programs acknowledge the value of developmental education. That value is clearly demonstrated in the history of student success after participation in a developmental reading program.

In a broader sense, the literacy problems indicated by limited comprehension experienced by many college students might require far more work than taking one or two developmental reading courses or some tutorial sessions. To address the literacy problems at the postsecondary level, mainstream faculty must also play a role in assisting students as they engage in content area reading and writing. Shared staff development activities where developmental and mainstream educators learn about better ways to help students learn may be one small step toward assisting students. Tutorial programs where colleges and high schools work together to improve pre–college learning may be another community-based solution.

Conclusion

Developmental courses, workshops, and centers have coexisted with college education in the United States for more than a century despite the constant complaints and embarrassment that Americans have expressed; they are likely to remain with us for a long time. A review of the history and some key research suggests that developmental education is a valuable asset. The message sent by the history and research must be shared with the entire community. It may take an informed community to make it even more valuable. Within the colleges, developmental and mainstream faculty can collaborate for stronger, more effective courses that follow the student throughout his or her studies. Between colleges and secondary schools, both can develop and use strategies that can make the transition between the two smoother and more productive. Faculty and administrators from both high school and college can learn about the effectiveness of developmental education and lobby for it so that it remains in place to do the work it is intended to do. The stigma can be removed and its value can be understood and promoted.

REFERENCES

Biggs, S.A. (1995). Establishing credit and credibility for your college reading courses. *Forum for Reading, 25,* i–iii.

Boylan, H.R., & White, W.G. (1994). Educating all the nation's people: The historical roots of developmental education—condensed version. In M. Maxwell (Ed.), *From access to success* (pp. 3–7). Clearwater, FL: H & H Publishing.

Breneman, D.W., & Haarlow, W.N. (1999). Establishing the real value of remedial education. *The Chronicle of Higher Education, 45*(31), B6–B7.

Carnevale, A.P., & Sylvester, K. (2000). As welfare rolls shrink, colleges offer the best route to good jobs. *The Chronicle of Higher Education, 46*(24), B6–B7.

Carriuolo, N. (1994). Why developmental education is such a hot potato. *The Chronicle of Higher Education, 40*(32), B1–B2.

Casazza, M.E., & Silverman, S.L. (1996). *Learning assistance and developmental education: A guide for effective practice.* San Francisco: Jossey-Bass.

Duignan, W.L. (1992). Student reading level and college success. *Research & Teaching in Developmental Education, 8*(2), 95–103.

Fleischauer, J.P. (1996). Assessing developmental reading courses: Do they have an impact? *Research & Teaching in Developmental Education, 12*(2), 17–74.

Kirsch, I.S., et al. (1993). *Adult literacy in America: A first look at the results of the national adult literacy survey* (2nd ed.). Washington, DC: Office of Educational Research and Improvement, U.S. Department of Education.

Maxwell, M. (1979). *Improving student learning skills.* San Francisco: Jossey-Bass.

McMillan, J. (1997). Well-regarded remediation program in Texas faces an uncertain future. *The Chronicle of Higher Education, 43*(19), A35–A36.

Napoli, A.R. (1993). *Report on the developmental reading and testing program at Suffolk Community College.* New York: Suffolk Community College.

Schmidt, P. (1998). A clash of values at CUNY over remedial education. *The Chronicle of Higher Education, 44*(28), A33–A34.

Shattuck, R. (1997). From school to college: We must end the conspiracy to lower standards. *The Chronicle of Higher Education, 43*(45), B6–B7.

Spore, M.B. (1997/1998). High aspirations: Portraying experiences with underprepared college students. *Forum for Reading, 28,* 25–38.

Stahl, N.A., & King, J.R. (1999). A history of college reading. In R.F. Flippo & D.C. Caverly (Eds.), *Handbook of college reading and study strategy research* (pp. 1–23). Mahwah, NJ: Erlbaum.

Walberg, H. (1996). U.S. schools teach reading least productively. *Research in the Teaching of English, 30*(3), 328–343.

Wyatt, M. (1992). The past, present, and future need for college reading courses in the U.S. *Journal of Reading, 36*(1), 10–20.

Metacognitive Awareness and Monitoring in Adult and College Readers

Steve D. Rinehart and Jennifer M. Platt

Researchers in the fields of developmental cognitive psychology and reading have attempted to use the concepts under the label of metacognition to examine good and poor reader differences and the use of reading and learning strategies. Metacognition, in general, refers to both the knowledge (awareness) and the control (monitoring and correction) which a learner has over his own thinking and learning activities (Baker & Brown, 1980; Flavell, 1976; Paris, Lipson, Jacobs, Oka, Debritto, & Cross, 1982). Flexibility and efficiency are essential to this learner-control interaction (Brown, Campione, & Day, 1981; Moore, 1982). Although the majority of metacognitive research has been concerned with school-age children, research has also provided us with important information about the college-age and adult reader. The major purpose of this article is to review metacognitive studies of older readers and to draw conclusions and implications for strategy instruction. Additional findings from other reading ages will also be presented.

Metacognition is both old and new. Even in early 20th century considerations of metacognition (viz., Dewey, 1910; Thorndike, 1917), reading exemplified cognitive activities in which reasoning and flexibility were precursory to learning-thinking efficiency. The essence of such early insight was that reading, like other cognitive activities, involved skills of self-awareness and self-control, which then led to efficient reasoning. For example, Dewey's system of inducing reflective thinking was basically a call for metacognitive training. The aim was to induce active monitoring and critical reasoning, which would result in critical comprehension (Brown, 1982).

Metacognition and Reading

Baker (1982) defines metacognition as being composed of two overlapping components:

Originally published in Forum for Reading *(1984), volume 15, number 2, pages 54–62*

1. Awareness of what skills, strategies, and resources are needed to perform a task effectively; and

2. Ability to use self-regulatory mechanisms to ensure the successful completion of the task.

Many of the difficulties of the inefficient reader may be due to deficits in metacognition, as evidenced by a lack of awareness and control of the cognitive demands of a task. Baker and Brown (in press) found that metacognitive deficits among young children, learning disabled students, and poor readers have been evidenced in each of the following areas viewed as crucial to effective reading:

1. Understanding the purpose of reading

2. Modifying reading strategies for different purposes

3. Considering how new information relates to what is already known

4. Evaluating text for clarity, completeness, and consistency

5. Dealing with failure to understand

6. Identifying the important information in a passage

7. Deciding how well the material has been understood.

The ability to employ appropriate strategies and monitor their use is an important part of reading. The idea that students should play an active role in the selection of strategies and in monitoring their performance during reading has recently received increased attention (Brown, 1980). As illustrated in the above seven areas, the poor reader may be evidencing difficulty because of deficits in metacognition.

Although most researchers in this area are careful to emphasize that proficient reading is mostly automatic—and that monitoring is an automatic mechanism rendering the "clicks" of comprehension (Anderson, 1980, p. 497)—it is metacognitive awareness that guides effective selection and usage of activities for "debugging" (Brown, 1980). Thus, metacognition in reading involves awareness of the reading process (Myers & Paris, 1978), how a reader monitors and regulates ongoing processes (Baker & Brown, 1980; Garner & Kraus, 1981–1982), sensitivities to one's own abilities, and evaluation and correction strategies (Brown, 1982; Paris et al., 1982).

It is an individual's awareness of the cognitive process that enables modification of the process to suit a goal (Flavell, 1976). Lack of insight into the reading process and lack of metacognitive awareness may result in less ability to integrate learning variables. Although we are not absolutely sure what to attribute it to, good comprehenders seem flexible, more aware of what good comprehension entails (Golinkoff, 1975–1976). Proficient readers are apparently better able to take control of their own comprehension and learning and regulate metacognitive variables. They are better able to know what they know and to monitor that awareness.

The major source of evidence that novice or poor readers have metacognitive deficits comes from awareness and monitoring studies. Researchers have tapped the reader's awareness with interviews and questionnaires and have assessed the reader's monitoring of ongoing comprehension with evaluation and regulation tasks.

Awareness

Younger and poor readers evidently are less aware that they must attempt to make sense of what they read. They seem to focus on decoding words rather than obtaining meaning from text (Garner & Kraus, 1981–1982; Moore & Kirby, 1981). They differ in their awareness of strategies for getting meaning and in their regulation of strategies when they do experience difficulty (Canney & Winograd, 1979; Forrest & Waller, 1979). For example, Myers and Paris (1978), in an often cited study, investigated children's metacognitive knowledge of reading variables. They interviewed 8- and 12-year-old readers about their reading abilities, the parameters of reading tasks, and cognitive strategies used in reading. The variables were based on Flavell and Wellman's (1977) delineation of person, task, and strategy variables as the three major categories of metacognitive knowledge. The second graders in the study displayed less sensitivity to the semantic structure of paragraphs, goals of reading, and strategies for "debugging" than the older readers. The younger readers, like the second graders in Canney and Winograd's (1979) study, perceived in general that reading was "an orthographic-vernal translation problem rather than as a meaning construction and comprehension task" (p. 688).

In a recent study, based in part on the Myers and Paris (1978) investigation, Jacobs (1982) found that metacognitive knowledge and monitoring of reading improves with age. She found fifth graders more aware than third graders of purposes and functions of strategy in both monitoring and intervention. The poor readers demonstrated performance gains in comprehension from intervention based on their deficiencies.

Adult poor readers may also reveal a lack of metacognitive knowledge. Gambrell and Heathington (1981) used an interview design to tap good and poor readers' metacognitive differences in awareness of task and strategy variables. They questioned 28 adult poor readers and 28 adult good readers. The adult poor readers lacked sensitivity to both task and strategy dimensions of reading. They reported fewer strategies, had more misconceptions about such strategies, and were not as aware of how and when to use them. The poor readers had less understanding of textual elements. For example, only 43% of the poor readers were able to relate that a paragraph or story had some kind of order, while 96% of the good readers revealed their knowledge that a paragraph or story had structure. Only 21% of the poor readers gave a meaning-centered response when asked about the purpose of reading, in contrast to 79% of the good readers.

In this study, questions about knowledge of strategy variables were related to purposes for reading, reading mode, reading skills, and reading comprehension failures, much like the Myers and Paris (1978) questions. Gambrell and Heathington also asked questions related to motivation, structure of text, and prior knowledge. Following are a few examples of questions related to strategy variables:

> If you're telling someone about something you've read, what do you try to tell them, all the word, just the ending or what?
>
> Which would be easier to do, read word for word or for general meaning?
>
> What makes someone a really good reader?
>
> When you are reading, what do you do if you don't know a word?

Only one third of the poor readers were able to give an answer to the last example above. In fact, the poor readers' knowledge of task and strategy variables, especially strategies, was much like the second graders in the Myers and Paris (1978) study. They seemed to perceive reading as a process of decoding rather than one of comprehending. Several misconceptions about the reading process were also evident. For example, 57% of the poor readers reported that it was easier to read word for word than for general meaning, a response much like the second graders. They also reported that reading aloud was more efficient than reading silently. They did not seem to be aware of independent, internally generated strategies. Such results demonstrate that adult disabled readers, too, may have a deficient understanding of the reading process.

Monitoring

Monitoring involves evaluation of one's comprehension success, regulation of the process, and self-correction when necessary (Baker & Brown, 1980). The majority of monitoring studies, as with awareness studies, have been concerned with elementary and secondary students. This research has revealed that young and/or novice readers are less able to monitor their understanding during reading and studying and to implement regulation and correction strategies when confronting comprehension problems.

Various measures have been utilized to identify the metacognitive differences existing among readers. Readers have been asked to rate the certainty of their response to a comprehension question. Older or better readers have been observed to be more successful than younger or poorer readers at rating such felt understanding (Forrest & Waller, 1979).

Several studies of self-corrections during oral reading have also revealed metacognitive differences among readers. Even the youngest good readers correct semantically inconsistent errors, but do not correct those that are semantically acceptable (Clay, 1973; Weber, 1970).

DiVesta, Hayward, and Orlando (1979) investigated metacognitive monitoring strategies by using a cloze technique. Their findings suggest that younger and poorer readers do not efficiently employ the strategy of using subsequent text for comprehension monitoring.

Another type of interview or questioning format for measuring metacognitive monitoring involves a reader's self-report during reading. From analyzing these reports, investigators have found strategy differences due to reading ability. For example, better readers across levels seem to adjust their reading behaviors according to task purposes (Hare & Smith, 1982; Smith, 1977).

Research indicated that readers differ by both age and ability in judging their own understanding (Brown, 1980; Markman, 1979; Steward & Tei, 1983). Using self-report techniques, Hare and Pulliam (1980) tested the hypothesis that college students' metacognitive behavior would predict their reading achievement scores. They asked students to introspect about their behavior as they read an expository article. Their data suggest that high scoring readers are more actively involved in reading. Collins, Brown, and Larkin (1980) gave their subjects five difficult texts and asked them to report the processing they used as they made sense of the passages. They found that skilled readers used a variety of strategies, such as evaluating for plausibility, completeness, and interconnectedness, in interpreting the text.

Readers who do not effectively monitor their understanding may fail to comprehend and make adjustments (Garner, 1980; Garner & Anderson, 1980). Researchers have asked if mature readers detect inconsistencies as they monitor text and what they do if comprehension fails. Baker (1979), for example, investigated comprehension monitoring in college-age readers. The college students were to read and recall intentionally introduced confusions. Each passage contained one of three confusions: inappropriate, illogical connectives; ambiguous referents; and inconsistent information. Subjects were not informed of the existence of the confusions before reading. Subsequent to answering recall questions, they were asked to reflect on whether or not they noticed the confusions, how they interpreted them, and how the confusions affected their comprehension. Subjects did not detect 62% of the confusions. Additionally, less than 25% were noticed during the reading. The retrospections, however, indicate that many failures to report problems were due to fix-up strategies, rather than failure to monitor initial comprehension. For example, students reported that they often deliberately omitted or altered confusing information. They made inferences to resolve confusions, even without realizing that they had done so.

In a later study, Baker and Anderson (1982) asked college students to read expository passages containing either main point inconsistencies, detail inconsistencies, or no inconsistencies. The investigators found that the majority of college students monitored their understanding of reading passages as demonstrated by their modifications in processing strategies. Students spent more time on sentences containing information that they found to be inconsistent with information they already possessed, and they looked back more often at the sentences that contained inconsistencies. Those students who did not identify the inconsistencies in the text may have failed to monitor their comprehension or may have constructed an explanation or interpretation of the text that satisfied their previous knowledge and experience.

Study monitoring is similar to comprehension monitoring. To be successful, students need to monitor their mental processes while studying (Locke, 1975). Metacognitive research has explored this study monitoring with college students.

A fruitful activity in this regard has been with summarization strategies. Brown, Campione, and Day (1981) pointed out that summarizing textual material may be a complex task requiring considerable skill. They have identified the following rules: delete redundancy, delete trivia, provide superordinates, select topic sentences, and invent topic sentences where missing. Brown and Day (1983) investigated summarization abilities of fifth-grade, seventh-grade, tenth-grade, and college-level students. Developmental differences apparently existed on the more complex rules. Invention was almost never used by fifth graders and by college students on only half of the appropriate occasions. The junior college students, who were remedial studiers, like the seventh graders, had great difficulty with the invention rule. This study indicates that while skilled students may successfully use summarization, remedial college students may find it difficult and improve with only the most explicit instruction.

Related to the ability to summarize textual content is the ability to identify the levels of importance of instruction in textual material. Brown and Smiley (1977) found that seventh-grade to college-age readers who were asked to study prose passages until they could remember the details were generally able to select the most important idea units to use as cues for later retrieval. The college readers, however, exhibited the greatest degree of sensitivity to the relative importance of textual information. They shifted their attention to idea units of intermediate importance in a repeat trial on the same passage.

Self-questioning seems to be another effective strategy that sophisticated readers use as they process text. Research findings suggest that hypothesizing questions is a means for metacognitive monitoring (Andre & Anderson, 1978–1979), but that it may be a late developing strategy. Garner and Alexander (1982) found that only half the college students they studied used the strategy. Moreover, they found that when the college students in their project did anticipate what questions might be asked about a passage they were reading, they significantly outperformed students who verbalized using other comprehension strategies. Self-questioning apparently serves to facilitate monitoring, regulation, and test readiness estimation as students interact with text. It seems that mature students possess sensitivities to textual idea relationships and implement interactive strategies such as summarization and self-questioning.

Conclusion

Metacognitive development differences appear to exist among all levels of readers but also among readers at all age levels. This review has supported the notion that metacognitive skills develop over time, that young children may be confused about the reading process, and may have trouble monitoring comprehension. High school students may demonstrate similar deficiencies. Adult and college readers usually monitor their comprehension but still may be deficient in some regards. They may lack awareness of some process, task, and strategy variables. They may also lack a sensitivity to the hierarchy of ideas found in text. Such insight may be essential for optimum processing. Furthermore, they may lack specific processing strategies, such as summarization.

In spite of the apparent strength of these findings, current controversy exists about the methodology used to measure metacognitive skills. Winograd and Johnston (1980), reviewing the error detection tasks discussed earlier, suggest that most readers are capable of exhibiting a wide range of metacognitive abilities and it is the subtlety of those abilities that may cause complications in accurate measurement. Additionally, a reader's performance might be affected by interactions between task demands and individual differences, such as affective factors (Erickson, Stahl, & Rinehart).

Despite the apparent shortcomings of awareness and monitoring studies, insights into metacognitive functioning have been gained. More expenditure of thought and effort is required as we consider the possibility of teaching the skills identified in awareness and monitoring studies to those who may qualify for direct instruction (Brown, in Golinkoff, 1975–1976). The findings in regard to the adult reader offer encouragement and indicate the need for further research. Most of the research has been done with younger readers, yet the findings clearly indicate that adult and college readers may have metacognitive deficiencies. Furthermore, older readers as well as children have benefited from strategy instruction.

The general intent of this review has been to demonstrate how knowledge of one's cognitive processes, the orchestration of strategic effort, and the monitoring of one's cognitive activities can enhance reading performance. Findings indicate that older readers exercise more awareness of their own learning processes and greater self-control or monitoring of performance. However, results demonstrate that although adult and college readers monitor their comprehension, they may be deficient in other ways, such as in a lack of awareness of task and strategy variables.

Strategies can have been taught, maintained, and used to facilitate learning in a variety of settings (Day, 1980; Manzo, 1969; Paris et al., 1982; Raphael, 1981; Smith & Alley, 1981). Adult and college readers who evidence metacognitive deficiencies may be the most promising candidates for strategy training since they appear to be more aware of and capable of monitoring their mental processes while reading.

REFERENCES

Anderson, T.H. (1980). Study strategies and adjunct aids. In R.J. Spiro, B.C. Bruce, & W.F. Brewer (Eds.), *Theoretical issues in reading comprehension*. Hillsdale, NJ: Erlbaum.

Andre, M.E., & Anderson, T.H. (1978–1979). The development and evaluation of a self-questioning study technique. *Reading Research Quarterly, 14*, 605–623.

Baker, L. (1979). Comprehension monitoring: Identifying and coping with text confusions. *Journal of Reading Behavior, 11*, 365–374.

Baker, L. (1982). An evaluation of the role of metacognitive deficits in learning disabilities. *Topics in Learning and Learning Disabilities, 12*, 27–33.

Baker, L., & Anderson, R. (1982). Effects of inconsistent information on text processing: Evidence for comprehension monitoring. *Reading Research Quarterly, 17*, 281–293.

Baker, L., & Brown, A.L. (1980). *Metacognitive skills and reading* (Tech. Rep. No. 188). Urbana, IL: University of Illinois, Center for the Study of Reading.

Baker, L., & Brown, A.L. (1983). Cognitive monitoring in reading. In J. Flood (Ed.), *Understanding reading comprehension*. Newark, DE: International Reading Association.

Brown, A.L. (1980). Metacognitive development and reading. In R.J. Spiro, B.C. Bruce & W.F. Brewer (Eds.), *Theoretical issues in reading comprehension*. Hillsdale, NJ: Erlbaum,.

Brown, A.L. (1982). Learning how to learn from reading. In J.A. Langer & M.T. Smith-Burke (Eds.), *Reader meets author: Bridging the gap*. Newark, DE: International Reading Association.

Brown, A.L., Campione, J.D., & Day, J.D. (1981). Learning to learn: On training students to learn from texts. *Educational Researcher, 10*, 14–21.

Brown, A.L., & Day, J.J. (1983). *Macrorules for summarizing texts: The development of expertise* (Tech. Rep. No. 270). Urbana, IL: University of Illinois, Center for the Study of Reading.

Brown, A.L., & Smiley, S.S. (1977). Rating the importance of structural units prose passages: A problem of metacognitive development. *Child Development, 48*, 1-8.

Canney, G., & Winograd, P. (1979). *Schemata for reading and reading comprehension performance* (Tech. Rep. No. 120). Urbana, IL: University of Illinois, Center for the Study of Reading,

Clay, M.M. (1973). *Reading: The patterning of complex behavior*. Auckland, New Zealand: Heinemann.

Collins, A., Brown, J.S., & Larkin, K.M. (1980). Inferences in text understanding. In R.J. Spiro, B.C. Bruce, & W.F. Brewer (Eds.), *Theoretical issues in reading comprehension*. Hillsdale, NJ: Erlbaum.

Day, J.D. (1980). *Training summarization skills: A comparison of teaching methods*. Unpublished doctoral dissertation, University of Illinois, Urbana.

Dewey. J. (1910). *How we think*. Boston: Heath.

Divesta, F.J., Hayward, K.G., & Orlando, V.P. (1979). Developmental trends in monitoring text for comprehension. *Child Development, 50*, 97–105.

Erickson, L.G., Stahl, S.A., & Rinehart, S.D. *Metacognitive abilities of above and below average readers: Effects of conceptual tempo, passage level, and error type*. Manuscript submitted for publication.

Flavell, J.H. (1976). Metacognitive aspects of problem solving. In L.B. Resnick (Ed.), *The nature of intelligence*. Hillsdale, NJ: Erlbaum.

Flavell, J.H., & Wellman, H.M. (1977). Metamemory. In R.V. Kail & J. Hagen (Eds.), *Perspectives on the development of memory and cognition*. Hillsdale, NJ: Erlbaum.

Forrest, D., & Waller, T. (1979). *Cognitive and metacognitive aspects of reading*. Paper presented at the meeting of the Society for Research in Child Development, San Francisco.

Gambrell, L.B., & Heathington, B.S. (1981). Adult disabled readers' metacognitive awareness about reading tasks and strategies. *Journal of Reading Behavior, 13,* 215–222.

Garner, R. (1980). Monitoring of understanding: An investigation of good and poor readers' awareness of induced miscomprehension of text. *Journal of Reading Behavior, 12,* 56–63.

Garner, R., & Alexander, P. (1982). Strategic processing of text: An investigation of the effects on adults' question-answering performance. *Journal of Educational Research, 75,* 144–148.

Garner, R., & Anderson, J. (1980). Monitoring-of-understanding research: Inquiry directions, methodological dilemmas. *Journal of Experimental Education, 49,* 70–76.

Garner, R., & Kraus, C. (1981–1982). Good and poor comprehender differences in knowing and regulating reading behaviors. *Educational Research Quarterly, 49,70–76.*

Golinkoff, R. (1975–1976). A comparison of reading comprehension processes in good and poor comprehenders. *Reading Research Quarterly, 11,* 623–657.

Hare, V.C., & Pulliam, C. (1980). *College students' metacognitive awareness of reading behaviors*. Paper presented at the annual meeting of the National Reading Conference, Washington.

Hare, V.C., & Smith, D.C. (1982). Reading to remember: Studies of metacognitive reading skills in elementary school-aged children. *Journal of Educational Research, 75,* 157–164.

Jacobs, J. (1982). Children's reports about cognitive aspects of reading comprehension. Paper presented as part of symposium. (See Paris et al., 1982, this reference list.)

Locke, E.Q. (1975). *A guide to effective study*. New York: Springer.

Manzo, A.V. (1969). The request procedure. *Journal of Reading, 13,* 123–126.

Markman, E.M. (1979). Realizing that you don't understand: Elementary school children's awareness of inconsistencies. *Child Development, 50,* 643–655.

Moore, P.J. (1982). Children's metacognitive knowledge about reading: A selected review. *Educational Research, 24,* 120–128.

Moore, P.J., & Kirby, J. (1981). Metacognition and reading performance: A replication and extension of Myers and Paris in an Australian context. *Educational Enquiry, 4,* 18–29. (Cited by Moore, 1982, this reference list.)

Myers, M., & Paris, S.G. (1978). Children's metacognitive knowledge about reading. *Journal of Educational Psychology, 70,* 680–690.

Paris, S.G., Lipson, M.Y., Jacobs, J., Oka, E., Debritto, A.M., & Cross, D. (1982). *Metacognition and reading comprehension*. Symposium presented at the annual convention of the International Reading Association, Chicago.

Raphael, T.E. (1981). *The effect of metacognitive awareness training on students' question answering behavior*. Unpublished doctoral dissertation, University of Illinois, Urbana.

Smith, E.M., & Alley, G.R. (1981). *The effect of teaching sixth graders with learning difficulties a strategy for solving verbal math problems* (Res. Rep. No. 39). Lawrence, KS: University of Kansas, Institute for Research in Learning Disabilities.

Smith, H.K. (1977). The response of good and poor readers when asked to read for different purposes. *Reading Research Quarterly, 3*, 53–84.

Steward, O., & Tei, E. (1983). Some implications of metacognition for reading instruction. *Journal of Reading, 27*, 36–47.

Thorndike, E.L. (1917). Reading as reasoning: A study of mistakes in paragraph reading. *Journal of Educational Psychology, 8*, 323–332.

Weber, R.M. (1970). A linguistic analysis of first-grade reading errors. *Reading Research Quarterly, 5*, 427–451.

Winograd, P., & Johnston, P. (1980). *Comprehension monitoring and the error detection paradigm* (Tech. Rep. No. 153). Urbana, IL: University of Illinois, Center for the Study of Reading.

Reading as Assignment Versus Reading as Art: Reader-Based Criticism Applied to Freshman Composition

DeWitt Clinton

> I was quickly running down the dusty brown dirt road. At every noise I nervously looked all about. The smell of fire was thick in the air and my skin was burning from the summer night's heat. Sweat was streaming down my face stinging my eyes with every step. I ran past freight car after freight car until I finally came to the end of the train. Suddenly I was staring at the face of a large man with an automatic rifle. I didn't know what to do so I quickly.... The annoying ring of the telephone caused me to jump up out of my seat. The setting around me wasn't a railway in some foreign land but my dorm room where I had been reading a short story. I got up and answered the phone which happened to be for my roommate who was at class at the time. After this short interruption I sat at my desk and was once again in front of this armed man.[1]

What's going on here? Why is a student writing about the impressionable impact of a story instead of analyzing the plot of a Holocaust survivor's story of Auschwitz? After all, what is literature for in the university classroom but to identify and code types of human behavior and dramatic situations? Isn't a story or novel designed to lead us to a universal theme where we can discuss an author's intention? Textual and authorial responses to literature have been the mainstay of undergraduate and graduate classes for so long that one can hardly imagine literature having any other dimension. But do we read, as children and adults, to figure out how something is made, or who makes it? Does the business traveler with a bachelor's degree in business administration pick up a novel by Danielle Steel or John Grisham in an air-

---

[1] Introductory paragraph of a freshman essay by Christopher Price, writing about the process of reading Tadeusz Borowski's short story "This Way for the Gas, Ladies and Gentlemen." University of Wisconsin–Whitewater, May 1994.

Originally published in Forum for Reading *(1997–1998), volume 28, pages 16–24*

port bookstore to simply analyze plot or structure between St. Louis and Chicago? I don't think so. This traveler, whom we have educated in our freshman composition class, is looking for a brief escape either into the world of romance, of high tech military escapades, or perhaps of the dramatic courtroom where so many of today's popular characters are found.

Yet in the freshman composition classroom where literature is introduced, discussed, and analyzed, what are we offering to this future traveler? Discussions of unreliable narrators? Examinations of various types of plots as a way of "understanding" what the author designed? Character analyses? Is this what our air traveler looks forward to? Is our future business traveler remembering to separate plot from narrator from character, or is the student learning to integrate all these artistic fictional devices into one whole work of literature? I am beginning to question this time-honored system of teaching fiction, or literary arts, in this fashion.

Our soon-to-be business executive simply wants to experience the novel. She will want to feel "transported" during her flight. If her experience is at all satisfying, she will buy another novel on her next trip, or finish her selection by her bedside, enjoying the moment or two of being swept away by the situation, by the voice of the narrator, or by the characters' situations. But our students come to the freshman English classroom with the profound belief that literature is a text that must be dissected. As a result, literary analysis is all that a student expects after reading a text. The task, no matter how sophisticated, is boring, repetitive, and one which will most likely elicit the comment, "We did that last year." Are there any alternatives to this serious and deadening phenomena which 18-year-olds must endure? Reader-based criticism, reader-oriented criticism, or reception theory offers an insight that nearly every one of my students would not have imagined possible in a course based on literary interpretation. Students are amazed to find that *they* are the true inheritors of literature, and that their "experience" of reading a text is not only valid, but may be even more interesting or "real" as they like to say, than textual or authorial criticism. Is that possible?

If as instructors and interpreters of literature, we continue to advise our students that art is an object to be examined with rational processes, then perhaps our answer is, "No," that "Art is and always will be something to be looked at." But in the last few decades, a number of German and American critics have been looking at the recipient of all this literature, the forgotten reader. An immediate response to considering the reader might be a guarded, "well, yes of course, but...." Yet when we set aside "the art made by the artist," and all the accompanying accouterments of literary criticism, what exactly is left to examine which might illuminate freshman minds, to write essays about? This art played out in the reader's mind is the new ground for a perspective on what literature actually "does."

In reader-based criticism, the art becomes an event; the reading becomes an experience to be felt and processed; the end result of this attention to the actual benefactor of literature is something quite new and refreshing to both critics and students. This phenomena has been obvious to anyone who reads. Literature would have disappeared long ago had it not been for this pleasure principle which intelligent readers yearn for all their lives.

Writing from the Rezeptionsasthetik school of "reader critics" based in West Germany at the University of Konstanz, George Poulet (1969) writes, "The extraordinary fact in the case of a book is the falling away of the barriers between you and it. You are inside it; it is inside you; there is no longer either outside or inside" (p. 54). Literature, in the eyes of Poulet and many of the new reader-based critics, is no longer an object under consideration, an object to be deciphered, but an event experienced in multiple right hemispheric modes of a reader. This is why our student at the beginning of this essay is trying his best to escape the horrors of Auschwitz; he believed he was there, transported by the awful words of Borowski's account. For the most part, reader-based critics are concerned with the creative transformation of text into event. As a result, they offer few practical notes on how to adapt this dynamic and evolving "reader event" into the classroom.

Synthesizing work about reader response by Iser, Rosenblatt, and Holland, Appleyard (1990) writes,

> The story is not the same as the text on the page, nor is it simply the reader's uniquely personal response to the text. Rather the story is an event that has roots both in the text and in the personality and history that the reader brings to the reading. The text is a system of *response-inviting structures* [my emphasis] that the author has organized by reference to a repertory of social and literary codes shared by author and reader.... The reader brings expectations derived from a literary and life experience to bear on the text, and the text feeds back these expectations or it does not. The reader filters this feedback through characteristic defenses, imbues them with fantasies, and transforms the event into an experience of moral, intellectual, social and aesthetic coherence. (pp. 9–10)

As both writer and teacher, I have also been absorbed with the current interest in applying recent left/right brain research to the creative process, particularly as it applies to both freshman composition and creative writing classes. Fusing information of right hemispheric thinking with reader-based criticism, we can develop an analogous critical rubric which offers a challenge to the predictable responses of both student and instructor.

Reader-based criticism as applied to freshman composition provides an opportunity for the instructor to explore the full range of sensory perception, that part of the mind which creates the "traveling" phenomena which determines the level of excitement in the reader. Analogic reactions to the text allow the reader/student to draw upon recollections and similar situations. These "para fictional experiences" allow the student reader to become part of, or to become, a living, breathing observer or participant in the fabricated art, compared, somewhat, to a possibly deeper "subtext." With both "text" and "subtext" running simultaneously in the mind, some readers report that they like or dislike a story even more. Finally, attitudinal responses determine how a reader reacts to the dramatized situation, causing a range of responses from empathy to complete disgust. All three of these reader applications create an entirely new response in the classroom, allowing students to see and recognize that art is personal, direct, and can shape critical thinking in remarkable ways.

Isn't reading reenvisioning what an artist first envisioned? Isn't the reader's perception of the story greater when it is processed through the powerful sensory organs of the right hemisphere of the brain? If we enjoy the experience of reading, isn't it because we see it happening in our own mind's eye, with our own senses interpreting an artist's vision of an experience? Readers often forget where they are, having been transported by only the suggestion of a visual description, or by overhearing or becoming part of a conversation. If the student reader is engrossed by the experience, subtler senses begin to develop; they can begin to taste the cold sausage, smell the stench of cattlecars, touch the abandoned child, and feel overwhelmed with despair they thought could never happen to them. These responses are only a few of the many sensory impressions students have admitted to having after reading Borowski's chilling account at Auschwitz.

Observing students in a different situation yet who responded in a like manner, Probst (1992) concludes,

In both of these instances the students were writing, not "about," the literature, but "from" it. The literary work was the catalyst or prompt, but the students, as they pursued their own thoughts, departed from the literary work, writing about their own lives. Clearly, they were not being "responsible to the text" in any New Critical way.... They had assimilated the literary work and the task of writing into the fabric of their lives so that they could understand better their own experience. It would be difficult to argue that they would profit more by writing an analytical/critical expository essay on some aspect of the text. (p. 119)

Another reader-based strategy designed to involve students is to explore how the literature is comparable or likened to their own experiences. For example, why does Flannery O'Connor's Grandmother character in "A Good Man Is Hard to Find" become the determining factor in whether or not the story creates a strong appeal or a deep resentment? A few students have remarked about how their own grandmother is exactly like the fictional grandmother. As a result, the story is enhanced or better in their eyes. On the other hand, some students have never gotten over disliking their grandmothers. For them, this story serves as a catalyst for old resentments. Many students can either relate to the story, or at least generate interest in it. Nearly all of them have taken a miserable automobile ride with their parents, and as a result, they read one text, and create another, deeper text of old memories. Both are fused simultaneously into a rich experience that is, for the most part, singular and unique to the reader. Who would have imagined in this day of multiculturalism the negative backlash by freshmen readers against an illegal Jamaican immigrant by the name of Jasmine, a character from Bharati Mukherjee's story of the same character title? In an unscientific poll of three sections of my freshman English course, the majority of students, including women, found Jasmine to be unlikeable, ingratiating, and far too amoral an immigrant to be taken seriously by aspiring American-born young adults. Few, if any, admired her courage; few saw their own ancestors in her creative adaptations to a foreign society; as a result, few deemed the story to be of much merit. Students were not interested in how the story was designed, how the story became a contemporary adaptation of the American dream, or how this story evolved into a more developed short novel. Few cared to look into the author's own experiences to see how art imitated life. No, the students just didn't "like" the story; few wanted to even have to talk about it, their biases and prejudices so profoundly caught up in our nation's discussion of Third World immigration.

Yet these attitudes which deeply affected the merit of "Jasmine" were mild compared to the outrage, disgust, and even silence when the same group of readers offered reactions to David Leavitt's short story "Territory." Most of the male students were angry that I had assigned this story of gay lovers. Women also reacted negatively, and hoped the class could spend as little time with the story as possible. As a group of reactionary readers, we couldn't even begin to talk about plot, about the mother-son relationship, or about any larger family themes. The students balked at having to read, to "experience in their heads," the backyard smooching scene which provoked strident, angry reactions with many of the heterosexual students.

In a textual- or authorial-based discussion, these attitudes become extraneous, incidental, peripheral. While they may be included in a discussion, when it is time to write, most students will be asked to rationally examine the artifice of "Jasmine," or "Territory," and as a result, considerable intrusive biases will be put aside in favor of reasoned, intelligent arguments. But the readers *are* angry, hostile, even belligerent. One of the best reader-response essays coming out of our reading of "Territory" was a pensive, affective "subtextual" analysis of a student's relationship to her lesbian sister whom she had disrespected for years. By reading "Territory," her own family experiences came under scrutiny, and the responsive essay became somewhat cathartic. Should the same reader have been instructed to react to the artful design of the story, or compare that story to a more heterosexual depiction, such as in Anton Chekov's "Lady with the Pet Dog"? Instructors have been doing that for years. Perhaps we can at least consider how valuable, how meaningful these varied reader responses actually are, and how central they are to the reading process.

Sensory perceptions, hatreds, biases, even old family stories of uncles as camp guards become central in the reading of provocative literature such as Borowski's (1991) short story "This Way for the Gas, Ladies and Gentlemen." The readers are simply not interested in discussing the narrator's perceptions, the careful and artistic design the author created of progressive horrors, or even that the author later committed suicide for having witnessed German atrocities. No, what the students want to talk about is how that story became so "real." For many, if not all, were either in tears, enraged, or nauseated by the treatment of human beings in Nazi concentration camps. Many talked about having actually smelled the "Portuguese sardines, bacon from Lublin...and authentic sweetmeats from Salonica" (p. 151).

One student regurgitated after reading the story. Many expressed how they felt powerless to help as witnesses to the unloading of endless numbers of cattle cars. Rage and anger became fundamental responses to the story. Many students expressed their idealism, that this could never happen again, despite hearing information about ethnic cleansing and abortion centers in Bosnia-Herzegovina. My student, Christopher, concluded his essay, the introduction of which appears at the beginning of this essay, with the following argument:

> The awful experiences of the holocaust were vividly played out in my mind. I read the story during a quiet afternoon after I was done with all my classes. I was in a good mood and read through the story rather quickly. While reading the story I became angered by the atrocities of the Nazi concentration camps and the total disregard of human life. Through Borowski's description of life at Auschwitz during World War II I feel that I can better understand the horrific occurrences of the holocaust than if I read a factual account. By writing a fictional story he made it easier for the reader to become engulfed by the story and experience more fully the horrors of what he went through. Instead of pitying Borowski and the terrible life he experienced, the reader feels as if he was in the camp and experiencing the horror himself.[2]

If art, particularly fiction, was intended to be a reexperiencing of an event in a reader's mind, then perhaps we need to look more carefully, and creatively, at the potential for bringing that "experience in the head" into the reader's reactionary or response prose. Freedman (1991) agrees. She argues,

> Students can be empowered rather than alienated by literature and composition courses when they are encouraged to trust—and then re-define—their emotional and interpretive impulses. It is liberating for them to see that as Mariolina Salvatori puts it, "Reading is construction, the composing of *oneself* [my emphasis] and the text through interaction with it." (p. 79)

While textual and biographical responses will always be a component of a literary response, we need to explore this new approach, for we may be astounded to realize that, despite our professional penchant for analysis, a reader of the text was always intended to be central, and integral to the textual narrative. Sensory, analogic, and attitudinal re-

---

[2] Closing argument of Christopher Price's essay, May 1994.

sponses may provide an essential "missing link" in our freshman writing classes. The challenge is to find creative ways to analyze this very mysterious, highly personal yet fundamental element of the total reading experience.

REFERENCES

Appleyard, J.A. (1990). *Becoming a reader: The experience of fiction from childhood to adulthood.* Cambridge, UK: Cambridge University Press.

Borowski, T. (1991). This way for the gas, ladies and gentlemen. In A. Charters (Ed.), *The story and its writer: An introduction to short fiction* (3rd ed., pp. 149–162). Boston: Bedford/St. Martin's Press. (Original story translation copyright 1967)

Freedman, D.P. (1991). Case studies and trade secrets: Allaying student fears in the lit comp classroom. *College Literature, 18*(1), 77–83. [Freedman quotes M. Salvatori (1983). Reading and writing a text: Correlation between reading and writing patterns. *College English, 45*(7), 657–686.]

Poulet, G. (1969). Phenomenology of reading. *New Literary History, 1,* 53–68.

Price, C. (1994). *On reading.* Unpublished essay, University of Wisconsin at Whitewater.

Probst, R.E. (1992). Writing from, of, and about literature. In N.J. Karolides (Ed.), *Reader response in the classroom: Evoking and interpreting meaning in literature* (pp. 117–127). White Plains, NY: Longman.

Reading, Writing, and Reality:
A Cultural Coming to Terms

Andrea R. Fishman

She appeared during office hours one day, the tall, tentatively graceful young woman from my 9:00 a.m. section of Effective Writing II, the second semester introductory composition course devoted to research writing.

"Can I talk to you a minute?" she asked, hovering in the doorway.

I pushed my chair away from the desk. "Sure, Lisa. C'mon on in. Sit down."

Lisa sat as tentatively as she stood. Barely perched on the edge of the chair she said, "I need to talk to you about something you said in class yesterday. It's really bothering me."

I could not imagine what I had said to produce the consternation evident in Lisa's dark eyes, not something I said in English 121, anyway. "Okay," I nodded, realizing she was waiting for permission to confront me.

"Did you mean what you said about truth? That there's no such thing as objectivity?" Lisa blurted out without further preface, more plea than question.

Oh, I thought. That. To me almost a throwaway line, intended to reassure students that when their research yields seemingly irreconcilable contradictions, they are on the right track, that in the exploration of such contradictions their writing will flourish. I knew that taken seriously, the idea of objectivity as an impossible stance challenges what most students want to believe. That notion prompts some wonderful discussion occasionally, but few students (high school, first year, or upper division) had ever wanted to continue talking about it after class. Certainly not the next day in my office.

"Yes, I meant it," I smiled, trying to loosen the tightness on Lisa's brow.

"But Professor, that can't be true!" she almost literally cried. "Some things have to be true!"

With that, Lisa launched a long, painful discussion of what she, in her words, "believed [her] whole life" and how my statement had to be wrong because it jeopardized her understanding of the world and

Originally published in Forum for Reading *(1996–1997), volume 27, pages 1–17*

everything in it. Her experiences, notably those with parents and preacher, had taught Lisa about Truth, with a capital T. And that was how she read the world, at least until college suggested another, different truth about her readings.

It is this other different truth I propose to explore here—that reading is about more than decoding and comprehending marks on a page. That reading is about worlds before it is about words. It is about how the world teaches each of us to read all the texts we encounter and produce—print and live, looked at and lived. And it is about how all our worlds are not the same and may as likely collide as merge, conflict as cooperate when students from various worlds come together in the college composition classroom, with each other and with us.

Of course, the notion of reading the world before the word is not original with me. Paulo Freire, one of the seminal thinkers about liberatory literacy, coined that elegant phrase. I want to extend and apply it, however, to people who may or may not be politically oppressed, or at least to people whose oppression is more diverse, more diffuse, and more difficult to both identify and remedy. I want to extend and apply it to the people many of us teach in our college reading or English classes—people like Lisa.

Before I return to Lisa, however, I want to consider a group of people who choose what some would call oppression but who find their chosen constraints more liberating than the paradoxically constrained freedom of their critics. I want to consider the Pennsylvania Amish, their small conservative culture, and their definitions of reading and writing the word and the world. After looking away at the Amish, we may look back to see our own classrooms differently.

Reading the (Amish) World

Consider seven-year-old Glenn, son of an Amish dairy farmer. He is a second grader at Meadow Brook, a typical one-room, eight-grade Amish school. Like second graders everywhere, Glenn is learning to read. One day he and his classmates read "On the Farm," a section in their health textbook about a child who develops an allergic reaction after eating too many strawberries. Glenn's teacher, Verna, conducted a typical question-and-answer lesson about the text. The questions are all Verna's, the answers the six second graders', responding anonymously by calling out when and if they think they know.

Q: Are strawberries good for you?

A: Yes.

Q: What could happen if you ate nothing but strawberries?

A: [no response]

Q: Does anybody know?

A: You would get as red as a strawberry.

Q: And would you itch too?

A: [no response]

Q: What do we call that?

A: [no response]

Q: Starts with an *H*.

A: Hyperactive.

Q: You'd get hives. That's what we call it when you get all red and itchy. What else were they working, besides picking strawberries?

A: [no response]

Q: Were they working anything else, Wilma?

A: Yes.

Q: What were they working?

A: [no response]

Q: Were they spraying trees?

A: Yes.

Q: What do we spray trees for?

A: [no response]

Q: So the insects don't get at the fruit?

A: [no response]

Q: Yes, that's why we spray. Look at the picture. What are they doing?

A: Picking apples.

At this point, Glenn speaks for the first time, objecting to his classmate's answer. "That's not farm work, picking apples," he says, telling the truth about work on his family's dairy farm. Yet Verna goes right on, as if Glenn never spoke:

Q: Look at the boy feeding cows in the picture. How many second graders ever gave cows something to eat?

A: [All but James raise their hands.]

Glenn never says another word.

In this lesson, all the children (but particularly Glenn) learn what it means to read books in school. Reading text at Meadow Brook means seeing what is on the page without regard for what is in your mind or your life beyond that print. "Say Yes to Books" might well be Verna's slogan (literally and figuratively) meaning not just "Do Read!" but "Don't Guess!" and, above all, "Don't question or disagree." "Just read as the second graders do. Accept, believe, and agree with what the author tells you. You may think you know better or differently, but don't. Don't think. Read." This message is clearly communicated in Verna's class.

Meadow Brook students understand and learn this lesson well. By the time they are in the upper grades, they are all successful readers. Consider this geography lesson, collaboratively constructed by Verna and her seventh and eighth graders, the oldest students in the school. The questions are Verna's. Students' anonymously called-out answers are in parentheses.

Who can tell me what the Sahara is? (a desert)

Does it get more or less than ten inches of rain? (less)

What part is covered with sand dunes? (three quarters)

What do they use to get water out of their wells? (pulleys)

How deep are their wells, about? (200 feet)

Is that average for around here, or are they deeper? Anybody know how deep their own well is? (275 or 285 feet)

Yes. And that's deeper. Now I want you to tell me about the lives of the people. Where do they live, and what is their work? (in tents; herding goats)

Why don't they build houses? (they move a lot)

Why do they have to move? (no response)

Because it gets too dry? (yes)

What other animals do they have in the Sahara besides goats? (camels)

What are *oases*? (no response)

How does an oasis work? (no response)

If we're in the desert and we get to an oasis, how do we know we've gotten to one? (see trees and water)

What works against them when they try to grow things? (sand storms)

What happens to the crops? (they're ruined)

Must everybody move away then? (yes)

These children know how to read. Despite the opportunity Verna creates for response from places beyond text, these students know such talk is peripheral. Talking about your family's well is not reading. These students know what counts as reading in school and what good readers do. They know what counts as learning and what good learners do: They recall what they know quickly, anonymously, and in ways that facilitate success of a group's lesson, not an individual's performance. That is what matters in their culture, how their culture reads the world (as a place of correctness and anonymity, community and conformity) so that is how their culture defines reading the word and teaches them to read.

Writing the (Amish) World

Correctness and anonymity, community and conformity shape Amish writing and Meadow Brook writing pedagogy as well. Much writing is done at Meadow Brook, much of it similar to what goes on in mainstream schools, elementary through college. One variety is writing in service of reading, answering end-of-chapter text questions on paper instead of out loud. Consider Meadow Brook's eighth graders, its senior class, as consummate student readers writing about what they have read.

The story is in their basal reader, *Our Heritage*, called "The Joker." It tells of boarding school boys who learn a predictable lesson about playing practical jokes on schoolmates. The text asks five questions about the story. Each question that follows is followed by the answers the three eighth graders wrote and submitted to Verna:

"What was the joke the boys played on Eddie Davis?"

• Daniel: moved the furniture into Charlie's room

• Richard: moved his furniture in another room

• Davie: hid his stuff

"Why did they choose Eddie to play [the joke] on? What does the word gullible mean?"

- Daniel: they could make believe things that aren't so, easily tricked
- Richard: He was afraid of Charlie easy to be tricked
- Davie: He didn't get mad at him, easily fooled

"What type of person was Dennis Conron? Use parts of the story as evidence for what you say."

- Daniel: short and cheerful
- Richard: cheerful looking boy
- Davie: Short cheerful little boy

"Do you feel Dennis could be blamed for Eddie's accident? Write a paragraph explaining your feelings on this."

- Daniel: yes
- Richard: yes
- Davie: yes, because he did it

"Did Eddie ever understand the joke? Explain."

- Daniel: yes, because the joker did it
- Richard: yes, they told him all about it
- Davie: yes, *because it says* (italics added)

This is the Sahara lesson written down. As they had in their geography lesson, these eighth graders confront direct recall questions with follow-up questions designed to help answer the first. Where textbook questions go beyond direct recall to require evidence, explanation, or opinion, however, these students respond barely if at all. They provide short yes-or-no answers wherever possible. They have learned that what matters to readers and writers is what "it says," as Davie put it. Right answers exist. They are best when attributed to the text and the same as everyone else's. Embellishment is not necessary; accuracy is. Once again correctness counts, serving community and conformity, serving the culture in which the writing occurs.

This cultural definition of what counts as reading, writing, and learning continues in two other mainstream-familiar genres: the secondary-source report and the composition. Upper grade students at

Meadow Brook participate in "nature study," a subject for which these fifth through eighth graders write what they call their "'nature study books." For these "books," Verna distributes six purple ditto master pages with a particular flower's name and outline on one side, the other side blank for student writing about that particular plant.

Fifth grader Katie Mae, Daniel's sister, wrote the following report on forget-me-nots for her booklet:

> Forget-me-not, name given to plants of the genus Myositis, belonging to the family Boraginaceae (q.v.). They are found in temperate zones in all parts of the world. A number of species are common in ditches and damp meadows of the United States. The true Forget-me-not, M. scorpioides, has creeping perennial roots with ascending stems bearing small sky blue flowers. The most popular horticultural Forget-me-nots are varieties of M. sylvatica, admired especially for the brilliancy of their blue flowers. They are used extensively for ground cover in gardens and borders, and beside pools and streams. A dark blue species, the Azores Forget-me-not, M. azorica, requires greenhouse cultivation in temperate regions. The romantic name is derived from the last words of a legendary German knight drowned while attempting to retrieve the flower for his lady. The End

Readers distressed that a culture can define writing as copying (or what we call plagiarism) are reading through the same cultural lens I first used when I encountered the institutionally supported copying that counts as researched writing at Meadow Brook. For it is not just in Katie's nature study booklet that I saw copying, it is in all her classmates' booklets, too. And it is in the seventh and eighth graders' geography reports, and in every other use of secondary sources by anyone at Meadow Brook School.

As my eyes adjusted to the Amish view of writing, however, I saw something I had overlooked before: plagiarism is only plagiarism if your culture sees it that way. And your culture will see copying as a crime only if it values originality, if it considers style and ideas "things" that can be "owned," and if it believes imitation is the sincerest form of flattery only to the extent to which imitators credit models—none of which describe the Amish view of the world.

It is other, more Amish-appropriate beliefs that produce definitions of literacy and learning which send children to copy Funk and Wagnalls verbatim:

Belief #1: Truth is immutable, unchanging, and found in books, beginning with the Bible. Because of this, no one tinkers with truth; no one presumes to "put it into [their] own words." The resulting definitions?

- Reading = finding the text-bound truth
- Writing = putting on paper the text-bound truth
- Learning = acknowledging the truth as it is read, as it is written

Belief #2: Right and wrong answers exist for every question, including the question, "What is the truth about Forget-me-nots?" It is important to be right, important not to be wrong. Therefore,

- Reading = finding the right answer
- Writing = recording the right answer
- Learning = focusing on right answers, to the exclusion of all other possible ideas which, by definition, must be wrong

Belief #3: Time is valuable; it should never be wasted because there is too much work to be done and too little time in which to do it. Therefore, it is a waste of time to restate something already perfectly well stated. Reading, writing, and learning, then, mean identifying, echoing, and remembering information in the most time-efficient manner (i.e., by reciting or copying it verbatim).

Belief #4: Perhaps the most significant belief of all—Originality is prideful. It is an attempt to say, "Look at me; see what I've done; notice how much better I am than everyone else." No Amish person—woman, man, or child—would ever want to say that, so no Amish student would ever want to claim that he or she writes as well as a published writer does, as a book does. So even if they do not use MLA or APA or any other baroque academic citation system, Amish children are *not* saying, "Look what I wrote," when they hand in a copied page. Rather, they are saying, "Here are the facts, here is the truth about this topic, read and presented as accurately and efficiently as I could." Implicit definitions: Reading, writing, and learning are matters of copying—not copying to claim, or dissemble, or stand out, but copying to find, acknowledge, and remember the truth and to implicitly credit texts as the source of that truth.

Therefore, plagiarism—or more accurately in Amish culture, copying—is not only the sincerest form of flattery; copying is the truest, most accurate, most time-effective way to read, write, learn, and even to be.

What about the second written genre, the composition? Here are two: one by fifth grader Katie, author of "Forget-me-not," the other by her eighth-grade brother, Daniel.

My Dog [by Katie]

My dog is little. He's mostly black but has a little white.

He's not too old yet. His name is Rover. He is a fat puppy!!!! His good habits are, he barks when people come, he does not run away, he is not scared of people. He runs up to them and bits them.

His bad habits are, he runs after cars, trucks and other things. He follows us to school, he gets Moms things, he likes to chew on soft things. When I go out to milk he comes and likes to chew on my shoe strings. The End

Rex [by Daniel]

He is brown and black mixed. He is about six feet tall. I have him around half a year.

His good habits are he doesn't kick and his bad habits are he tries to bite you. He doesn't follow me around. I didn't have him long enough to see how he got along with other horses.

The future of him is Rex and I are going to live together in an old shack.

What are the cultural beliefs and definitions of literacy and learning implicit in these compositions and their assignment? Again, they reflect the Amish values of correctness, conformity, and community:

Belief #1: Some topics (i.e., scenes or stories in the world) are appropriate for consideration in speech or writing, and some are not. Children must learn to read the world accordingly, to comprehend the culture's concept of appropriateness, so teachers must assign topics that model such culturally appropriate reading as Verna did: "Write a composition about your pet."

Belief #2: Right and wrong ways exist for doing everything, including writing. Students must learn how many paragraphs to write; they must learn what to put in them—which is exactly what we see in these papers. Verna told her students to write three paragraphs: in the first one, "give a description of your pet"; in the second one, "give his good and bad habits"; and in the third one, "give his future." Daniel did exactly as instructed, right down to saying "the future of him is...." Katie, however, did not understand or did not relate to "give his future." She did know, though, that she needed more than two paragraphs, so she negotiated the terms of the assignment, splitting Rover's description and habits into two paragraphs each.

Belief #3: Time and efficiency are again paramount. Writing should be done and gotten over with. Three paragraphs suffice, so learn to write no more, no less. Students will try to learn that, even if they must negotiate the terms of the assignment to do it.

Reading and Writing Realities on Campus

As readers realize, these beliefs and their resulting definitions of reading and writing, or literacy at Meadow Brook, do not differ significantly from those found at more culturally mainstream schools—right-answer orientation to reading, not only of history or health text but of literature; writing assignments that are really just fill-in-the-very-large-blanks tests; research paper assignments that produce plagiarized accuracy which, when pointed out to students, bring some variation of the response, "But I thought that was what you wanted." Our students think that some minor variation on plagiarizing is what they are supposed to do, even though we inveigh against it. Students think that is what it means to read and write the word because that is how they have learned to read the world.

This is what frustrates many of them and many of us. We all see the vast amount of reading required by college professors. We see syllabi calling for hundreds of pages each week. We see a highlighter market expanded from only yellow to a rainbow of neon colors suggesting that something called "reading" occurred on every page where their trail appears. Where did our students get the idea that highlighting important points equals reading? Where did they get the idea that few points on a page are *not* important? What does our basic, K–12 school culture believe and teach them? That truth is found in books? That everything in books is true and important? That right and wrong answers exist? That students have too much work to do to waste time stopping to think? Could that be how students learned to read and write papers not only with highlighters but also with Xerox machines?

It would be easy to agree that this is the case in many high schools. It would also be easy to object strenuously to those teachers' unexamined definitions of reading and writing. It is more difficult, however, when we examine those definitions in light of the competing cultural beliefs that prompt our own definition of plagiarism rather than simply its practice.

Most of us define plagiarism as something negative because our culture believes ideas can be original, can be owned, as can ways of expressing them. In fact, we believe the best ideas are original and the best writing styles are too. Further, we believe that the purpose of higher education is higher order thinking, that college students must learn *not* to accept everything they are told, must learn to distinguish between the important and unimportant, to identify relevant truths, and to cope with competing belief systems. For these reasons, we tell students: "Say it in your own words!" "Think for yourself!" "Don't just summarize—analyze, synthesize, evaluate. This is college, not high school."

We say these things and we believe them. At the same time, however, we require citation and quotation marks. As academics, we are trained and required to bow to all our predecessors, to recognize our intellectual debts, to couch our own thinking in tentative, derivative terms. Not until we have earned "terminal" degrees may we say other than "it seems," "it may be that," or "a case could be made for...." So as we initiate our first-year students into academia, we may say "This is college"—meaning, "Think for yourself." But we also say in many more powerful ways (including in our assignments and our grades): "Get it right," "get it all," and "get it from authoritative sources"—meaning, "Get it from someone else, from someone else's text."

The corollary of this intellectual paradox is a pedagogical one. We say college students can and should learn to work collaboratively, to participate in what Bruffee (1993) calls (in 1984 terms) the "conversation of mankind." We say that classrooms are places where real discussion should happen. Real intellectually involving, intellectually challenging talk should be supported, not traditional initiation/response or question/answer teacher talk as modeled by Verna and her students, but real participatory conversation among peers facilitated by a mentor.

But how can we have that talk, have real collaboration among people who enter our classrooms from so many cultural backgrounds? From places with so many competing, contradictory definitions of reading and writing, of what it means to teach and to learn? In other words, what exactly are our students unprepared—or underprepared—to do?

I suggest they are unprepared not only to read hundreds of pages a week but, more significantly, they are unprepared to think about why they should do that reading in the first place—to think about what counts as reading, or what it means to write. I suspect that many of them have Amish-like understanding of what it means to find and use textual information—Amish-like expectations of being told what to do and how, a sense that theirs is not to wonder why but just to do as they are told—or drop out.

Imagine putting siblings Sarah, Daniel, or Katie Mae in a classroom and telling them to work with peers, to learn collaboratively. What a pointless, if not impossible, exercise for them! Why should people work together to do what can most efficiently be done alone? Why sit side by side and talk when you should be getting your work done? Unless a task is truly collaborative (something individuals could not possibly do or do efficiently alone) group work is nothing more than a shared scavenger hunt. Or in the words of some of my students when first introduced to collaborative learning, "This is the blind leading the blind." Many of my students, like Daniel and Katie, believe only I (the professor, the teacher) can see.

Neither my students nor Amish students believe that outside of school, however. What counts as reading in school is not necessarily the same as what counts as reading outside school or simply outside the curriculum, even for the same readers. Daniel's sister Sarah illustrates this difference when she reads at home. First she reads the world to choose texts differently; then, she reads the world to read words differently.

When Sarah started "running with the young folks" (the Amish term for the semiformal, semistructured socializing their older teenagers do), she started reading *True Story* and *True Confessions* magazines. Purchased at the local drugstore, these magazines with their stories of unrequited love and troubled relationships, their sad endings and sad-der-but-wiser heroines, fascinated Sarah, who learned to read at Meadow Brook School.

I was amazed and even a bit appalled that Anna allowed her daughter to read these publications, which Sarah in no way tried to hide from her mother. "She likes reading about other girls' experiences," Anna explained to me. "Sometimes she can't believe that people could treat each other the way they do in some of those stories. I told her, 'There are some things in there we don't believe,' and she said, 'I know that.'"

At home with her mother or in the community with her friends, Sarah is not reading "The Joker" or other *Our Heritage*-type stories. She is reading *True Story* and *True Confessions*— texts she could never bring to school, texts that speak to her life of "girls' experiences," texts to which she has very powerful personal responses. When she discusses these texts with others, it is not to review facts or summarize what "it says" but to discuss why people behave as they do, what they believe, the relationships between belief and behavior, and how some people's truths are not others. This is collaborative learning and higher order thinking.

Some readers may be distressed by what seems the naive acceptance of *True Story* and *True Confessions* narratives as, in fact, true. I know I was appalled that they "believe that stuff" which is exactly what I said to Anna: "You believe that stuff?"

"Don't you?" she asked in return.

"No," I replied quickly, but my assurance faded in the face of her truly ingenuous question and my own internal questioning: "How do I know it isn't true?" How in this world of Lorena Bobitt, the Menendez brothers, Tonya Harding, Susan Smith, Kato Kaelin, and O.J. Simpson can I know those magazine stories are not true? How in this world of Oprah and Phil, Montel and Maury, Sally Jesse and Ricki and all their guests can I know what is truth and what is fiction? And if reading is culturally defined as "finding a moral lesson for my life in the text," as it seems to be outside of school for the Amish, why should anyone want to draw hard and fast genre lines at all? Or media lines, for that matter?

Consider film. Now a discipline of its own, film study requires that students read film as text, and many teachers at all levels use movies in the classroom. But what do we think it means to read movies? Consider how the Amish read them. When the Harrison Ford movie about the Amish, *Witness*, was being filmed literally in the neighborhood near Meadow Brook School, Anna read the almost daily articles about it in her local newspaper. One day, however, she was particularly distressed. The newspaper had recounted a scene in which Ford, a Philadelphia police officer dressed as an Amishman, gets angry at a tourist who wants to take his photograph. The newspaper described the action: He tells the woman that if she dares to photograph him, he will take her brassiere and wrap it around her neck. Anna was appalled.

"No Amishman would do that!" she exclaimed.

"But he's not Amish. He's a Philadelphia cop," I pointed out.

"But he's dressed Amish. People will think he's Amish."

I tried to explain how movies work, how people will understand the fiction within the fiction. How we separate the real world from the movie world, and accept the movie on its own terms for the purpose of the theatrical experience. Something called "suspension of disbelief," I told her. "Does that help?" I asked.

Anna just shook her head. "No, that doesn't help," she insisted, as much about the world's reading as her own.

It was not until much later that I realized the absence of fiction as a way of construing the world in reading or writing precludes film "fictions," too. Suspension of disbelief is a cultural construct, one designed for our hours in the theater, applied to our hours in books. It is a sophisticated rationalization for what Anna and Sarah do when reading the word or the world all the time, an intellectual excuse for entering into life in personal ways.

So how do the young folks, Anna and Sarah, define reading? The most striking feature of their definition is that reading is something to discuss with other people, with friends or parents. You tell them how exciting stories are or that you "can't believe" that people could do what the people in this or that story do to each other. You talk about, and ultimately agree on, how awful that is. You talk about, and clearly agree on, how wrong that is as far as "we" are concerned. Reading outside school is about agreeing, but not necessarily with the text. Reading outside school is about readers questioning, about readers thinking. It is still right-answer oriented, but right answers are searched out and consensus reached among readers, not through instruction from one reader to the rest. Reading outside school has room for everyone. When Anna, Sarah, and I talk—share, compare, or debate our very different readings of the world and the word—that is collaborative learning and higher order thinking none of us could do alone.

Perhaps the most startling "truth" I learned from the Amish resulted from reading the world, not the word. One day, Sarah and Daniel came running into the house after school, afraid they were going to be late. "Late for what?" I asked Anna. "For the sleepover," she replied nonchalantly.

It took a minute for me to really hear what she said. Then I did an aural double take. "The sleepover?" I said, sure I had misheard or she had misspoken. "Sarah and Daniel are going to the same sleepover?"

Anna looked at me, honestly confused by my confusion. "Sure."

"You're letting them go to a *co-ed* sleepover?" I pressed. Anna continued looking at me but said nothing. She did not seem to get my point.

"I would never let Matthew go to a co-ed sleepover," I said flatly, referring to my son who is Daniel's age. "No one I know would ever even have co-ed sleepovers." I paused. "Aren't you worried about what they'll do?"

"No," Anna slowly shook her head. Then she smiled, suddenly realizing what I meant. "Our kids would never do that," she laughed. "If anyone even tried any funny stuff, everyone else would stop them."

Peer pressure works both ways, she was suggesting, depending on the culture of the peers. Frankly, I did not believe her. Adolescents are adolescents, I thought to myself. Hormones are hormones, in Amish bodies or otherwise. I could not envision reading the "facts" of human biology any other way.

A few months later, however, I saw a different story unfold. It was late summer and I had driven all of Anna's family to the cabin we owned at a nearby lake. One of the lakeside concessions rented pedal boats, and the children were eager to try these contraptions, so Anna and I stood in line to rent several for their use.

The line was long. August is hot in central Pennsylvania, and there are very few beaches where people can cool off, so we were surrounded not only by other families but also by groups of teenagers in assorted shapes, sizes, and bathing suits. In front of us, in fact, was a teenage girl in one of the smallest bathing suits Anna or I had ever seen. It was the first season of the string bikini, and neither of us could keep from staring.

Suddenly, Daniel appeared. He wanted to ask his mother a question. This 16-year-old boy saw what we were staring at, looked once, looked away, and never looked back. He had a brief conversation with Anna, then returned to the family picnic table without another word. I could not believe it. And I said as much to Anna. Daniel certainly noticed. Why didn't he look?

"He was probably embarrassed," she told me.

"Embarrassed? Because of me?" I wondered.

Anna laughed. "No, it had nothing to do with you, or even with him. He was probably embarrassed for her," she explained, nodding toward the nearly naked young lady. "He probably felt sorry for her. Wondered what kind of person would let herself be seen like that. It's really sad, you know."

Anna's reading of the situation, and Daniel's, were clearly unlike mine. It never occurred to me that a 16-year-old boy would look away from a beautiful, nearly naked young woman. It never occurred to me that hormones did not necessarily rage through adolescents, causing them to behave in unavoidable, inevitable ways. It never occurred to me that my culture's definition of adolescence was one among many. It never occurred to me, in other words, to read the world through a lens other than the one my culture had surreptitiously slipped over my eyes.

It is this lesson about reading the world, about each of us writing our own version of life and truth, that may be the most important notion I posit. The question of how I define reading and writing, teaching and learning, for example, depends on what my culture has taught me to believe is true. And I refer to the cultural amalgam of all my cultures—of my campus and my department, of my academic discipline and my kindergarten through doctorate education, of all that I learned in my very particular experiences as a child, a teenager, a woman. How my definitions interact with those of my students determines the culture we will create together in the classroom we share. Which brings me full circle to Lisa and her Meadow Brook–like definitions of reading and writing as the search for Truth, with a capital T.

I wish I had had a tape recorder in my office that day. I wish I could recall everything Lisa said and everything I said, but I cannot. All I remember is the pain in her eyes and my sense of myself as both the cause of and possible cure for that pain. All I remember is trying to explain the notions of competing interpretations and concurring interpretive communities of the human conversation that has been going on for centuries: How what I bring to a text as a middle-aged, divorced, Jewish woman born and raised in New York City is different from what she or my male colleagues or even my other female colleagues may bring. How all the books in the library cannot be bibles; how maybe none of them are. How the science lab, lecture hall, and library are not churches. How she certainly can, and should, search for truth; consider competing possible truths; accept, debate, or discard what others posit as truth. How she is author of her own truth. How what she thinks, her deliberation and decision-making processes matter as much as anyone's in our classroom. How difficult I know it is to even imagine believing something contrary to what her parents and home community believe. How all I expect is her conscious and conscientious participation in the process of reading and writing the world as well as the word. How all I expect is exactly what she came to my freshman English classroom unprepared to do.

These are not just my expectations, however. They are the purpose of higher education, too. Colleges and universities exist not only to help students develop skills and find jobs, but to help them find and create meaning in their lives, in their work, and in their worlds—for themselves and for others as well.

REFERENCE

Bruffee, K.A. (1993). *Collaborative learning: Higher education, interdependence, and the authority of knowledge.* Baltimore: Johns Hopkins University Press.

SECTION II

■ Research

Although theory, research, and pedagogy are closely related interactive elements that concern literacy professionals, research is the vehicle that facilitates the systematic examination of those issues and questions we have about the field. Researchers generally set out to do one of the following as they design and implement studies: (a) identify the problems they believe interfere with the achievement goals we set for learners, (b) increase their understanding of how literacy functions, and (c) determine which literacy efforts are most effective given a set of specific conditions (Shanahan, 2002).

We, the editors of this volume, believe that theory and informed practice can influence the types of questions we raise and the problems we address in the research we conduct. However, we are aware that even well-conceived research is just one among the various intervening variables or factors that shape the pedagogy practiced in college classrooms. Political climate, institutional policies, and the status of teacher knowledge and commitment are some of the factors that interact in ways for which we cannot always account to determine the quality of instruction and learning that students experience. Yet, without the influence of ongoing research, teachers, administrators, and other decision makers would find it difficult to provide a rationale for and have confidence in the practices evident in many college reading, writing, and study skills programs.

Research in college literacy addresses issues related to teaching, learning, and assessing areas of reading and study skills and written composition. The articles presented in this section include comprehensive reviews of literature, informal reports of practices that represent the early stages of potential full-blown investigations, and formal reports of studies. The articles also explore attitudes and perceptions students and teachers have about literacy and emerging computer use.

This section begins with literature reviews. Eanet and Camperell describe quantitative and qualitative research that suggests how students manage literacy tasks. They identify student-perceived problems, discuss conclusions they drew from the research, and raise questions they believe are important for practitioners to consider as they assist students on a daily basis in the classroom. The article by Bartel explores the search for what readers determine to be important in texts as they read and mark text for the purpose of learning and remembering. The practice of directing students to find the main ideas in texts yet providing them with little or no guidance as to how to do it has left countless students frustrated and anxious about reading. Bartel's review explores the underlying thinking that guides readers to mark texts in ways that accurately reflect importance (or what often can be marked as main ideas) and likely to lead to improved comprehension and learning.

Next, qualitative studies are presented. Henrichs's investigation describes proficient students' reading behavior and the potential use of information gained from proficient readers to assist less able readers. Her use of interviews and selected reading of content texts yielded data that challenge teachers to consider tailoring instruction to specifically assessed needs.

The next two are examples of descriptive, naturalistic research that provide readers with extensive contextual information. Laine explores students' perceptions regarding the reading and writing relationships in a paired course through an analysis of field notes, interviews, and student writing. The naturalistic, real-classroom setting of the study provides a model that can be easily adapted for teaching and learning. Guenther and Anderson also take a naturalistic approach in their investigation of an instructor who assumed the role of student to learn more about what it means to study successfully in a specific content course. Like Laine's study, their work provides an instructor-as-learner perspective. These descriptive studies are designed to uncover issues and problems that instructors and learners experience in college classes.

The remaining articles in this section are best described as quantitative; they increase our understanding of how processes and activities work and/or suggest what can be effective practice in specific conditions. Orlando, Caverly, Swetnam, and Flippo address the problem of study from a text-reading perspective. Through the use of student and faculty questionnaires and follow-up faculty interviews, they have determined the amount of time required for reading, the role of reading as compared to other class activities, and the relationship of assigned reading to course examinations. Hayes's study investigates the relative effectiveness of three study tasks for learning factual information. His comparison of the use of composing, self-questioning, and study guides has yielded results practitioners can consider as they engage in ongoing instructional decision making.

Next, de la Pena approaches English as a foreign language (EFL) students' reading of expository text. Two studies are reported, one that provides a description of student responses to instruction that focused on grammar, and the other that details what happens when students receive text structure guidance. Each approach has provided information about EFL students' summarizing efforts. O'Hear and Ashton explore the relation between main ideas in text and readability. Their results have implications for textbook writers and classroom instructors. This section continues with Hamer's description of an instructor's attempt to infuse writing activities into a reading class.

The section concludes with two investigations that reflect emerging trends in the field. Valeri-Gold and Commander explore the possibility that one of the many factors that may negatively affect underprepared college readers is their belief that reading is a feminine activity. This study, like the other descriptive investigations, identifies a problematic area that may need to be addressed if those attitudes interfere with student literacy growth and development. Scales's article details the use of technology in 1994. Her update reminds us of the rapidly expanding developments in technology and their impact on teaching and learning in the college classroom.

In summary, articles describing research in this section vary in methodology, content, and author perspective. The two literature reviews provide information that focuses on student notions of what it means to study and learn. They also offer the reader a strong basis for exploring and designing advanced studies in how-to or process learning in areas like text marking. The qualitative and quantitative studies address proficient reader characteristics, reading and writing relationships perceptions, difficult study, text demands, study guides, summarizing strategies and EFL learners, main idea clues, in-class writing, sexist attitudes and reading, and classroom computer use. Authors of these articles represent a range of teaching and research experiences. Like the others, this section offers a wealth of ideas for literacy specialists.

REFERENCE

Shanahan, T. (2002). What reading research says: The promises and limitations of applying research to reading education. In A.E. Farstrup & S.J. Samuels (Eds.), *What research has to say about reading instruction* (3rd ed., pp. 8–24). Newark, DE: International Reading Association.

Students' Conceptions of Learning, Their Motivations, and Their Approaches to Study

Marilyn G. Eanet and Kay Camperell

A rich body of research from Great Britain, Sweden, and Australia relevant to the concerns of college reading specialists has scarcely been discussed in the American literature. This body of research about learning in higher education offers us another perspective and, perhaps, fresh insights on the issues which most concern us helping students become both academically successful and effective learners. The purpose of this paper is to provide a brief introduction to this body of work and to present and discuss three conclusions from this literature that we find particularly useful to our thinking about instruction in college reading and study skills.

Overview of the Research

The British and Swedish researchers who have focused on the broader issues of student learning in higher education include Marton, Hounsell, and Entwistle (1984) and their colleagues. Their work has been done within a research framework that is different from those that have been typically used in this country—a qualitative or "phenomenographic" approach. This approach is different from more traditional research in terms of the researcher's focus or process, the perspective taken, and the attention given to contextual and content validity. We will briefly address each area in turn.

1. Process orientation—the research examines directly the *process* of student learning instead of looking at *effects* of student learning such as student performance on a criterion measure, in a course or in a program.

2. Perspective—learning is examined from the *students' perspective*, using students' perceptions of their college learning experience

Originally published in Forum for Reading *(1989), volume 21, number 1, pages 50–56*

as the most significant part of the data base. This information was obtained through the use of interviews, questionnaires, and inventories which were systematically collected and analyzed. (In some cases, follow-up experiments were devised to test the understandings learned from this data.)

3. Contextual validity—the focus of the research has been on "natural study"; i.e., what students actually do as they study actual content in real courses in higher education.

4. Content validity—attention has also been given to how students' approaches differ across disciplines.

In justifying his choice of a less traditional methodology, Entwistle (1984, p. 12) points out the limitations of the traditional perspectives of educational psychologists. He claims that such research, rooted in an external view of the student, tends to "blame" the student for low achievement (i.e., the student lacks ability, is not organized, does not apply strategies). Further, Entwistle believes that traditional research fails to account either for individual differences in studying or for the complete context in which learning takes place, both factors obviously worthy of consideration.

These research efforts have involved a community of scholars at different universities and colleges in different countries for a period of well over a decade. This fact has provided opportunity for the development of the underlying ideas in different research settings. While Entwistle and Märton (1984) see this "cross-pollination of ideas" as a strength of the work, at least one critic describes the degree of collaboration involved with some of the work as "incestuous" (Wilson, 1981).

Whatever advantages or disadvantages the magnitude and breadth of these research efforts have for its ultimate validity, they do pose several for its readers. First, it was impractical, if not impossible, to examine primary documents both in terms of accessibility and sheer volume. Therefore, this article is based on more accessible secondary sources, usually written by the original researchers. Second, understanding specific terminology was sometimes difficult: some concepts evolved over time, changing meaning but not labels. Also different researchers used different terms for very similar concepts. Thus, this article is not a critical review of the research; it is a discussion of a few key concepts that seem to be both adequately substantiated and reasonably well accepted across the board.

An additional quality of this work that we found appealing was the fact that the consideration of affective factors such as intention and motivation has been an integral part of a number of the studies. These studies include Gibbs, Morgan, and Taylor's (1984) case study explorations of "educational orientation"; by which they mean the student's personal context for learning—the student's "aims, values, and purposes." Using a more traditional approach, the Australian researcher John Biggs (1984) has examined the relationship between students' motivation and their learning strategies.

American researchers interested in learning about and affecting student learning such as Dansereau and Weinstein (see, for example, articles by each in Segal, Chipman, & Glaser, 1985) have focused on identifying effective learning strategies and training students in the use of these strategies. Such work is based in psychological research on memory, learning, and cognitive processes, and it uses a more traditional methodology and perspective (that of the outside, objective observer). The research being discussed here, which is based on a different perspective (the view of the learner) and a different research paradigm (social anthropological), has the potential to provide different, perhaps even complementary, insights.

Three Useful Conclusions

Three conclusions reached by these researchers particularly relevant to college reading specialists are

1. Many students have a predilection for either a deep or surface approach to studying.
2. The way students conceptualize learning influences how they approach learning.
3. Students adopt learning strategies according to the motives that they bring to learning.

Deep vs. Surface Approaches to Studying

Studies examining students' purposes as they study have concluded that the major distinction that students express as they describe how they learn is between the intention to understand and the intention to memorize (Gibbs, Morgan, & Taylor, 1982). Märton and Säljö (1976) labeled this distinction as being between a "deep" or "surface" approach, terms that they chose because of the metaphorical resemblance to Craik and Lockhart's (1972) "levels of processing" concept. The idea is somewhat analogous to Ausubel's "meaningful" or "rote" learning, and Entwistle prefers the terms "understanding" vs. "reproducing," but the underlying conceptualization is basically the same.

What are the characteristics of a surface approach? Students who use it see the learning task as the goal to be accomplished; they fail to relate the various aspects of the task to each other or to other tasks. They seem to avoid seeking either personal meaning or other meaning that the tasks might have, and they rely heavily on memory, reproducing surface aspects of the task. In contrast, students who take a deep approach seek the meaning inherent in the tasks, integrate aspects of the task into the whole, make the task personally meaningful, and even try to theorize and hypothesize about the task (Biggs, 1984).

In terms of reading, a student taking a surface approach would focus on the text itself reproducing "what the author says," while a student taking a deep approach would focus on the author's intentions and be able to discuss what he/she thinks the author means and the implications of that meaning. Or as Märton and Säljö put it, the fundamental difference between the approaches is one of "whether students interpreted the text itself as what was to be learned, or conceived the text as *the means* through which they sought to...change their conceptions about historical developments, economic processes, or whatever" (1984, p. 50).

Although the research establishes that many students have a favored approach, they can and may use the other approach on occasion. For example, approach can be induced by task demands. In reading instruction, we often try to induce a deep approach by asking "higher level" questions about the text, or by requiring integration tasks such as summary writing. While such tasks are well-intentioned and sometimes helpful, they have their limitations. Students may indeed learn to summarize and give the impression of taking the deep approach when in reality they may have only shifted tasks: The new task becomes "reading to write the summary," not reading to grasp the meaning and alter one's conceptions about the topic as would be characteristic of a genuine deep approach (Märton & Säljö, 1984).

Study out of genuine interest tends to induce a deep approach, and lack of interest, perceptions of threat or anxiety about the task correlate with a surface approach (Märton & Säljö, 1984). Märton and Säljö also suggest that in the context of everyday studying, a deep approach relates primarily to the realization that the facts that one is studying refer to some aspect of the real world and that by studying one can improve one's understanding of it.

Svenson points out that the student who uses a deep approach is rewarded with the "pleasure of understanding" (Svenson, 1984, p. 69). The student who uses the deep approach is also generally rewarded with academic success, although there are exceptions to this. These exceptions may occur when the evaluation is set up, either deliberately or through ignorance, to reward surface learning. Also, certain content, in the sciences or engineering, for example, may require much more attention to surface factual and procedural learning in the early stages of mastering a topic (Svenson, 1984). But, in general, taking a deep approach appears to be concomitant with a higher quality of learning outcome (Märton & Säljö, 1984; Van Rossum & Schenk, 1984).

Conceptions of Learning

One way the researchers have probed the reasons for the surface/depth differences in study approaches is by asking students exactly what they mean by learning. Answers to this question fall into one of five categories:

1. Learning means an increase of knowledge.
2. Learning means memorizing.
3. Learning means the acquisition of facts or procedures to be used in practice.
4. Learning involves abstraction of meaning.
5. Learning is an interpretation process aimed at the understanding of reality (Gibbs, 1983).

These responses can be further categorized by recognizing that 1 and 2 present the *how* and *why* of the surface or reproductive approach (one increases knowledge by memorizing), and 4 and 5 represent the *how* and *why* of the deep or constructive approach (one abstracts meaning from learning materials in order to understand reality). In an experimental situation, Van Rossum and Schenk (1984) found the expected relationship between first-year university students' conceptions of learning and their uses of either a deep or surface approach to studying. That is, most students who saw learning as memorizing or increasing knowledge took a surface approach with the assigned reading tasks, and, conversely, students who held the view that learning was abstracting meaning in order to better understand reality tended to use a deep-level approach.

Because the emphasis in phenomenographic research is on understanding rather than explanation, the idea that some students probably take a deep or surface approach *because* it is congruent with their concept of learning is not explicitly stated by most of the researchers. However, Gibbs (1983), in an article discussing some practical applications that he has derived from some of this research, does draw that implication. Gibbs uses the idea that a student's learning approach might stem from the student's conception of learning to make a case against the teaching of study skills, per se. His argument is that a student can master a specific study skill, such as note-taking or previewing, which the student will then use in service of his/her own conception of learning. Thus Gibbs views study skills and strategies as neutral techniques— which are *assumed* to improve learning outcomes (examination scores, etc.), but which may have very little positive impact on actual learning.

Anyone who has worked in college reading and study skills for any length of time will probably identify with and provide abundant examples to support Gibbs's point; especially in the first year of college, we find students who have been taught a technique like SQ3R and who are "applying it" mechanically with a corresponding lack of either understanding or academic success.

Gibbs acknowledges that as a study counselor he does help students develop techniques for implementing study, and he also works to help students become more "cue conscious" to academic conventions and to various study task demands. However, he sees as his most important job, and the only one with lasting value, the task of helping students "learn how to learn," which he defines as "a developmental process in which people's conceptions of learning evolve" (p. 83).

Given that students do have differing conceptions about learning, an obvious question at this point is "why?" Where do these conceptions originate, and how are they formed? While Gibbs's developmental approach would suggest that conceptions of learning are concurrent with or even the result of students' intellectual maturity, he obviously feels that this development can be advanced through intervention such as the study counseling that he provides. Van Rossum and Schenk (1984) suggest that conceptions of learning are largely formed in a person's upbringing and in their prior educational experiences. For example, they account for the surface reproductive learning conceptions that they found in many first-year university students with the emphasis on memorization in secondary schools (in their case, in the Netherlands). We would suspect that the structure and values of the larger culture have considerable impact. The researchers cited thus far are all from either the British Isles or Northern Europe. A colleague who has taught in the Middle East reminded us that the first two conceptions of learning are typical of the educational purposes in more traditional cultures in which cultural reproduction is of primary concern. Certainly, we would predict that the third conception—learning as acquiring facts or procedures to be used in practice—would be more congruent with the beliefs of large numbers of Americans given the pragmatic and materialistic bias of much of our culture. This idea, in turn, suggests that a student's underlying motivation for being in college might also be influential in determining how that student conceives of learning and what approach is brought to academic tasks and learning materials.

Motivation and Study Approaches

There is evidence to suggest that students in higher education adapt study approaches according to the motives, or intention, that they bring to the learning situation.

John Biggs (1984) has evolved a multidimensional model of academic performance using both traditional and phenomenographic research. His construct is based on the idea that people's motives determine their strategies; there is a "psycho-logic" to how people view situations and what they decide to do about them (Biggs, 1984, p. 118). Formal learning situations, according to Biggs, generate three common expectations or motives: *Instrumental* (study to become qualified or certified for a specific job as easily as possible); *Intrinsic* (study to actualize one's interests and competence in an academic subject); and/or *Achievement* (study to obtain high grades regardless of interest). Biggs hypothesized that a student whose motive was instrumental would tend to take a surface approach to studying, the student with intrinsic motivation would take a deep approach, and the achievement-motivated student would take an organizing or strategic study approach (i.e., choosing whatever they feel will result in the highest grade). In research with Australian college and university students, Biggs found weak but positive support for this pattern. The students surveyed also rated themselves as to how well they felt they were doing academically, and this yielded interesting results. In general, students who perceived themselves as doing well were likely to choose and use appropriate strategies (i.e., those strategies consistent with their motives). On the other hand, students who were self-identified as low achievers did not exhibit congruence. For them, Biggs suggests, it is "any port in a storm" (p. 131). It is these latter students—those who don't employ strategies sensibly—that Biggs considers most likely to benefit from study skill instruction.

Gibbs, Morgan, and Taylor (1984) work with a construct which they call "educational orientation" that is very similar to Biggs's construct of motive. They define educational orientation as "the collection of purposes which form the personal context for the individual student's learning" (p. 169). They identify four major types of educational orientation: vocational, academic, personal, and social, each with subtypes indicating intrinsic or extrinsic interest. However, they are quick to point out that the orientation of any particular student is often a complex mix of two or more of the types.

With longitudinal case studies of Open University students, Gibbs, Morgan, and Taylor were able to demonstrate that students with different orientations go about studying differently. Like Van Rossum and Schenk (1984), they found evidence that the specific study approach was subservient to the student's conception of learning, and, most encouragingly, they were able to demonstrate that conceptions of learning may develop and study approaches move from surface to deep as students interact with course material, fellow students, and tutors (instructors). One such case was "Sally Brown," an adult student whose educational orientation was personal and intrinsic—she primarily wanted to gain self-confidence. At the beginning of the social science course that she took, Sally's conception of learning was Level 1—"gaining new knowledge," and she had a surface approach to studying. By the end of the course, she conceptualized learning as "being critical and relating ideas to one's own experience" (p. 186)—a definite Level 5 concept. She was also taking a more active and deep approach to studying (Gibbs, Morgan, & Taylor, 1984).

Gibbs, Morgan, and Taylor conclude that educational orientation is a useful construct in obtaining a full view of learning from a learner's perspective. They also suggest that understanding of this construct might be useful to instructors. Obviously most instructors have had a strong academic orientation in their own careers as students. It might be helpful for them to understand that students who bring vocational, social, or personal orientations to their studies are simply different—not deficient, lazy, or lacking motivation.

Summary and Reflections

We have examined three ideas about student learning in higher education that have come out of a qualitative, phenomenographic research approach focused on understanding the process of student learning from the student's perspective. The research has been done in Great Britain, Europe, and Australia. These ideas are that

1. Students tend toward either a deep or surface approach to studying.
2. There is a relationship between the way students conceptualize learning and the study approach that they take.
3. The motivation or "educational orientation" that students have for participation in higher education also influences the study approach taken.

Delving into this research has raised a number of questions for us. Is there a commonality in the way professors and students understand what it means to learn? Could the concepts of deep/surface approaches to study and the differing conceptions of learning be helpful in explaining the problems of transfer and application in skill/strategy training? Most important, what are the implications for the way that college reading and study skills might best be taught? Are we overly technical in our approaches? Do we go beyond task strategy consciousness to concerns with "real" learning? Are there teaching strategies or approaches that would aid us in doing a better job of encouraging students to take a meaningful, deep approach to studying? Gibbs (1983) offers some suggestions from his experience with adult learners. Certainly, the current research on learning strategies, with its concern for all aspects of metacognition, including motivation, appears relevant and hopeful (Weinstein, Goetz, & Alexander, 1988). However, in his critique of this research, Rothkopf makes two points with which the researchers reviewed in this paper would undoubtedly concur. First, just because a learning strategy proves efficient in a laboratory study does not provide adequate reason for its application in a practical setting. Second, any learning skills that are taught should transcend narrow academic demands and be applicable in the larger world (Rothkopf, 1988). We feel that some familiarity with the body of research introduced in this paper can help both practitioners and researchers to be conscious of the larger issues and to view the work on learning strategies within a broader perspective.

REFERENCES

Biggs, J.B. (1984). Learning strategies, student motivation patterns, and subjectively perceived success. In R. Kirby (Ed.), *Cognitive strategies and educational performance* (pp. 111–134). Orlando, FL: Academic Press.

Craik, R.M., & Lockhart, R.S. (1972). Levels of processing: A framework for memory research. *Journal of Verbal Learning and Verbal Behavior, 11,* 671–684.

Entwistle, N. (1984). Contrasting perspectives on learning. In F. Märton, D. Hounsell, & N. Entwistle (Eds.), *The experience of learning* (pp. 1–18). Edinburgh, Scotland: Scottish Academic Press.

Entwistle, N., & Märton, F. (1984). Changing conceptions of learning and research. In F. Märton, D. Hounsell, & N. Entwistle (Eds.), *The experience of learning* (pp. 211–228). Edinburgh, Scotland: Scottish Academic Press.

Entwistle N., & Ramsden, P. (Eds.). (1982). *Understanding student learning.* New York: Nichols.

Gibbs, G. (1983). Changing students' approaches to study through classroom exercise. In R.M. Smith (Ed.), *Helping adults learn to learn: No. 19, new directions for continuing education* (pp. 83–95). San Francisco: Jossey-Bass.

Gibbs, G., Morgan, A., & Taylor, E. (1984). The world of the learner. In F. Märton, D. Hounsell, & N. Entwistle, (Eds.), The experience of learning (pp. 165–189). Edinburgh, Scotland: Scottish Academic Press.

Märton, F., Hounsell, D., & Entwistle, N. (Eds.). (1984). *The experience of learning.* Edinburgh, Scotland: Scottish Academic Press.

Märton, F., & Säljö, R. (1976). On qualitative differences in learning: Outcome and process. *British Journal of Educational Psychology, 46,* 4–11.

Rothkopf, E.Z. (1988). Perspectives on study skills training in a realistic instructional economy. In C.E. Weinstein, E.T. Goetz, & P.A. Alexander (Eds.), *Learning and study strategies: Issues in assessment, instruction, and evaluation.* San Diego, CA: Academic Press.

Segal, J.W., Chipman, S.F., & Glaser, R. (Eds.). (1985). *Thinking and learning skills: Relating instruction to research* (Vol. 1). Hillsdale, NJ: Erlbaum.

Svenson, L. (1984). Skill in learning. In F. Märton, D. Hounsell, & N. Entwistle (Eds.), *The experience of learning.* Edinburgh, Scotland: Scottish Academic Press.

Van Rossum, E.J., & Schenk, S.M. (1984). The relationship between learning conception, study strategy and learning outcome. *British Journal of Educational Psychology, 54,* 73–83.

Weinstein, C.E., Goetz, E.T., & Alexander, P.A. (Eds.). (1988). *Learning and study strategies: Issues in assessment instruction and evaluation.* San Diego, CA: Academic Press.

Wilson, J.D. (1981). Student learning in higher education. New York: John Wiley & Sons.

What Research Has to Say About Instruction in Text-Marking Strategies

Beverly Bartel

Study skills courses offer a variety of approaches for learning at the college level. Course instructors suggest a diversified approach to remembering and learning content depending on the kind of test and the format of the class and the textbook. However, generally, within only a few semesters after completion of a reading/study skills course, students revert to the use of underlining and lecture notes as their preferred study methods (Nist & Kirby, 1989). Since underlining and note-taking are the methods of choice, the focus of instruction should be on how to make the preferred methods more efficient.

Overall, research on the effectiveness of underlining has suggested at best inconclusive results (Anderson & Armbruster, 1984). However, some studies have suggested significant effectiveness for text marking as a study strategy (Annis & Davis, 1978; Davis & Annis, 1979, Fowler & Barker, 1974; Glynn & DiVesta, 1979; Hartley, Bartlett, & Branthwaite, 1980). Comparing the results of underlining research is extremely difficult if not impossible because of extraneous variables that affect a study's focus (for example, assigning the skill without testing for preference or ability, using extremely brief passages that would discourage skill use, testing immediately without review, and using a narrative text which a student would often mark by annotation only).

Nevertheless, several general conclusions can be drawn about text marking from the results of these studies. First, because delineated material receives emphasis apart from the text it is more likely to be learned and remembered (Wallace, 1965). Second, students below grade seven are not efficient at selecting important information to be underlined (Brown & Smiley, 1978; Hartley, Bartlett & Branthwaite, 1980). Third, when underlined, information of high importance is retained better than information of low importance (Nist & Hogrebe, 1987; Rickards &

Originally published in Forum for Reading *(1993–1994), volume 24, pages 11–19*

August, 1975). Fourth, Nist and Kirby (1989) suggest that although college students prefer text marking, they often demonstrate inefficient and random marking patterns.

Baker and Brown (1984) conclude that efficient use of study strategies evolves from proficiency in the reading process. Students who demonstrate the ability to identify the important information while reading are presumably more adept at using that information in a study strategy. Mickler (1989) suggests that since the reader's comprehension of the text, in part, relies on the reader's relationship with the presentation of information within text structures, more instructional focus should be aimed at the location of important information within the text structure. Knowledge of text structure directly affects the reader's ability to comprehend and use expository text (Armbruster, Anderson, & Ostertag, 1987; Barnett, 1984; Gordon, 1990; McGee, 1982; Taylor & Beach, 1984). Therefore, a key to aiding students in the identification of importance as they mark text may lie in the reader's use of text structure when processing expository text.

Processing Importance During Reading

Because readers generally find the task of remembering all information found in the discourse impossible, when they process a text they identify some of the information as more important to remember than other information. The reader's purpose for reading the text and knowledge of the text itself both provide clues to important information while reading. Each discourse type has a recognizable semantic and schematic structure that readers employ when processing for importance (Kintsch & van Dijk, 1978; Meyer, 1975). The schematic structure relies on the discourse type (e.g., newspaper article, laboratory instructions, textbook chapter, or short story). The reader uses the discourse type to establish an informational hierarchy. For example, the reader may focus on a summary in a chapter, the first paragraph in a newspaper article, or an abstract in a journal article.

Familiarity with both the semantic content and schematic structure aids the reader in the process of identifying important information for later use. Knowledge of text structure aids in reading for important information because structural knowledge encourages top-down processing of the content (Meyer, 1975; Wittrock, 1981).

While readers generally remember the topic when reading expository text, they have difficulty identifying the important details that support the topic statement (Britton, Meyer, Hodge, & Glynn, 1980; Meyer, 1977). This is evident when examining textbook markings (Nist & Kirby, 1989).

Kintsch and van Dijk (1978) propose a theory of discourse processing that may provide insight into the difficulty students have identifying importance through text marking. According to Kintsch and van Dijk, importance is inferred through a process of selection, deletion, integration, and construction of micropropositions (units of information) into macropropositional form. During the reading process, the reader may select the information in a sentence as important, integrate the information in a sentence into information already stored, ignore the information in a sentence as unimportant, or construct a new inference from the information provided in a sentence. These processes form macropropositions and are guided by the readers' knowledge of the text structure. For example, high ability readers look for summary statements that aid in identifying importance, they realize that recipes generally order ingredients in order of use, and they know that an abstract for a journal article will focus the reader on the author's purpose and results. Therefore, identifying important information by using the text structure requires interactive processing between the reader and the text as a whole. Experienced readers bring a schema for the discourse type to the text which they use to infer what is important, what to ignore as unimportant, what to integrate into an expanded inference, and what to use in constructing a general statement of importance.

While text structure aids the reader in processing what is important, aspects of text structure may make identifying the important information difficult when text marking. Not only is the reader creating inferential summary statements (macropropositions) while reading, but often the author is also presenting the information in an implicit form. Baumann and Serra (1984) and Braddock (1975) demonstrated that almost half of the important information (main ideas) in expository text is information that is inferred. Further, they suggest that in some instances the information is inferred from information in more than one paragraph. Therefore, importance is often found on a level that transcends the individual sentences within a text.

Implications for Text Marking

In expository text, the important information often resides within and beyond a specific sentence or set of sentences. To fully grasp text meaning, inferences must be made. Aspects of both the reading process and the text's structure require that the reader employ chunks of text larger than a sentence. The reader uses a more holistic sense of the text when processing for importance by constructing macropropositions from paragraphs and/or passages and using knowledge of the discourse type.

Unfortunately, inferred main ideas and macropropositions that have been integrated and constructed during the reading process are not easily text marked. Although some of the important information in expository text can be selected for text marking because it is explicitly stated in sentence form, this is not true of all important information.

The problem for the reader who marks text by underlining information perceived to be important is to find a way to identify implied importance. One solution is to write brief summaries in the margins. While summary statements noted as marginal annotations or at the end of passages may relate inferred importance, this is a strategy that is not frequently employed by text markers (Nist & Hogrebe, 1987), and assumes an ability to concisely summarize text.

Tierney, Bridge, and Cera (1978–1979) found that the recall protocols of elementary school readers contained about 50% inferred information. If half of what readers identify as important is found through a process of drawing inferences from the text, restricting a text-marking strategy to underlining or highlighting explicit micropropositions will not be conducive to postreading review. Focusing only on the explicit statements will not provide a complete reconstruction of the important information. The reader needs a strategy that goes beyond "selection" and also allows for integration and construction. The reader needs to employ a strategy that allows for the holistic nature of discourse; a strategy that goes beyond the sentence to the paragraph, passage, and text as a whole. Summarizing can be taught (King, Biggs, & Lipsky, 1984; Taylor & Samuels, 1983). Perhaps text marking should consist of underlining *and* marginal annotations of summary statements in order to be effective as a study strategy.

When Perry (1959) gave postsecondary students a chapter from a history text and asked them to read it for important information, he noted that the students got bogged down in the introductory narrative passage and therefore were unable to efficiently utilize their time to review important concepts for the assessment that was to follow. Possibly, students did not possess a schema for the text structure of the chapter. Further, even if a schema was in place, they may have been unable to employ knowledge of text structure that might lead them to skim the narrative section for background and then focus on the concepts in the expository section. They assessed each sentence and each paragraph as being equally important. The students were employing a bottom-up processing strategy to mark information. The ability to view the chapter with a top-down processing strategy, using the text structure of the chapter to determine that the narrative section was of lesser importance to the total concept, would have aided the students in identifying the important concepts. Text structure can be taught to postsecondary students (Bartlett, 1989; Meyer, 1975). Knowledge of text structure facilitates the understanding of relationships between the concepts and the hierarchy established by the discourse type. The findings that suggest that knowledge of text structure can help students focus on important information in expository text, have strong instructional implications regarding practices related to underlining, highlighting, and other text-marking strategies.

Summary

Text marking is a study strategy that most students employ, but not always effectively. It is possible that many students are not identifying the most important information because they are applying the strategy on the micropropositional level. They are assessing each sentence for important information and making their selections at the sentence level. Important information is often accessed by constructing and integrating the information found at both the micropropositional and macropropositional level. Readers use the text structure to make inferences about importance from information found on the paragraph, passage, and whole text levels. Inferred statements are not easily marked in text. Conclusions drawn from this review of research suggest that readers need to be encouraged to use the text structure when identifying information in a text for later review and to make summary statements in the margins of their text when the important information is not explicitly stated in the text.

REFERENCES

Anderson, T.H., & Armbruster, B.A. (1984). Studying. In P.D. Pearson (Ed.), *Handbook of reading research* (pp. 657–680). New York: Longman.

Annis, L., & Davis, J.K. (1978). Study techniques and cognitive styles: Their effect on recall and recognition. *The Journal of Educational Research, 71,* 1–7.

Armbruster, B.B., Anderson, T.H., & Ostertag, J. (1987). Does text structure/summarization instruction facilitate learning from expository text? *Reading Research Quarterly, 22,* 331–346.

Baker, L., & Brown, A. (1984). Metacognitive skills and reading. In P.D. Pearson (Ed.), *Handbook of reading research* (pp. 354–394). New York: Longman.

Barnett, J.E. (1984). Facilitating retention through instruction about text structure. *Journal of Reading Behavior, 16*(1), 1–13.

Bartlett, B.J. (1978). Top-level structure as an organizational strategy for recall of classroom text. (Doctoral dissertation, Arizona State University, 1978). *Dissertation Abstracts International, 39,* 6641A.

Baumann, J.F., & Serra, J.K. (1984). The frequency and placement of main idea in children's social studies textbooks: A modified replication of Braddock's research on topic sentences. *Journal of Reading Behavior, 16,* 27–40.

Braddock, R. (1975). The frequency of topic sentences in expository prose. *Research in the Teaching of English, 8*(3), 287–302.

Britton, B.K., Meyer, B.J.F., Hodge, M.H., & Glynn, S.M. (1980). Effects of the organization of text on memory: Tests of retrieval and response criterion hypotheses. *Journal of Experimental Psychology, 6*(5), 620–629.

Brown, A.L., & Smiley, S.S. (1978). The development of strategies for studying texts. *Child Development, 49,* 1078–1088.

Davis, J.K., & Annis, L. (1979). The effect of study techniques, study preferences, and familiarity on later recall. *Journal of Educational Psychology, 47,* 92–96.

Fowler, R.L., & Barker, A.S. (1974). Effectiveness of highlighting for retention of text material. *Journal of Applied Psychology, 59*(3), 358–364.

Gordon, C.J. (1990). Contexts for expository text structure use. *Reading Research and Instruction, 29*(2), 55–72.

Glynn, S.M., & DiVesta, F.J. (1979). Control of prose processing via instructional and typographical cues. *Journal of Educational Psychology, 71*(5), 595–603.

Hartley, J., Bartlett, S., & Branthwaite, A. (1980). Underlining can make a difference—sometimes. *The Journal of Educational Research, 73,* 218–224.

King, J.R., Biggs, S.A., & Lipsky, S. (1984). Students self-questioning and summarizing as reading study strategies. *Journal of Reading Behavior, 16*(3), 205–218.

Kintsch, W., & van Dijk, T.A. (1978). Toward a model of text comprehension and production. *Psychological Review, 85*(5), 363–394.

McGee, L.M. (1982). Awareness of text structure: Effects on children's recall of expository text. *Reading Research Quarterly, 17,* 581–590.

Meyer, B.J.F. (1977). What is remembered from prose: A function of passage structure. In R.O. Freedle (Ed.), *Discourse production and comprehension* (pp. 307–336). Norwood, NJ: Ablex.

Meyer, B.J.F. (1975). Identification of the structure of prose and its implications for the study of reading and memory. *Journal of Reading Behavior, 7*(1), 7–47.

Mickler, M.J. (1989). Comprehending textbooks: Building the relationship between texts and readers. *Review of Research in Developmental Education, 7*(1).

Nist, S.L., & Hogrebe, M.C. (1987). The role of underlining and annotating in remembering textual information. *Reading Research and Instruction, 27*(1), 12–25.

Nist, S.L., & Kirby, K. (1989). The text marking patterns of college students. *Reading Psychology, 10,* 321–338.

Perry, W.G. (1959). Students' use and misuse of reading skills: A report to a faculty. *Harvard Educational Review*, *29*, 193–200.

Rickards, J.P., & August, G.J. (1975). Generative underlining strategies in prose recall. *Journal of Educational Psychology*, *67*(6), 860–865.

Taylor, B.M., & Beach, R.W. (1984). The effects of text structure instruction on middle-grade students' comprehension and production of expository text. *Reading Research Quarterly*, *19*, 134–146.

Taylor, B.M., & Samuels, S.J. (1983). Children's use of text structure in the recall of expository material. *American Educational Research Journal*, *20*(4), 517–528.

Tierney, R.J., Bridge, C., & Cera, J.J. (1978–1979). The discourse processing operations of children. *Reading Research Quarterly*, *14*, 539–569.

Wade, S.E., & Trathen, W. (1989). Effects of self-selected study methods on learning. *Journal of Educational Psychology*, *81*(1), 40–47.

Wallace, W.P. (1965). Review of the historical, empirical, and theoretical status of the von Restoff phenomenon. *Psychological Reports*, *63*(6), 410–424.

Wittrock, M.C. (1981). Reading comprehension. In F.J. Pirossolo & M.C. Wittrock (Eds.), *Neuropsychological and cognitive processes in reading* (pp. 229–259). New York: Academic Press.

Characteristics of Highly Proficient College Freshman Readers

Margaret L. Henrichs

n the wake of public outcry over problems in reading education, and in the rhetoric over their possible solutions, the issue of reading maturity seldom surfaces. Yet, included in the concept of reading maturity are those very abilities we wish to develop in our students: competence, knowledge of purpose, comprehension, a positive attitude, reader judgement, breadth of interest, and continued practice (cf. Gray & Rogers, 1956).

The recent attention toward the reader's self-awareness and personal control of the reading and learning processes (i.e., metacognition), has offered a new dimension to the concept of effective, mature reading. Clearly it is important that our students not only have the ability to read, but that they become proficient, mature readers.

Proficient reading has been a focus in rapidly expanding postsecondary developmental learning programs. College reading improvement courses fall into this somewhat heterogeneous category. Though the needs, objectives, structure, and facilities vary among these programs, the purpose remains the same: to offer a transition between the reality of today's college students as language users and the expectations for language use demanded by their colleges. Entering college students whose reading strategies do not conform to their college's expectations must quickly learn those strategies necessary for success.

Academic support programs at the college level meet a variety of students needs. In recent years two reading programs have developed simultaneously at a small, selective private college in the midwestern section of the United States. One program was designed to improve the language strategies for students considered "high risk" in terms of predicted college success. The other program was designed to meet the needs of the general college population who were often effective readers preparing for a business or professional school. Evaluative techniques and instructional strategies used for both groups of students were based on psycholinguistic theory, principles, and research.

Originally published in Forum for Reading *(1989), volume 20, number 2, pages 6–14*

Data from both proficient readers and the ineffective college readers over a seven-year period revealed that in some areas the groups are similar. For example, most of the students are fluent oral readers and all expressed a desire to read faster; however, there seem to be far greater differences between the groups in comprehension of both informational and aesthetic text. Further, differences were apparent in other areas such as attitude, motivation, knowledge of purpose, breadth of reading, interest in reading, personal control over the reading process, and, above all, confidence. In short, the data from the proficient college readers substantiate that found in a number of studies which describe strategies of effective mature readers.

Background

Maturity in reading is most often equated with growth in reading skills as measured primarily, if not solely, by standardized tests. Maturity, in fact, encompasses a wide range of characteristics. In the following study the concept of reading maturity is defined as related to but not synonymous with that of reading proficiency. Maturity in reading is presented in the broad sense. Reading proficiency is defined as the ability to use effective, efficient reading strategies in a variety of text. Because it is quite possible for college students to be proficient yet not mature readers, the study attempted to link both terms in the description of highly proficient college freshman readers.

In recent years there has been a growing interest by researchers in the reading strategies of mature, proficient readers. In a series of studies, Smith (1982, 1984, 1985) has described the strategies and behaviors that mature, experienced readers use when they encounter difficult text. In the first study, Smith (1982) found that experienced readers proceed on a trial-and-error basis but within a systematically organized repertoire of strategies. In the second study, Smith (1984) found that mature readers are not bound by a specific text but search out other sources when a text seems incomprehensible. These readers also diagram, paraphrase, and reorganize information to make sense of the print. In the third study, Smith (1985) concluded that the ownership of a task can affect a choice of learning strategies as well as comprehension. If students sense an ownership (i.e., when the task is personalized), they often seek other sources as an aid to understanding. Smith also found that study skills such as discovering the main idea, annotating, and outlining are used effectively by mature readers, but these tasks may be insufficient when students encounter difficult text. This was also true for the skill of summarizing.

Summarizing as an aid to studying is generally a statement or two of the main ideas at a higher level of abstraction than the passage itself (Anderson & Glover, 1981). Ann Brown and colleagues, in a series of studies (Brown & Day, 1983; Brown, Day, & Jones, 1983), stated that as readers mature, they develop a reliable set of rules for summarizing text. These rules involve selection (finding the main idea), invention (inferring the main idea), and superordination (putting details into larger categories). Brown and Day (1983) found that summarizing could be an effective aid to study if students were trained to apply macrorules for comprehending discourse to their summarizations.

Research data based on the Reading Miscue Inventory of the performance of readers of all ages (Goodman & Burke, 1973; Watson et al., 1979) have described the strategies that effective readers utilize and, thus, have helped create a new direction for reading instruction. Successful readers are confident; they know they can construct meaning through interaction with the text. Proficient readers sample the text, predict, confirm, and correct in the process of reading. They depend on cues found in the natural text: graphophonic, syntactic, semantic, which are intrinsic to all text. Effective readers skip words, guess, make analogies, and they are generally aware that their prior knowledge is closely related to understanding of text.

A number of evaluative and instructional strategies based on miscue research have been developed. Watson (1978) charted the Reader Selected Miscue, a procedure in which the reader, during silent reading, marks areas of comprehension breakdown within the text. After completion of the reading, a selection of the most troublesome miscues is made to be analyzed and discussed by the student and teacher. Weatherall (1982) described the process of Retrospective Miscue Analysis, a procedure built upon both miscue analysis and Reader Selected Miscue. Retrospective Miscue Analysis allows the students to listen to their taped oral reading and to reflect, describe, and analyze the causal nature of their reading miscues. Thus, both Reader Selected Miscue and Retrospective Analysis provide metacognitive insight into the subject's reading behaviors.

The relationship between metacognitive skills and proficient reading has gained the increasing attention of researchers in cognitive-developmental psychology and reading. Flavell (1979) defined metacognition as "knowledge and cognition about cognition phenomena," which means one's own awareness and knowledge of one's own cognitive processes and all its related aspects. Mature readers generally engage in comprehension monitoring, and if comprehension is occurring they are most often unaware of this process. It is generally when comprehension breaks down that these readers become aware of the metacognitive process. Effective reading requires some awareness and control of the cognitive activities in which the reader is engaged. Introspective and retrospective techniques as well as verbalizing thoughts while reading have been commonly employed in metacognitive research. Introspective reports produced by adults have shown that mature readers do possess some awareness and control of their comprehension process (cf. Collins et al., 1980).

Thus, a number of studies have described both study techniques and reading strategies of mature, proficient readers. These readers generally implement various techniques when learning from text, and, if a break in comprehension occurs, they seem able to utilize a number of regulatory strategies. The possibility of teaching study techniques and reading strategies of proficient college readers to less effective college readers provided the impetus for the following study.

Method and Procedures

Because of the probable differences in college freshman students' reading maturity and proficiency, it seemed reasonable and useful to develop a picture of just what it is that the highly proficient college freshman readers do when they encounter a variety of print, and why they believe they do it. The purpose of the study, thus, was to develop an historical, composite portrait, through case analyses of four highly proficient college freshman readers. These readers were to be studied in relationship to current research findings in language and the reading process, as well as in study strategies. The study design was intended to provide a database from which reading behavior, attitudes, interest, and experiences could be described, discussed, and analyzed. The intent of the study was also to probe the cognitive processes in two ways: to determine (1) what strategies the readers used while reading, and (2) how they acquired and stored information for future use. Because cognitive monitoring (awareness of one's own thinking and learning) assumes an essential function in comprehension, it was considered an integral part of this study. The communication of metacognitive insights of the proficient readers to less effective readers, and the development of instructional strategies for doing so were an underlying intent of the study.

In order to identify a group of freshman students who might be considered proficient, mature readers, established measures of academic achievement were used. The English Invitational Examination, a local evaluation, was given to those entering freshman who scored above 600 on the verbal section of the SAT or above 27 on the ACT. The English Invitational is used for placement in upper level English courses. Through the years students who qualified for this exam have ranked at the top of the entering freshman class in both college board scores and high school grade point averages. These students have been perceived by faculty to be both proficient readers and writers. Twenty-four students qualified for the English Invitational Examination in 1985, and it was from this group that the four subjects were randomly selected. Participation in the present study was on a voluntary basis, and the subjects received a fee.

The data for the present study were collected in two phases. Phase One included the use of the Reading Interview (Burke, 1978), the Reader Selected Miscue (Watson, 1978), and summary response information. An introductory sociology text was used for both the Reader Selected Miscue Analysis and for the summary response information. Phase Two data were collected and analyzed through the use of the Reading Miscue Inventory (Goodman, Watson, & Burke, 1987), and the Retrospective Miscue Analysis (Weatherill, 1982). A philosophy text was used for the Reading Miscue Analysis and for the Retrospective Miscue Analysis. Additional data concerning the reading behaviors of the four proficient readers were collected as they read and described their reading in a variety of text. Additional texts used in this study included math, science, poetry, and a comprehension section of a standardized reading test. The research instruments used in this study provided an organized structure in which to look at the highly proficient freshman college reader. Discussion following each procedure provided data of heuristic value in relation to the subject's comprehension and monitoring of comprehension.

Results

The results of the Burke Reading Interview provided extensive information and insight into the students' personal models of reading. Interview responses were examined within four categories which included metacognitive understanding and experience, strategy, task, and instructional variables.

Interview responses confirmed the students' models of reading and provided rationale for these models through metacognitive-metalinguistic information. The self-perception of the subjects as readers, family-supported early reading experience and instruction, coping with boredom in school, specific text reading strategies, the readers store of background knowledge, suggestions for instructional improvement, the interrelationship of the components of language, reading interests, and the common interest in mythology were among the items discussed using the structure of the interview response.

The Reader Selected Miscue procedure, using a sociology text, showed that with few exceptions, the four subjects monitored themselves beyond the word level in their reading. Individual discussion with each subject following the procedure indicated that these students were well aware of relationship between cognition and language, and its effect on the reading process. Their answers reflected a depth of metalinguistic understanding related to textual complexity. Further discussion centered around the notion of who owns the responsibility for text comprehension, the writer or the reader? The general agreement was that clear writing is the author's responsibility but the understanding of text rests with the reader. Looking at the reasons for difficulty in specific text indicates that these readers were insightful, sophisticated, and knowledgeable users of language.

Summary response data, both written and oral, were examined for the highly proficient readers in this study. Evaluation of text summaries were based on the macrorules devised by Brown and Day (1983). On written summarization of the sociology passage, only one subject identified the main idea and was able to adequately summarize the text. The other three subjects summarized the passage in a general manner without noting a main idea. It may be that written text summarization is a skill in which many proficient readers would profit from training.

On the oral retell from the philosophy text, however, all of the subjects readily generated the main idea, and they were able to put details into larger categories. Thus, on the oral summary task they showed their ability to apply both the rules of selection and superordination in the manner of mature readers.

The Reading Miscue Inventory (RMI) generated an abundance of information related to how the four proficient readers cope with the systems of language. It was also possible, through this structure, to examine their use of reading strategies. The RMI profile data provides a general summary of these subjects as readers. High scores were obtained by the readers in the three language systems. They paid close attention to the surface language structure which resulted in high graphic-sound relation scores. The majority of miscues were at a high level, that is, miscues that do not impede the flow of reading comprehension. This was reflected, in part, by high grammatical relations scores. Overcorrection was of some note in the scores of three readers, and this might raise the question of efficiency in oral reading. The lack of repeated miscues on the RMI indicates that these readers learn from the text. Though the text drew upon a vast store of background information, three of the students scored exceptionally high on meaning construction while one scored somewhat lower.

Though one student scored lower on meaning construction, his pattern of miscues indicates that he, like the other subjects, sampled text, predicted meaning, and attempted confirmation. This same student had the lowest score on overcorrection, which might signify that even in oral reading he is less concerned with surface features of language than he is in obtaining meaning; he is efficient as well as effective as a reader. All of the subjects showed exceptional control over language and, even in difficult print, they were effective readers.

A detailed retell guide was constructed for the philosophy selection used for the miscue analysis. The unaided, aided, and cued responses for each subject were appropriately scored. The readers' response matched or exceeded the text summary provided by a professor of philosophy with one exception; a concept of liberalism was not included in the readers' retell of the selection.

Elaboration on the retell response substantiates the readers' ability to describe their comprehension monitoring. Two questions were devised to provide this metacognitive information: (1) In the inquiry related to asking the expert, the subjects described their search for information to fill in the gaps not triggered by prior knowledge; (2) the specific text-related question revealed various strategies these proficient readers employ as they confront and attempt to assume control over difficult text. These strategies ranged from cursory activities related to the graphic-phonic information, to such cognitive activities as monitoring an inner voice while reading.

The information obtained through the use of the Retrospective Miscue Analysis attempted to seek answers to what highly proficient freshmen college readers do as they take control of the reading process. It further sought information as to whether it is possible to describe, in retrospect, metalinguistic insights from the subjects' previously taped reading for the Reading Miscue Inventory.

Discussion with the subject following a tape-stop was based on the causal nature of comprehension breakdown. Tape-stops often occurred a line or two after correct pronunciation of a word or string of words, a nonmiscue. Thus, the observed response in this procedure often differed from what might have been expected, based on typescript information. The readers monitored themselves at both the word level and beyond the word level on this procedure. Interaction between the subjects and the researcher following a tape-stop resulted in digression of discussion. This digression provided an analysis of the subjects' textual difficulties as well as additional insight into the readers' perception and understanding of the reading process.

In reading a variety of texts, the highly proficient freshmen college readers defined and examined their specific text-related strategies. Through the years these strategies have been developed and refined. While these readers may use similar tactics as they approach various texts, most of their comprehension strategies appear to be idiosyncratic and not easily categorized. For example, one student's reading strategies seemed to be related to those he had developed for math-science texts. The other three subjects developed more diverse techniques for reading various texts.

Discussion

This study of proficient readers confirmed all that we have learned, through current research, regarding language and the reading process. Early literacy was nurtured in the closeness of the family, where support and encouragement allowed ample space for the language growth of naturally curious children. As one of the readers described the experience,

> It wasn't just reading we [reader and sister] were in their [parents] laps and we'd follow along in the books exactly where they were reading. Our parents would point to a picture, repeat the sentence and just keep going, and we actually had the book memorized before we learned to read.

Going to the library with parents or grandparents to pick out a book was a "big deal" for these readers.

Early school reading instruction held a significant influence over all reading associated with school. School reading and home reading were seen as very different endeavors for three readers who had learned to read naturally, without school instruction, before they began school. For these students reading at home was not related to oral performance, it was less structured and it was generated by intense interests. School reading instruction broke into pieces the words the students already knew, attached sounds to them, and put them back together. Initially this new notion of what school reading was about interested the early readers for they were curious about language. Soon, however, school reading became dull stories in basal readers, so unlike the earlier preschool reading experiences. For the early readers there seemed to be a few less active years in reading development until an initiating experience or interest caused them to become avid readers. This took place in the upper grade school years. For these readers the strong early foundation in literacy provided the impetus for self-directed activities in language learning. It also provided a buffer to classroom boredom during the early school years.

Early school reading was characterized by correctness in oral reading, and this was considered important throughout the students' schooling because of its emphasis in the curriculum. Status in the early classrooms was often defined in terms of placement in reading groups. As the years went by, smoothness in performance seemed important for oral class reading of textbooks. Good reading was equated with good oral performance.

All four students expressed a love of learning. They knew at an early age that proficiency in reading and writing was not a goal in itself. Language development for them provided a means to thinking and learning about the world. They were never satisfied with the unknown, and would persevere until the unknown made sense. They did not accept failure in any sense and, as a result, they built unique, proficient reading and writing strategies to aid them in their thinking and learning. These students expressed the belief that they knew that they were in control of their own learning, that no matter how difficult the print might be they could master it.

As the school years passed there were favorite teachers who sparked an interest in their subject, and who encouraged the students to search out information beyond a textbook. School, for these students, seemed to meet its intention, that of a fountain of learning. The students' curiosity was alive; learning was relevant and exciting. They became mature, proficient language users in school and outside the classroom. All of the readers had an intense interest in mythology but their other reading interests were more diverse.

As college students, the proficient readers demonstrated the ability to describe in detail the relationship between their reading and thought processes. The data underscored the sophistication of these readers as language users as they read, and later described their reading in a variety of college texts.

Over the years these proficient readers had developed specific, idiosyncratic, comprehension strategies for dealing with a variety of texts and they demonstrated the ability to "change gears" in the manner of mature readers. The print itself seemed to generate mental recall of these strategies which resulted in an immediate, well-tried plan designed to make sense of a particular text. The texts used for the present study were new to the readers, yet the blueprint for comprehension appeared to be in place in all cases. Three students who had been early readers described their use of different sets of strategies for informational and aesthetic reading materials. These readers discussed various means of imprinting the information from math or science texts "on the brain," and these memorization strategies included some aspect of writing, such as diagramming and underlining. They described their reading in science and math texts as a slow, focused, step-by-step procedure through the text examples—a continuous building on prior knowledge.

In contrast to math and science reading, the proficient readers described poetry as "being like a puzzle." They often read a poem several times and their comprehension comes from analyzing pieces of the text. If something does not make sense, they look for underlying meaning. Footnotes, lectures, and criticism are used as needed for understanding. The subjects employed various strategies in taking standardized reading comprehension tests: focusing attention to their known problem areas, reading the questions first, mentally organizing passages into shorter units, and marking passages while reading.

One of the readers had developed reading strategies which were significantly different than those of the other readers. The comprehension plan of this reader was also well developed, and it was far more consistent within all texts. All texts were approached in a similar manner— they were conceptualized in a mathematical framework and then transcribed. This student emphasized the importance of learning to "systemize, outline mentally and then on paper," in order to first note the organization of a particular text and then to learn the concepts within that organization. It may be of interest to note that this student, though highly proficient, was not an early reader, had less interest in recreational reading, and seemed to project a more negative self-perception as a reader than did the other readers in this study.

All of the readers described a projection of themselves into "aesthetic" reading as in the philosophy text. This personal involvement resulted in taking a stance in the arguments presented in the text, and this was described as a comprehension strategy. The four readers seemed to possess an acute awareness of what they perceived to be their weaker intellectual or interest areas. Similarly, they were keenly aware of their considerable strengths and breadth of interests. Development of compensatory reading strategies for difficult or uninteresting print was based on these strengths. The use of various writing strategies, as well as focused attention on problem areas, text organization, "letting it simmer," judicious use of lecture notes and outside source material, reflection after reading, and asking the professor what sparked his or her interest in a particular discipline were noted as aides in understanding dull or difficult reading material.

Conclusions

The four subjects in this study represent the desired outcome of our educational system. No one would deny the ability, motivation, and the self-direction that these students possess. Their educational observations seem worthy of the attention of those who work with less effective students enrolled in college developmental reading programs.

Students participating in college developmental reading programs frequently describe negative early learning experiences. The proficient readers who participated in this study described positive learning experiences, but they were also sensitive educational observers with years of experience in this capacity. What have they learned along the way? The information they have provided underscores all that we have learned from recent research in language, literacy, and learning.

The students remembered early reading groups with embarrassed students who were poor oral readers. They felt that beginning readers should not have to cope with those negative stressors. They stated that "reading should begin where a child is at," and the reading materials should be both interesting and relevant to the child. The students cautioned against "reading that doesn't touch the brain." They said that though they were good test takers, standardized tests did not in any way measure knowledge. Discussion centered around the importance of reading in opening the door to learning. They stated that young children also need to be encouraged to write because writing helps to organize thinking and enhances the ability to learn. It also allows for creative expression. Above all, these students stressed that the child should not be "put down" as a learner.

Many students succumb to the educational system at all levels. They lose interest in school, and they experience an erosion of curiosity for learning. The subjects in the present study are highly successful college freshmen readers who have developed the attitudes and learning strategies necessary to ensure academic success. Less effective college readers might benefit from their insights.

Those who have the responsibility for developing college reading programs may, likewise, profit from the information provided by the highly proficient readers in this study. Instructors in these programs can discuss with less effective readers the metacognitive insights that able readers have as learners. They can also discuss the strategies and attitudes that effective readers have developed over the years which have contributed to their reading maturity and proficiency. It may be possible to match individual learning strengths with specific reading strategies.

Instructors can meet individual and group needs by developing a spectrum of reading strategies for a variety of college textbooks based on the information provided by the proficient readers. For example, less effective readers could benefit from listening to and discussing portions of the taped oral readings, retellings, and the retrospective analyses of the proficient readers in the present study. Less able readers could be taught to analyze their own reading strategies in specific text in the content of proficient reading. This could be accomplished by utilizing the research instruments of this study and the subsequent follow-up discussions. Summary strategies are important aids to reading comprehension, and based on the findings of this study, might well be taught to all students.

Less effective college readers are often helped in reading by discussions of the reading process, of relevant research in reading and study techniques, and of their own early reading experience. Learning effective reading strategies helps to improve college performance. Less able college readers can and do become mature, proficient readers and for some, the students in this study have provided the direction.

REFERENCES

Anderson, T., & Glover, J. (1981). Active response modes: Comprehension "aids" in need of a theory. *Journal of Reading Behavior, 13*(2), 99–109.

Brown, A., & Day, J. (1983). *Macrorules for summarizing texts: The development of expertise* (Tech. Rep. No. 270). Champaign, IL: University of Illinois, Center for the Study of Reading.

Brown, A., Day, J., & Jones, R. (1983). *The development of plans for summarizing text* (Tech. Rep. No. 268). Champaign, IL: University of Illinois, Center for the Study of Reading.

Burke, C. (1978). *The reading interview.* Bloomington, IN: Indiana University, The Reading Program.

Collins, A., Brown, J., & Larkin, K. (1980). Inference in text understanding. In R. Spiro, B. Bruce, & W. Brewer (Eds.), *Theoretical issues in reading comprehension.* Hillside, NJ: Erlbaum.

Flavell, J. (1979). Metacognition and cognitive monitoring: A new area of cognitive development inquiry. *American Psychologist, 34,* 906–911.

Goodman, K., & Burke, C. (1973). *Theoretically based studies of patterns of miscues in oral reading performance* (Final report). Washington, DC: Office of Education.

Goodman, Y., Watson, D., & Burke, C. (1987). *Reading miscue inventory: Alternative procedures.* Katonah, NY: Richard C. Owen.

Gray, W., & Rogers, B. (1956). *Maturity in reading.* Chicago: University of Chicago Press.

Smith, S. (1982). Learning strategies of mature college learners. *Journal of Reading, 26*(1), 5–13.

Smith, S. (1984). Reading texts without contexts: An analysis of problem solving by experienced readers. *Western College Reading Association Journal, 3*(2).

Smith, S. (1985). Comprehension and comprehension monitoring by experienced readers. *Journal of Reading, 28*(4), 292–300.

Watson, D. (1978). Reader selected miscue: Getting more from sustained silent reading. *English Education, 10,* 75–85.

Watson, D., Robinson, R., Chippendale, E., Nicholaus, C., & Jenkins, P. (1979). *Describing and improving strategies of elderly readers.* Columbia, MO: University of Missouri–Columbia, Department of Curriculum and Instruction.

Weatherill, D. (1982). *The reading strategies of average upper-elementary students observed through miscue analysis.* Unpublished doctoral dissertation. University of Arizona, Tucson.

A Qualitative Study of College Developmental Students' Perceptions of the Reading and Writing Relationships in a Co-Taught Paired Reading Course

Michaeline E. Laine

Educators and researchers such as Tierney and Pearson (1994), Bartholomae and Petrosky (1986), Elbow (1986), and Moffett (1983) agree that there are important relationships among reading, writing, listening, speaking, and thinking. Reading, like listening, is a receptive language skill, and writing, like speaking, is an expressive language skill. Both receptive and expressive skills are necessary and important for effective communication (Moffett, 1983). Learning depends on understanding information conveyed by others (reading and listening) and articulating information to others (writing and speaking). Both reading and writing skills influence students' abilities to learn and think.

Researchers and teachers have long known that there were relationships between reading and writing. For example, teachers generally agree that good readers tend to be good writers and poor readers tend to be poor writers. Also, the act of reading tends to be similar to the act of writing in that both processes involve the construction of meaning. Barr (1985), for example, asserts that "you learn to read by reading as a writer, and to write by writing as a reader" (p. 110). Schema theory has shown us that both readers and writers construct meaning by interpreting information in terms of prior knowledge and experiences (Anderson & Pearson, 1984).

We also know that readers and writers engage in similar thought processes. For example, readers survey or preview a passage, and writers organize or outline their thoughts. Readers make and check their predictions, and writers develop a first draft, then seek feedback and suggestions. Readers elaborate on or modify their predictions, and writers make revisions; readers monitor their comprehension to make necessary

Originally published in Forum for Reading *(1997–1998), volume 28, pages 1–15*

adjustments, and writers edit their work. Finally, readers evaluate their learning, and writers assess the effectiveness of their final drafts.

We know that instruction in both reading and writing can influence achievement (Shanahan, 1988). Research by Tierney, Soter, O'Flahavan, and McGinley (1989) suggests reading and writing in combination are more likely to facilitate critical thinking. It is clear that reading and writing should both be emphasized in all classrooms.

Finally, we know that social interaction enhances literacy learning (Goodman, 1984; McCarthey & Raphael, 1992; Vygotsky, 1986). Within the teaching/learning situation, this means that teachers guide and direct the individual activity of students, but do not force or dictate their own will on the students. Rhodes and Dudley-Marling agree that educators cannot force learning since learning is a student's prerogative (1988). Authentic teaching and learning come through collaboration by adults with students (Davydov, 1995). Teachers aim for the learner's "zone of proximal development...the distance between the actual developmental level as determined by independent problem solving and the level of potential development as determined through problem solving under adult guidance or in collaboration with peers" (Vygotsky, 1978, p. 86). Educators not only need to plan instruction for students but to involve them in the teaching and learning process.

Statement of the Problem

Given what we know about the teaching and learning of the communicative skills, do students perceive these relationships among reading, writing, listening, speaking, and thinking? Bartholomae and Petrosky, in *Theory and Method for a Reading and Writing Course* (1986), describe a paired reading and writing course, but do not address the developmental students' perceptions. The research question examined in this study is What are college developmental students' perceptions regarding reading and writing relationships in a paired course?

Setting

A large midwestern university offers a paired reading and writing course for academically underprepared college students. The course, titled Strategic Reading and Writing (SRW), is designed to model the type of instruction called for in current research and theory. Reading and writing are linked within the classroom for academically underprepared college students. In particular, placement tests in reading and writing suggest that these students are unprepared for the academic demands of freshmen English and other college courses. In SRW, a reading teacher and writing teacher work together to integrate reading and writing. Students enroll for one six-credit hour course. The reading component meets for 75 minutes each Tuesday and Thursday, and the writing component meets for 50 minutes each Monday, Wednesday, and Friday. During the reading sessions, the major focus is on strengthening comprehension, vocabulary, and learning strategies. These strategies are taught through reading passages from a textbook designed for developmental readers and writers. During the writing sessions, the instructor attempts to increase students' writing proficiency with the guidance of the instructor and two in-class tutors. The two components of the course are similar in format to the Reading Workshop and Writing Workshop outlined by Atwell (1987). In the writing component, students prewrite, draft, revise, edit, and rewrite papers. The teacher conducts minilessons on the conventions of writing, structures editing and revision groups for the writers, and conferences with individual writers. The topics of the students' papers are related to the reading assignments that are discussed in the reading sessions. The reading component is structured around 82 passages, poems, essays, and short stories written by students and professional writers. The text, *A Reader for Developing Writers* (Buscemi, 1993), is designed to illustrate principles and strategies that writers need to learn and includes a glossary, short biographies of the authors, explanations of reading, and writing, principles, questions for discussion, and suggestions for journal entries and full-length essays.

Methodology

Context

Within the context of Strategic Reading and Writing (SRW), students transacted with texts as they read, discussed, and wrote within a community of learners. This community included two instructors, two in-class tutors, and the students. In the reading section of SRW, the instructor introduced the reading passages from the text through pre-reading activities. Vocabulary development and comprehension strategies were emphasized. Prompts from the reading passages were the focus of freewriting in journals. The journals became the springboards for each of the four required papers.

In this course, the reading passages were also used to teach summary writing. In addition, the reading instructor also worked on study skills such as those related to test taking. The reading instructor demonstrated how reading passages contained components which were to be incorporated in their writing: introductions, main ideas, details of support, and conclusions. The goal of both the reading and the writing instructor was to help students internalize reading and writing relationships.

In the writing section, the instructors used the freewritten journals from the reading section as springboards for each of the four required papers. Writing instructors focused on the writing process: prewriting activities, multiple drafts, revisions, and editing. Each paper was completed in a two-week cycle. Tutors in the writing class on Monday and Friday each week provided individual assistance to the students. Each Wednesday the writing instructor taught minilessons designed to address difficulties that emerged from the students' writing (e.g., the conventions of grammar or techniques to write an effective introduction).

Participant Observation

I was both the teacher and the researcher in this study. As a reading instructor in this two-year open-access college, I have an understanding of the program and curriculum since I codeveloped the original curriculum. I selected a qualitative methodology to obtain students' perceptions of reading and writing relationships in this paired course. Reagan (1984), in her study on a paired reading and writing course, explains that "quantitative evaluations cannot adequately explain the results of various methods of pedagogical intervention nor describe exactly how they affect the student" (p. 9). My goal was to obtain the perspectives of individual students. What were their perceptions regarding the reading and writing relationships that were the bases of this integrated course?

Miles and Huberman (1984) and Spradley and McCurdy (1972) caution against reporting in a biased fashion. I made a conscious effort to report the findings in a nonjudgmental fashion even though I was the reading teacher in this integrated reading and writing course. I acted as an unobtrusive instrument as a participant observer to discover the perceptions of these students in this quarter-long paired course.

Participants

During the course of the study, the focus moved from all seventeen students to three focal students. Two white females and one black male dropped the course before the end of the quarter, leaving fourteen students: five black males, five white males, and four white females.

Focal students for this study were then selected on the basis of patterns that emerged during the early stages of data analysis. The criteria for selection were (a) students who were enrolled and attended from the first class meeting until the end of the quarter, (b) students who completed all of the reading and writing assignments (four journals, two summaries, complete drafts of papers one and four, final self-evaluation paper), and (c) students who were willing to participate in the study.

These criteria left seven possible informants to schedule for interviews. After final grades were turned into the department secretary, these seven students (two white females, one black male, and four white males) were scheduled for interviews. Six out of seven students participated in the interviews. From the six interviews, three male informants—David, Shawn, and Hugh—became the focal subjects of this study.

David, a 20-year-old white male from northern Ohio, was motivated, determined, and driven by his willingness to learn. David's motivation is driven by his need to succeed and a less than successful experience at a community college in his hometown. He did not view himself as a good reader or writer. In David's self-evaluation journal, he wrote, "I'm an awful writer and would love to improve my writing and reading." David also viewed himself as the "world's worst speller."

Hugh is a 19-year-old white male from Long Island, New York, whose self-confidence radiates from his body language and an ever-present effervescent smile on his face. Hugh was the most vocal of the students in the class and had a sincere eagerness to learn in spite of his learning disability. One of Hugh's characteristics is that he had a questioning mind; no topic was off limits. Hugh asked numerous questions such as, "What do you do when you get writer's block?" "Why does a summary need to be written in a hundred words or less?" With his questioning mind, desire to learn, and command of oral language, Hugh became a catalyst for class discussions.

Shawn is an 18-year-old black male from an affluent section of northern Ohio. Shawn was playful by nature; his playfulness came out in interactions with Hugh. Shawn believed that he had control of his learning. During the interview, he stated, "I think, it [learning] was what you put into it. If you put something into it, you will get something out of it." Shawn was eager to put something into his learning by coming prepared for class as a willing and self-motivated student.

Data Analysis Procedures

Fieldnotes provided information about the social interactions among the students, instructors, and in-class tutors within the classroom environment. Interviews supplied more information because the students' perceptions were articulated. Several artifacts also provided further evidence of the students' perceptions. These included (a) the reader/writer self-evaluation in journal one, (b) the two essay test questions related to the reading and writing concepts they had learned in the paired course, (c) the entry about giving advice to someone in journal seven, and (d) the final in-class self-evaluation journal entry.

Results

In this section, I explore the three dominant themes that emerged from the triangulated data. Through the use of triangulated data, I support each theme and summarize my findings. The data documented that students were reading like writers and writing like readers. The data (classroom observations, interviews, and written work) provided insights into the three focal students' personalities and reading, writing, and thinking abilities within this community of learners in a co-taught paired reading and writing course. Each data set provided a valuable lens. For example, David was very quiet in the classroom, but very talkative during the interview. Shawn was vocal and talkative in the class and interview. Hugh was a very dominant voice in both the reading and writing classes but was reflective during the interview.

Each subtitled section will use triangulated data from the focal students to support that particular theme. David, Shawn, and Hugh were selected because they turned in the written materials designated in the data collection phase of this study, participated in the interview, and were the most informative.

Theme One: Writing Improved by Reading, Writing, Listening, and Speaking

For these three students, the speaking and listening components of the communicative process were interwoven with reading and writing.

Speaking gave them opportunities to express their thoughts, hear the opinions of others, and negotiate meaning. Moffett (1983) argues that most problems facing English language arts teachers do not concern spelling, punctuation, and word recognition nearly so much as thinking and speaking. He suggests that teachers provide young adults with abundant practice in oral composing and oral comprehension. The results of this study support Moffett's research in that oral language helped these three students develop their reading and writing strategies.

One of the most vivid examples of students perceiving the relationships between reading, writing, listening, and speaking became known as the "debate thing." With more than 26 years of teaching experience, I have learned that each class takes on a life of its own. For this class, this life was what the students called the "debate thing." The concept of the "debate thing," as opposed to simple discussion of the reading passages, developed in an attempted discussion of Maya Angelou's (1969) "The Boys" (as cited in Buscemi, 1993).

The Debate Thing

To start the discussion of "The Boys," the students were asked to write something about the reading passage. They were asked to write whether they liked or disliked the reading or if they had a question about the passage. According to Gullette (1992), by having the students write a few sentences on a topic or question, it implies to the student that the topic is serious and complex. While the students were involved in this activity, Hugh and Shawn talked to each other, laughed, and started to write. They had started to develop a relationship. Shawn saw this relationship as fun, one in which he could "disagree with Hugh on everything." It was a relationship based upon mutual respect, but they agreed to disagree about any topic under discussion just for the fun of it.

Sharing what was written was instrumental for this class and activated students' schema about Maya Angelou and her story "The Boys." The discussion centered on Maya Angelou's and students' experiences with racism and discrimination. The student-directed question and answer exchange developed about interracial dating, stereotyping, acceptance, and generalizations. Hugh and Shawn started into a major debate about whether Shawn was prejudiced. The students came to a consensus that "we" are all prejudiced in some way. Finally, Shawn stated, "I was raised that blacks should not date whites because of the problems it can bring. It is not fair to the children." The discussion worked its way into the problems for interracial children.

The emotional volcano erupted when Geoff, a nonfocal informant, stood up, pounded his fist on the table, and yelled, "My father is black, and my mother is white so do not tell me there are problems with the children. I am fine. You people do not know what the hell you are talking about." The classroom became absolutely silent. Hugh looked over at Geoff, smiled, and stated, "I like you, Geoff, and I am glad that you are here." Shawn and Geoff had a whispered, verbal exchange, smiled, and seemed at peace with each other.

At this point, the end of the scheduled class was near, and I needed to bring a sense of closure to the class session. I stated, "Today's discussion should have enabled you to think and to write about the issues of discrimination, racism, and stereotyping. There were many emotional issues brought up in today's discussion. When you write, you need to show your emotions and let your reader know what you are thinking." As the students left the classroom, they were talking to each other about concepts in this class discussion.

Before the start of the next reading class, Hugh entered the classroom and asked me, "Are we going to have that debate thing today?" Before I answered, Shawn interrupted, "Yeah, are we going to have that debate thing again? I am ready." Therefore, the "debate thing" became part of the normal life in the reading class. Also, as I coded fieldnotes and triangulated data, the "debate thing" emerged as integral part of the class and data.

These three focal and vocal subjects all perceived a connection between oral and written language. They perceived classroom discussions, the "debate thing," and discussions in editing and revising groups as important ways to become better writers. From the students' perceptions, the oral activities aided in their thinking, learning, reading, writing, and communicating with each other. Rosenblatt (1978) argued that writing emerged from transactions among reader, writer, and text; the end result of these transactions was better writing. Through the use of oral language activities, the three focal subjects transacted with text as they activated schema to combine new knowledge with old. By orally sharing their thoughts and ideas, these three focal subjects were able to clarify their thoughts, which enabled them to decide on a focus for their papers. Even though David and Hugh felt that the "debate thing" sometimes got out of hand, it helped them to learn about other people's opinions, giving them a clearer sense of audience. From the analysis of the interviews, written work, and classroom observations, David, Shawn, and Hugh were influenced by what other people thought. They perceived that the "debate thing" influenced their writing—what they wrote, how they wrote, and how they read the writing of others. The elements of Atwell's Writer's Workshop (1987)—prewriting, collaboration, peer revision, editing groups, and author's chair—were important for all three informants. It was important, for example, for David to see how others wrote within guidelines. This gave him a framework to follow when he wrote. Writer's Workshop helped David gain confidence and place his own difficulties in perspective. He realized, for example, that he was not the "world's worst speller." David viewed writing as a process, which included brainstorming, reading others' writing, reading models and examples, drafting, and working in peer revision and editing groups.

Shawn also saw merit in the revising and editing activities. He perceived reading and looking at text as a learning experience. He believed that this work improved his writing. Shawn used his experiences with the reading passages to help pick out important information and organize his own writing.

Hugh used Writer's Workshop to edit and revise his writing and the writing of his classmates. He perceived reading, writing, and learning to be related processes and that he was a participant in transactions among texts, readers, and writers.

Theme Two: Development of a Sense of Audience and Purpose

David, Shawn, and Hugh perceived that they needed to write so that readers would clearly understand their written texts. The three focal subjects wrote with a real audience in mind. They wrote about experiences and ideas that they wanted to share. They wanted their writing to activate the imaginations of their readers. Britton, Martin, McLeod, and Rosen (1975) characterized this as writing to an internalized audience. For my three focal learners, this internalized audience grew out of the reading, writing, listening, speaking, and thinking that took place among their peers in this course. This theme emerged from interviews with the three focal subjects, their written work, and classroom observations.

These focal subjects wanted their writing to be picturesque, have the readers use their imaginations, and get the readers attention. David and Shawn felt that they involved the reader more effectively through the use of supporting details. Hugh perceived that sentence variety and sentence structure helped him write better sentences to help the reader. Therefore, for David, Shawn, and Hugh, better writing helped their readers have a more enjoyable experience. They wrote with a sense of audience and purpose because they were starting to internalize a sense of audience (Britton et al., 1975).

Theme Three: Writing as a Form of Thinking

The students perceived that reading and writing were ways of thinking. Sometimes, their thinking was metacognitive in nature, in that they monitored their own writing processes. In other situations, they came to see writing as a generative process.

These focal subjects perceived that thinking was part of their reading and writing. For David as a reader and writer, thinking involved two dynamics: reflective thinking and sharing his thinking with others. Shawn started to think of himself as a writer as he worked to organize his thinking, which helped him organize his writing. Hugh organized his thinking and writing by asking questions. During the interview, Hugh stated, "I know what questions to ask myself when writing a paper and what to look for. For example, is there a good thesis statement, a backup statement? Now, I think about supporting details." For these students, reading, writing, listening, speaking, and thinking were interrelated elements within a recursive and dynamic process.

Conclusions and Implications

Conclusions

The focus of this study was to describe the perceptions of college developmental students regarding reading and writing relationships in a co-taught integrated course. The study was driven by my need to learn more about my students and their perceptions regarding reading and writing relationships. As a teacher, with more than 26 years of experience, I still struggle to help my students find their voices and develop a sense of responsibility for their learning. I wanted to be a participant observer and learn about their perceptions of the reading and writing relationships in our co-taught course. Action research was the avenue for me to follow to answer my questions. It also helped me mature as a teacher, researcher, and scholar.

Students' perceptions, a vital element in the classroom, are largely neglected in the research literature. Many developmental students, in particular, lack motivation and self-esteem; thus, they seldom perceive themselves as competent readers and writers. Developmental courses, like Strategic Reading and Writing, provide strategies for students to hold on to as they prepare for freshman English and other college courses. Also, this course specifically provides students with opportunities for academic success within a community of thoughtful learners.

The students in this study felt safe enough to ask questions and allow others to see their shortcomings. But, more important, these students came to realize that they were not alone; there were others in college who were academically underprepared and had similar struggles with reading and writing. Hugh and Shawn, for example, were at opposite sides of most issues; however, they always sat next to each other when we discussed issues and engaged in the "debate thing." They took pleasure in the social aspects of the class and in these academic confrontations. These three students' perceptions primarily focus on reading and writing relationships but extend to perceptions of themselves as a readers and writers within a community of learners. These three focal subjects have learned specific concepts about writing by developing their metacognitive abilities through the use of reading, writing, listening, speaking, and thinking activities. The following are conclusions based upon the perceptions of David, Shawn, and Hugh. The data suggest that the focal students perceived the following:

- They monitored their writing processes.
- Discussing topics, brainstorming, debating, and other oral prewriting activities helped them determine what they wanted to write.
- Closely examining reading passages helped them to look for the thesis and details of support when they read. This, in turn, helped them include these elements in their own writing.
- The discussions in the reading section helped them to develop their ideas for papers in part because they learned about other people's opinions. Learning the opinions of others helped them to form their own opinions and express those opinions in their writing.
- Oral language stimulated their thinking and helped them develop more complex concepts.
- Writing for an audience helped them improve as writers.
- The act of writing stimulated their reflective thinking. This, in turn, helped them generate new text.

- The recursive writing process of prewriting, drafting, revising, drafting, and editing helped them to develop their thinking and writing.

- Working with their peers helped them revise and edit their papers. They learned that other students also had difficulty with some of the conventions of writing.

- They felt a sense of security in that they knew the people in the class, learned with them, and developed friendships and bonds. The students felt supported by their teachers, tutors, and peers. They believed that this sense of security was of value; as a result they felt free to express their opinions while discussing the reading passages.

- They started to recognize themselves as writers. As they recognized that they were becoming competent writers, they also perceived that they were losing some of the emotional baggage and negative feelings they had about themselves as readers and writers.

Implications

This co-taught integrated course provided students with a structure for reading and writing. One unexpected finding in this study was the expression by the students of the high value they placed on discussion. In retrospect, I should have expected as much, given the orality of most cultures. Students perceive that these oral language activities help them think through arguments and understand the reading passages; therefore, the reading passages and especially the discussions are a vital part of the writing process.

After I collected data for this study, I began to use a variation of the Socratic method in our class discussions, the question-and-answer formula employed by Socrates in Plato's *Dialogues*. This method has merit in that the students interact and share their ideas with each other. The teacher is not the catalyst for discussion, but keeps the conversation moving in a productive direction.

The importance students place on choice was also apparent from the study. As a result, I plan to alter the final weeks of the syllabus to include additional readings of the students' choice. By the seventh week of the 10-week quarter, students are not required to read passages that relate to future writing tasks. In the future, I plan to have students do self-selected reading from either the text or a novel of their choice. Because the best way to improve reading is to read. I will provide students with yet another opportunity to read for the sake of reading, and to make some connections to authentic writing.

Finally, audience became an important emerging theme in this study. Another pedagogical change I can make is to have the students' essays created on a website. This would expand the audience for their writing and make their communicative efforts even more authentic.

REFERENCES

Anderson, R.C., & Pearson, P.D. (1984). A schema-theoretic view of basic processes in teaching comprehension. In P.D. Pearson (Ed.), *Handbook of Reading Research* (pp. 225–253). New York: Longman.

Angelou, M. (1969). The boys. Excerpt from *I know why the caged bird sings*. In S.V. Buscemi (1993), *A reader for developing writers* (2nd. ed., pp. 247–250). New York: McGraw-Hill.

Atwell, N. (1987). *In the middle: Writing, reading, and learning with adolescents.* Upper Montclair, NJ: Boynton/Cook.

Barr, J.E. (1985). Writing and reading: A marriage between two equals. In E.M. Clark (Ed.), *New directions in the study of reading* (pp. 103–110). Philadelphia: Falmer Press.

Bartholomae, D., & Petrosky, A.R. (1986). *Facts, artifacts, and counterfacts: Theory and method for a reading and writing course.* Portsmouth, NH: Boynton/Cook.

Britton, J., Burgess, T., Martin, N., McLeod, A., & Rosen, H. (1975). *The development of writing abilities, 11–18* (Schools Council Research Studies). London: Macmillan Education.

Buscemi, S.V. (1993). *A reader for developing writers* (2nd ed.). New York: McGraw-Hill.

Davydov, V.V. (1995). The influence of L.S. Vygotsky on education theory, research, and practice. *Educational Researcher, 24,* 12–21.

Elbow, P. (1986). *Writing with power: Techniques for mastering the writing process.* New York: Oxford University Press.

Goodman, K.S. (1984). Unity in reading. In A.C. Purves & O. Niles (Eds.), *Becoming readers in a complex society* (83rd yearbook of the National Society for the Study of Education Part 1, pp. 79–114). Chicago: University of Chicago Press.

Gullette, M.M. (1992). Leading discussions in a lecture course: Some maxims and exhortations. *Change, 24*(2), 32–39.

McCarthey, S.A., & Raphael, T.E. (1992). Alternative research perspectives. In J.W. Irwin & M.A. Doyle (Eds.), *Reading/writing connections: Learning from research.* Newark, DE: International Reading Association.

Miles, M.B., & Huberman, A.M. (1984). *Qualitative data analysis.* Newbury Park, CA: Sage Publications.

Moffett, J. (1983). *Teaching the universe of discourse.* Boston: Houghton Mifflin.

Moffett, J., & Wagner, B.J. (1983). *Student-centered language arts reading, K–13: A handbook for teachers.* Boston: Houghton Mifflin.

Reagan, S.B. (1984). *The effect of combined reading-writing instruction on the composing processes of basic writers: A descriptive study.* Paper presented at Conference on College Composition and Communication, New York. (ERIC Document Reproduction Service No. 243 134)

Rhodes, L.K., & Dudley-Marling, C. (1988). *Readers and writers with a difference: A holistic approach to teaching learning disabled and remedial students.* Portsmouth, NH: Heinemann.

Rosenblatt, L.M. (1978). *The reader, the text, the poem.* Carbondale, IL: Southern Illinois University Press.

Shanahan, T. (1988). The reading-writing relationship: Seven instructional principles. *The Reading Teacher, 41,* 636–647.

Spradley, J.P., & McCurdy, D.W. (1972). *The cultural experience: Ethnography in complex society.* Prospect Heights, IL: Waveland Press.

Tierney, R.J., & Pearson, P.D. (1994) Learning to learn from text: A framework for improving classroom practice. In R.B. Ruddell, M.R. Ruddell, & H. Singer (Eds.), *Theoretical models and processes of reading* (4th ed., pp. 496–513). Newark, DE: International Reading Association.

Tierney, R.J., Soter, A., O'Flahavan, J.F., & McGinley, W. (1989). The effects of reading and writing upon thinking critically. *Reading Research Quarterly, 24,* 134–173.

Vygotsky, L.S. (1978). *Mind in society: The development of higher psychological processes* (M. Cole, V. John-Steiner, S. Scribner, & E. Soubermen, Eds. and Trans.). Cambridge, MA: Harvard University Press. (Original work published 1934)

Vygotsky, L.S. (1986). *Thought and language* (A. Kozalin, Trans.). Cambridge, MA: MIT Press. (Original work published 1934)

Studying Hard for a College Level Geography Course: A Case Study

Joseph W. Guenther and Thomas H. Anderson

Which studying strategies does a college student use to attain high marks in a difficult course? A community college study skills instructor investigated this question by enrolling in a regional geography course and monitoring the strategies he used to study for the course.

Prologue

The investigation was prompted by a concern (Anderson & Armbruster, 1982; Casale & White, 1980) about the suspected lack of generality or "workability" of some common studying strategies, for example, the SQ3R family reading strategies (Pauk, 1984; Robinson, 1945) and the Cornell method for note-taking (Pauk, 1984). Also of concern was the fact that most studying strategies are taught as if they were content free in practice. If this is true, the structure of the to-be-learned network of ideas, the procedural knowledge in a content area, as well as the ways an instructor lectures and constructs tests, would play only a minor role, if any, in the student's selection and application of studying strategies.

With these concerns in mind, we decided that the study skills instructor would enroll as a serious student in a college level regional geography course. The arrangements to take the course were simple and informal. The instructor asked permission from his colleague to attend the class with the intent to develop a studying strategy specifically modified to meet the needs of students in that course. The geography instructor, who often referred students in need of special assistance to the study skills instructor for help, agreed to the plan and welcomed this interest in his course. In addition, the study skills instructor hoped that he would be able to attract students who were having trouble with the course and tutor them from an "informed" advantage. That is, he would be able to teach them effective studying strategies from the vantage point of having gained a good grounding in the content area.

Originally published in Forum for Reading *(1987), volume 19, number 1, pages 7–18*

Initially, we thought that our biggest contribution to the typical, struggling students' dilemma would be to help improve their ability to read their textbook. We had several ideas, based on what we knew about the structure of the content area, and the usefulness of these structures (e.g., knowledge structures and text structures) when reading expository text.

The plan did not develop as we had anticipated. We will describe what happened, and attempt to explain it in a framework garnered from certain cognitive psychology notions.

Setting

The subjects in this investigation were three college level instructors and four course sections (approximately 100 undergraduate students) of regional geography. They ranged in age from 18 to over 60 and had enrolled in the course as part of their regular college curriculum. The first author is a reading/study skills instructor at the community college where the investigation took place. The second author is an educational psychologist and senior scientist at the Center for the Study of Reading at the University of Illinois. The first author was taking an independent course of graduate study with the second author while the study unfolded. The third instructor taught the regional geography course at the community college.

The instructional materials and activities were typical of a college level introductory course. They included a comprehensive textbook, a study guide, lectures, and tests. The course syllabus assigned the first four chapters (a total of 242 pages) of the textbook throughout the semester. The Dale-Chall (1948) readability index estimated the textbook to be about the 13.5 grade level.

The students were given a study guide to accompany each of the six unit tests. The study guide was an instructor-modified version of the guide provided by the publisher and discussed in the teacher's manual. As part of the study guide, the instructor gave the students a grid or "frame" (Armbruster & Anderson, 1984) that represented the kinds of topics that are discussed when studying the geography of regions.

The students took six unit tests which covered general geographic concepts (in the introduction) and the regions of Europe, Australia, the Soviet Union, North America, and Japan. The first five unit tests had 50 multiple-choice, true-false, and fill-in-the-blank questions. The sixth was a combination of 30 such items and a blank map of Asia, on which the students filled in the names of each of the countries.

The class sessions consisted of three weekly lectures of 50 minutes each for 16 weeks, followed by a final exam. The instructor used these lecture periods to introduce and elaborate on new concepts, with the help of maps, charts, and a globe. The instructor was aware of the fact that the text was too difficult for many of the students, so he used this period to explain the more difficult concepts, as well as to cover most of the material that would be on the tests. He also helped the students answer any study guide questions not answered in the textbook but left most questions for which the text provided information for the students to answer themselves. After each test, a copy was made available for analysis purposes.

During that semester, we met weekly to discuss the strategies employed during the week and any ideas or observations noted in the weekly log and recent (or upcoming) tests.

Results

What happened in this course? A detailed account of the strategies employed by the study skills instructor is given for each test.

Unit Test 1: Geography Concepts

Initially, the study skills instructor followed the course syllabus and read the assigned text pages for unit one. This unit included information on broad geographic concepts such as location of a place on a map or globe, the division between the physical landscape and the cultural landscape, and the interaction among such elements within those landscapes such as climate, soils, vegetation, hydrology, economics, culture, politics, race, language, and religion. Geography encompasses a wide domain of ideas, and it attempts to integrate these widely separated human concepts into one discipline. The domain of geography can be divided as follows:

    I. Cultural landscape, including

        A. race

        B. language

        C. religion or value system

        D. economy

  E. political structure
    1. internal security
    2. external security
 II. Physical landscape, including
  A. landforms
    1. mountains
    2. hills
    3. plains
    4. plateaus
  B. hydrology
    1. rivers
    2. lakes
    3. groundwater
    4. rainfall
  C. climate
  D. vegetation
  E. soils
  F. mineral resources

  Each of these topics was discussed in great detail. It was not light reading by any means, with readability samples ranging from 12th to 16th grade on the Dale-Chall scale. While reading the introductory chapter, the skills instructor encountered problems in applying the SQ3R method he had been teaching in his study skills course. The procedure for using the SQ3R version (Paul, 1985; Robinson, 1970) is described as follows:

1. **Survey the text**, reading summaries at beginning and end, glancing at headings, pictures, captions and other graphics to get a flavor for the content and to build advance organizers.
2. **Ask questions** by turning headings into questions or by generating general questions of one's own.
3. **Read** the text to answer the question.
4. **Recite** the answers by covering the text, exposing only the headings, saying aloud all that is remembered, and finally, checking oneself afterward for accuracy.
5. **Review** immediately after reading and periodically thereafter.

To begin with, the survey step of SQ3R had limited value when reading this chapter. For example, the title of the chapter, "Introduction: Regional Geography of the World," gave little helpful information to a novice who did not already have a good background in regional geography. Although there are many pictures and maps in the chapter, surveying them would tend, at first glance, to leave a reader more muddled than before opening the book. The pictures, maps, and charts provided no advance organizers; they were simply illustrations for the text, with no obvious meaning independent of it.

The headings included "Concepts of Regions," "Concepts of Culture," "Vegetation Patterns," "Water, Essence of Life." The latter heading was followed by five pages (about 600 words per page of text, maps, and pictures). One could survey such headings and be able to conclude only that the chapter was about geography, and that geography had something to do with culture, vegetation, and water.

What about the second step of SQ3R, the question step? What kind of questions might one ask from such headings? "What are vegetation patterns? Why is water the essence of life?" While these are respectable questions, they fail to penetrate very deeply the content information. Forming these questions is limited severely by the students' background knowledge. How about a question which in effect is answered throughout these sections, "How do rainfall patterns affect vegetation patterns and vice versa?" Freshman community college students are not analytical enough to ask such a question at this stage of their study. Yet this is the question that they would supposedly be answering as they completed the third step of his SQ3R, the "read" step.

The read step of SQ3R asks a reader to actively search for answers to whatever questions he has posed either from the headings or, in the absence of headings, from his own understanding of what he was about to read, based on the interaction between background knowledge and what was just read.

The recite step is not practical for this textbook, for the same reason that makes the question step impractical: There is too much text between headings and too little information in the headings. For example, the headings, "Food Production" and "Japan in the Post-Industrial Era" were each followed by about 1,100 words of text.

The review step is always practical, provided the student was able to read the text with meaning in the first place. Who could deny that review of some form or other is necessary for optimal test performance? Robinson (1970) does not specify the direction of that review, and we suspect that the kind of review one undertakes would make a difference. We return to this issue in our discussion section.

A strategy that quickly replaced the SQ3R strategy was one in which information from the study guide helped in the "Q3R" steps. Here, the student questions the text with study guide questions, reads to answer the questions, recites the answer by covering up the question, and reviews the study guide periodically. The course instructor had foreseen the difficulty his students would have with the text, and even included the page numbers on which specific answers could be located. This facilitated the use of the study guide.

Another strategy typically recommended to students is to "read the chapter before the lecture." Was this a realistic or useful "axiom"? In fact, even the study skills instructor with perhaps 20 years of formal education and a demonstrated ability to read textbooks, put discretion before valor and modified this axiom to "preview the chapter before the lecture, but keep it open during lectures." This, along with another new axiom of "keep the study guide handy during lectures and while reading the text," turned out to be quite useful.

What happened during lectures? The course instructor's lectures ranged from topics related to the world vegetation map to the soil map to the precipitation map to the climate map and back, painting with a broad brush from the arctic to the tropics. Often, one would discover, at the end of an anecdote or brush stroke, the answer to one of the study guide questions—even one not available in the textbook chapter.

Did the researcher use the Cornell note-taking format (Pauk, 1984) he taught in his study skills class? Although he eventually followed Pauk's suggested step of reading over lecture notes directly after class while they were still fresh in mind, and could still be expanded, he did not use this note-taking convention in toto. He used a more complicated strategy, instead. He divided his attention among these processes: listening to the instructor, summarizing important points in writing, glancing through the chapter, and looking at the charts handed out by the instructor.

This division into several processes seemed to be important because there were times when the instructor would refer to tables or maps in the book or on handouts. During these discussions, the study skills instructor decided it was important to have these charts and maps in front of him. These pictures, charts, graphs, and maps served to illustrate the "text" of the lecture. He also kept his study guide handy and open to the topics currently under discussion in the class. He frequently made notes in his study guide when it seemed better to write them there than with the summaries he periodically wrote in his lecture notebook.

This strategy was modified later in the course to reflect the pattern of what information from lecture, chapter, and study guide was important and was likely to appear on the test. In summary, the study skills instructor developed his own systems to study for the test. It included these steps:

1. Preview or lightly skim the text relative to concepts about to be discussed in the lecture.

2. Attend lectures for explanation of and elaboration on key concepts and to build background by listening in preparation for actually reading the chapter.

3. Use the question of the study guide to focus one's attention within the textbook, reading to find answers to questions as in the "question" and "read" steps of SQ3R.

4. Write out the answers on a separate sheet of paper, using lecture notes, the chapter, and handouts as resources for finding these answers.

5. "Recite" and "review" by asking the original questions of the study guide and trying to write the answers from memory. Check these answers against those developed in step four. Repeat this step until all the questions are mastered.

An analysis of the first test showed that the study guide, although very useful as an aid to reading the chapter, was helpful on only 32 out of 50 questions, a mere 64% of the test. Another 24% of the test questions was covered in lecture and in the chapter, and the remaining 12% could be answered only from information presented in the lecture. The researcher scored 92% on this first unit test, missing several questions about map concepts covered in the lectures. The researcher resolved to take more thorough notes in class, and added another step to his studying procedures, for example, expanding lecture notes as soon as possible after the lecture, while the ideas were still fresh in his mind.

Unit Test 2: Western Europe

This was the next of five units on regions of the developed world. Using the model (grid) for regional geography proposed by the instructor, the researcher drew up the following grid to summarize, sort, and categorize the facts about Western Europe into a meaningful framework:

1. Name of country:

2. GNP:

3. Per capita income:

4. Strengths of the country:

5. Weaknesses of the country:

A.	B.	C.	D.	E.	F.	G.	H.
country	climate	resources	agriculture	industry	religion	language	cities

As many facts as possible were written into the appropriate categories for each country, which were themselves grouped into their appropriate regions (Nordic, Mediterranean, Low Countries, etc.). The researcher answered the questions on the study guide before filling out the grid. He then went through the chapter on Europe to glean out information which seemed important (test-type materials). This was written in the form of summaries and raw notes, such as a list of important cities, their products, and their importance to the rest of the country. Then, as much as possible of this information was squeezed onto the grid. He felt that the process of constructing the grid was an important step in learning the information, because it required a structuring of the ideas. Also doing it helped decide which among many possibilities were the most important.

To study the grid in preparation for the test, the researcher masked the information below the headings, and tried to recite a few lines at a time. He checked his performance by uncovering the few lines just recited to see if he was correct.

He then constructed a proactive test of 50 questions, based primarily on information from the study guide. Also, he wrote the answers to these questions on a separate sheet. His rationale for this was that the questions could help him to memorize the material by asking and answering them until he mastered them. He patterned his questions after those in the study guide, and based the content of the questions on what the model for studying geography would predict to be important. Again, just writing the questions seemed to be useful in learning the material, and answering them was a good final review.

The researcher scored 96% on this test. Only eight of 50 test questions came from the study guide. Information on the grid and practice test were in 32 of 50 items, or 64%. Information on eight of the questions not predicted was on rivers and was not in the above sources. The researcher failed to include rivers, an essential element of the physical landscape, on his grid. Of the remaining questions not found in the above sources, four were covered only in lectures and six were covered only by the text. The next adjacent test, whatever its form, would have to include rivers and landforms.

Unit Tests 3 to 6

For test 3, Eastern Europe and Australia, the researcher adapted his study method to the information presented in the unit and, rather than using his grid, he gleaned testworthy information from the text, and made up a practice test. He scored 98% on this test.

For test 4, the Soviet Union, the researcher answered the study guide questions and then drew a rough regional map of the Soviet Union and summarized information by region into a table. He scored 90% on this test and suspected that had he prepared more extensive adjunct texts and tests; he may have increased his performance on this test.

For test 5, North America, the researcher again drew a table with information organized by principal region, and then went back to the text to add to his table any information he thought might be testworthy. He scored 94% on this test.

For test 6, Japan and Asia, the researcher summarized information in a table according to the core regions. He studied it by asking study guide questions and additional questions of his own, and answering them until he knew them by heart. He studied the Asia map by writing the names of Asian countries onto a blank map until he knew them all. He scored 98% on this test. His average on the five tests was 95.6%, second highest in the class.

Discussion

We now introduce a theoretical framework to help explain our observations of this studying scenario. We conceptualize the process of studying as having two major components: state variables and processing variables.

The **state variables** are those related to the status of the student and the to-be-studied text at the time of studying. Important student state variables include knowledge of the learning criteria, prior knowledge of the content area, and motivation. Important text state variables include content covered, organization or structures, and other features that affect the "readability" of the prose. The **processing variables** are those involved in getting the information from the written page into the student's head. Processing variables include the initial focusing of attention, the subsequent encoding of the information attended to, and the retrieval of the information as required by the criterion task. Studying is a function of the interaction of state and processing variables. A discussion of some of these components and a review of related research follows.

Although state variables include several student- and text-associated variables, "knowledge of the criterion event" is the one that is rather uniquely related to studying. Results from several lines of research (reviewed and reported by Anderson & Armbruster, 1982) generally support the hypothesis that the more specific the knowledge about the criterion event, the greater the effectiveness of studying. In those conditions where the criterion task is known exactly, performance is much higher than that found in a control condition. The effectiveness of studying decreases as knowledge of the criterion task decreases. Finally, when the nature of the criterion task is only vaguely known, facilitative effects are difficult to demonstrate.

Knowledge of the criterion task may be a necessary condition for optimal studying, but it is obviously not a sufficient condition. Knowledge of the criterion task must be accompanied by processing of the relevant information. Because there are so many ideas that students encounter while studying, it is folly to think that they all could, or even should, be learned and remembered. Therefore, the prime tasks of students are to focus attention and engage in encoding activities in a way that will increase the probability of undertaking and retrieving the "high pay-off" ideas and relationships. In other words, the students must select the segments of text and lectures that contain the most important ideas and ensure that they are well understood and likely to be remembered.

Which cognitive processes actually occur when students focus attention and concentrate hard are mostly conjecture at this point. Two theoretical frameworks, however, suggest in a very general way some processing variables relevant to studying. These are the "principle of encoding specificity" (Tulving & Thomson, 1973) and "the principle of levels of processing" (Anderson, 1970, 1972; Craik & Lockhart, 1972).

According to the principle of encoding specificity, the way in which information is encoded determines how it is stored. This in turn determines which retrieval cues will effectively access it. This principle calls attention to the important interaction between initial encoding and subsequent retrieval operations: The optimal form of processing is ultimately dependent on the nature of the retrieval task. The implication of the encoding specificity notion for studying is that studying will be facilitated to the extent that students know the performance requirements of the criterion task and encode the information in an optimal form to meet those requirements. If students know the exact questions to be asked, then naturally they should "perform" the answers to those questions. If students do not know the exact questions, but know the general type of questions, they should focus their studying on the class of appropriate responses to tasks of that type.

Processing the information in a form as close as possible to the requirements of the criterion task is only part of the problem. The students must also be concerned with the qualitative nature of the processing: They must ensure that the requisite information is processed in such a way that it is stored and available when needed to perform the criterion task. A theoretical framework pertaining to the qualitative aspects of the processing effort is the "principle of levels of processing" (Anderson, 1970, 1972; Craik & Lockhart, 1972).

According to this principal, stimuli are analyzed in a hierarchy of processing stages, from an analysis of physical or sensory features to an extraction of meaning. The durability of memory traces is a function of depth of processing, where greater depth implies a greater degree of semantic analysis. In other words, what is stored in memory is determined by the kinds of operations performed on the input. The implication of the levels of processing notion for studying is that performance on criterion tasks requiring comprehension recall will be facilitative to the extent that students attend to, interact with, and elaborate on the underlying meaning of the text.

Together, then, the principles of encoding specificity and levels of processing suggest that studying will be effective if students process the right information in the right way, where right information is defined with respect to the criterion task and right way connotes a relatively deep or meaningful level of involvement with the text.

Students can and do engage in a variety of covert and overt activities to help them process the right information in the right way. Most of the common studying techniques, such as underlining, note-taking, summarizing, and outlining are commonly used because teachers and students alike intuitively believe that these methods of studying will aid in learning and remembering the required information. Unfortunately, empirical research fails to confirm the purported benefits of the popular strategies.

Anderson and Armbruster (1982) reviewed the research on the common studying techniques and concluded that any of them can be effective if its use is accompanied by focused attention and encoding in a form and manner appropriate to the criterion task. Some techniques have more potential than others, however, for promoting the deeper processing suited to criterion tasks requiring greater comprehension and/or recall. These techniques include outlining (Barton, 1930), networking (Holley & Dansareau, 1984), mapping (Armbruster & Anderson, 1982), and schematizing (Camstra & van Bruggen, 1984). These techniques force students to identify, or impose, relationships that convey the meaning of ideas. Not surprisingly, the techniques that are likely to yield the highest learning benefits also have the greatest costs in student time and energy.

To illustrate how this framework of studying can be useful in understanding the strategies used in this case study, we have divided our discussion into three parts: (1) How was knowledge of the criteria gained? (2) How was attention focused on the textbook? and (3) What kinds of encoding activities were used?

How did he gain knowledge of the criteria? His drive, almost compulsion, to learn information about the criteria was a major component of his studying activities. The two major sources of this information were the study guide and the lectures. As noted earlier, the questions on the study guide were always taken seriously and were viewed to be potential items on the tests. Answers to them were carefully constructed and learned in preparation for the tests. Also, the main ideas from the lectures were used as keys to important information. In addition, a third source of information was the geography grid. Main headings in that grid suggested categories of information that were likely to occur for each geographical region. Note that the textbook was not much help in this task. The headings were too general, or they required too much prior knowledge to understand what they meant.

How did he focus attention to relevant areas in the textbook? Remember that there were about 40 pages of reading for each unit test. This typical segment of reading assignment presented about 8,000 idea units of information (based on 600 words per page and three words per idea unit). In addition to the individual idea units, there were pictures, charts, and other graphics. The number of potential "meanings" among the interactions of these components was astronomical. Reading to learn it all was impossible.

Instead, he read for specific purposes. These included finding answers to the study guide questions, locating information to construct grids and tables, and searching for information that would help him elaborate certain important ideas. In a sense, the textbook was seen as an encyclopedia of information rather than a discourse with a structure and organization that was unique to the discipline of geography.

What kind of encoding activities did he use? He engaged in a variety of encoding activities. Taking notes during lectures and writing answers to the study guide were two of the more "straightforward" activities—ones that every student is admonished to do. Recall that he is often engaged in these two activities simultaneously while attending to the lecture. He often used the study guide as a note-taking device.

Being aware that the benefits of simply taking notes during a lecture (compared with listening only) are not very robust (Anderson & Armbruster, in press), he always engaged in another layer of encoding activities in which information from his notes were used. This information was used to construct grids and tables, speculate on the items that would appear on the next test, and write "adjunct" texts and tests. Each of these study aids (grids, tables, texts, and adjunct tests) was simply a stylized version of the important information. The grids and tables used spatial clues (rows, columns, and cells) to help show the organization of the information while the adjunct text used the conventions of written language (list notations, paragraphs, and discourse markers) to help do this.

The techniques of preparing a speculation test encouraged him to think about the ways in which text item formats might be used to organize and highlight information. He considered the type of information that might naturally be included in matching items versus that which might be included in short-answer, fill-in-the-blank types of items. Also, he was able to predict some of the "foils"—reasonable wrong alternatives—that would be included in multiple choice items. This activity seemed very consistent with the kind suggested by the encoding specificity hypothesis discussed earlier.

Another class of encoding activities concentrated on committing information from the study aids into the student's memory so that it could be quickly and accurately retrieved. These included memorizing, reciting, and practicing. While the processes involved in constructing the aids were thought to be beneficial learning activities, the job did not appear to be complete until they could be reconstructed from memory.

Our "hard studying" instructor employed rather traditional techniques to help remember the material. Basically, he memorized the material by repeatedly reading and rehearsing it to himself. Then, a mask was placed over some or all of it, and he tried to say it aloud. Finally, as a test of his memory he would practice reproducing it by writing it down. The general objective was to be able to reproduce the study aid materials, if necessary, during the exam so that he could refer to that information.

This process of learning the content in preparation for an exam was not unlike a problem-solving task. The problem was to do well on the test and the solution path was the result of a "means-end" approach (Gagne, 1985). That is, he struggled to approximate the criterion task using all the clues that were available and then tested himself against those criteria. By using an iteration process, he varied his processing strategies as the criteria were better understood after each test.

The typical studying strategies that are taught students are more "forward" in their conceptualizations than those employed here. That is, the general strategies used by experts in a process or content area (Gagne, 1985) are referred to as "working forward" strategies. Those such as SQ3R are often taught to give the impression that if you use them, you will be studying like an "expert" and will consequently do well on the test. Anderson and Armbruster (1982) reviewed research findings and concluded that SQ3R has only a mixed history of success as an "expert" technique. Using it does not guarantee that the student will be successful.

Casale and Kelly (1980) and Manzo and Casale (1980) recognized that students often do not adapt expert strategies to the specific requirements of a course and have developed a Problem-Solving Approach to Study Skill (PASS) techniques as an alternative. This technique purports to teach students how to address realistically the variety of problems that contribute to their studying failures.

Perhaps there are no "expert" techniques. Each studying context presents a set of clues that can enable the student to acquire knowledge about the criterion events, focus attention on relevant text information, and engage in encoding activities. It becomes a problem-solving task to decide which among the many possibilities constitute the path of maximum payoff with minimum effort—an unapologetic objective of all busy students.

Recommendations

We do not see the need to abandon the teaching of how-to study courses, which include major segments of "expert" systems. In fact, we are rather convinced that the "expert" systems are probably as good or better than what is being employed by most students considered to be "at risk," or are highly likely to flunk the course.

We think, however, that more effort should be spent in making students active problem solvers within the serious game of doing well in a course. This effort might include the following suggestions:

1. Teach them that it is all right to use all legitimate sources to find out what might be on the next test. These include asking the professor, searching for last semester's tests, and asking other students and asking other instructors.

2. Teach them how to use all available study aids (textbooks, lecture notes, study guides, etc.) that are likely to be used in a course, but help them determine early in a course which one(s) is (are) the most effective. Then encourage them to concentrate on it (them).

3. Convince them that finding a good studying partner or two can be helpful in several respects. (In general, problem solving is more effective with several solvers than with just one.) First, different ways of organizing the information may emerge; second, more heads and hands are available to construct the grids, tables, and test items; third, more help is available to help untangle confusing information; and fourth, someone else can help determine whether the information has been memorized or not.

4. Teach them to learn to study within an authentic course context. Content-free studying techniques make about as much sense as learning to read without using text, learning to play the piano without a piano, or learning to tie one's shoes without shoestrings. How-to-study sections of typically tough courses should be offered to students at risk. These adjunct sessions should focus on the important processes of learning the course information as well as on the content itself. How-to-study instructors could teach these adjunct sessions after they begin feeling comfortable with (not an expert in) the course content.

5. Provide close tutorial support with "at risk" students while they attempt to encode important information in preparation for a test. Many of them may have never successfully memorized much information in their lives and they need to get the feel of what it's like to learn something new the "hard" way.

REFERENCES

Anderson, R.C. (1970). Control of student mediating processes during verbal learning and instruction. *Review of Educational Research*, 2(40), 349–369.

Anderson, R.C. (1972). How to construct achievement tests to assess comprehension. *Review of Educational Research*, 42, 145–170.

Anderson, T.H., & Armbruster, B.B. (1982). Reader and text—studying strategies. In W. Otto & S. White (Eds.), *Reading expository material* (pp. 219–242). New York: Academic Press.

Armbruster, B.B., & Anderson, T.H. (1984). Mapping: Representing information text diagrammatically. In C.D. Holley & D.F. Dansereau (Eds.), *Spatial learning strategies: Techniques, applications, and related issues* (pp. 189–209). New York: Academic Press.

Barton, W.A. (1930). *Outlining as a study procedure*. New York: Teachers College, Columbia University.

Camstra, B., & Bruggen, J.V. (1984). Schematizing: The empirical evidence. In C.D. Holley & D.F. Dansereau (Eds.), *Spatial learning strategies: Techniques, applications, and related issues* (pp. 163–187). New York: Academic Press.

Casale, U., & Kelly, B.W. (1980). Problem-solving approach to study skills (PASS) for students in professional schools. *Journal of Reading*, 24, 232–238.

Craik, F.I.M., & Lockhart, R.S. (1972). Levels of processing: A framework for memory research. *Journal of Verbal Learning and Verbal Behavior*, 11, 671–684.

Dale, E., & Chall, J.S. (1948). A formula for predicting readability. *Educational Research Bulletin*, 27, 11–20, 37–54.

de Blij, H.J., & Muller, P.O. (1985). *Geography: Regions and concepts*. New York: John Wiley & Sons.

Gagne, E.D. (1985). *The cognitive psychology of school learning*. Boston: Little, Brown.

Holley, C.D., & Dansereau, D.F. (1984). Networking: The technique and the empirical evidence. In C.D. Holley & D.F. Dansereau (Eds.), *Spatial learning strategies: Techniques, applications, and related issues* (pp. 81–108) New York: Academic Press.

Manzo, A.V., & Casale, U. (1980). The 5 C's: A problem-solving approach to study skills. *Reading Horizons*, 20, 281–284.

Pauk, W. (1984). *How to study in college*. Boston: Houghton Mifflin.

Robinson, F.P. (1970). *Effective study*. New York: Harper & Row.

Text Demands in College Classes: An Investigation

Vincent P. Orlando, David C. Caverly,
Leslie A. Swetnam, and Rona F. Flippo

Reading for a purpose is one of the major tenets emphasized when preparing students to read in the content areas. That purpose, however, often turns out to be a vague exhortation by a teacher to "read to understand" or "read to answer this question." Brown, Armbruster, and Baker (1986) concluded that reading for different purposes and tasks seems to be a skill that good readers develop on their own, and that the adjustment of effort in response to task demands is the essential element of effective studying.

Brown (1985, 1980) has argued that recognition of the task demands and adjusting one's reading are important metacognitive skills separating less mature readers from more mature ones. She has postulated that an effective reader uses three stages in learning: (a) *planning* which study reading strategy will fit the task demands before learning, (b) *monitoring* the effectiveness of the application of the strategy during learning, and (c) *checking* that one has satisfied the task demands after learning. Knowledge and understanding of the task demands are predicted in all three of these stages.

Research by Schallert and Tierney (1982) found that high school students generally have little awareness of the task demands of reading in the content areas. Also, Smith and Feathers (1983a; 1983b), Mikulecky (1982), and Greenewald and Wolf (1979, 1980) indicated that little reading is required of high school students. Greenewald and Wolf (1980) further indicated that of the little reading that is done, students are rarely called upon to use print as their only or even primary source of information. Further they stated that little sustained reading is taking place in the typical secondary classroom. Moore and Murphy (1987) stated that other researchers reached similar conclusions regarding the relatively minor role that reading seemed to play in the lives of secondary students, and indicted that secondary teachers do make reading assign-

Originally published in Forum for Reading *(1989), volume 21, number 1, pages 43–48*

ments but seldom expect students to develop understanding from the passages. In fact, they state that "teachers assign a portion of text to be read, but later, through lecture or discussion, they present the concepts the students were to have learned. Thus, many students can participate adequately in class without reading" (Moore & Murphy, 1987, p. 9).

At the college level, though, it is reasonable to assume that print materials are a major source of information. Apparently no previous research has explored the task demands at the college level. The major thrust of this study, therefore, was to determine the reading demands placed upon freshman students in college and university classes and to determine students' perceptions of these demands. Specifically, our purposes were to examine college classes to discover (a) the amount of required reading, (b) the purpose of this reading in relation to other class activities, and (c) the relationship between the assigned reading and course examinations.

Method

Subjects

Data were collected from 256 first semester freshmen enrolled in four classes at a large, western, urban college. Two sections of an introduction to psychology class (82 and 95 students) and two sections of an American history class (42 and 37 students) were sampled. The four professors used for this study were tenured full-time faculty members holding the rank of associate or full professor.

Procedure

A 20-item questionnaire was administered to all students in each of the four sections by the investigators approximately a week after midsemester. This provided the students with the opportunity to have experienced at least one examination prior to our survey. A similar questionnaire was completed by each faculty member while the students completed their version. The faculty survey was verified by a follow-up interview which expanded on the questions from the survey.

Material

In order to describe the reading demands of college freshmen, a 20-item questionnaire developed and piloted in previous research was used (Caverly, 1984; Caverly & Orlando, 1985). This questionnaire surveyed three areas of focus in this study: (a) the *amount* of reading required in terms of number of books, number of pages per assignment, and number of pages per course; (b) the *purpose* of reading in daily course activities in terms of whether the text presented concepts discussed in class, presented concepts not discussed in class, or presented viewpoints differing from those presented in class; and (c) the *relationship* between the assigned reading and course examinations in terms of the level of the questions (i.e., recall, interpretive, or applied), the type of questions asked (i.e., subjective or objective), the source of test questions (text material, or class activities such as lectures or discussion), and the role reading the textbook played in preparing for course examinations compared to class lecture notes and the amount of the textbook read prior to the examination. Closed-end questions were used almost exclusively except for responses dealing with number of pages read, percentage of assignments read, and the source of test questions which required that students and professors list a percentage for each source.

The question asked in the faculty survey were identical to those given to the students.

Results

Amount of Reading

A great deal of similarity existed among all classes in the total number of pages of required reading. The professors in each class indicated that the reading assignments were between 600 and 750 pages per semester. All professors used a textbook, with both history professors supplementing their text with a book of primary source readings. Most students were able to accurately report the number of texts that were assigned and the length of the reading assignments.

Purpose of Reading

Differences were noted both among faculty descriptions of the purposes for the reading in their classes and also between student perceptions and faculty descriptions of the purpose of reading in a particular course. History professor one indicated that reading was used for three purposes: (a) to introduce concepts which would be covered in class; (b) to review concepts in class; and (c) to introduce new concepts not covered in class. History professor two indicated that reading was used to introduce new concepts not covered in class, and to provide a different point of view about ideas presented in class. Psychology professor one indicted that reading was used to review concepts discussed in class, and to introduce new concepts not covered in class. Psychology professor two indicated that reading was used to review concepts covered in class, and to provide a different point of view. Each of the four purposes provided in the survey was chosen by one or more of the professors.

Three of the four groups of students, however, perceived that reading was used only to introduce or review concepts covered in class. History professor two's students were the only group that did not select these purposes, and they were in strong agreement with their professor that the purposes of the reading were to introduce new concepts not covered in class, and to present different points of view. While the other three professors cited at least two purposes, their students concurred *only* with the introduction or review of concepts covered in class purposes mentioned above. These students seemed to stick with a more traditional role of reading as an introduction and review tool, while their professors seemed to be expecting the reading to serve extended purposes (presentation of concepts and views not covered in class).

Relationship of Reading Assignments to Course Examinations

Both history professors indicated that their tests were subjective, while both psychology professors indicated that their tests were objective. Students in all classes concurred.

When asked at what level the test questions were written, both history professors indicated that questions asked students to recall and/or interpret what was learned. Students in both classes agreed that they were asked to recall what was learned. In addition, students of history professor two felt that the test questions required application (rather than interpretation).

Psychology professor one indicated that students were asked only to recall what was learned, and his students agreed. Psychology professor two indicated that her test questions served three purposes: recall, interpretation, and application of what was learned. Her students agreed that they needed to recall and apply what was learned, but did not believe that interpretation was necessary.

Professors and students were asked to indicate the percentage of test questions taken from text material versus class activities (lecture and discussions). Three professors indicated a near even split; history professor one 50/50; history professor two, 40/60; and psychology professor one, 60/40. Psychology professor two reported that 85 percent of the test material could be found in an overlap of lecture and text information. Professors were not asked to distinguish between test material found only in the text or only in the class activities. However, it is assumed that overlap would exist between these two sources. Although student responses varied within these classes, there was a relatively high correlation between student and faculty perceptions of the sources of the test questions.

Students were asked how they prepared for examinations. In three of the classes, strong agreement was shown between the professors' expectations and the students' perceptions about how to study for tests. Except for psychology professor two, all professors indicated that students should read text material and take class notes to study; their students almost unanimously agreed. Professors in these three classes also felt that reading should occur on a regular basis at least once a week; their students concurred. However, when professors in these three classes were asked how much of the assignments they perceived students had actually read, they predicted that students read only about 60 percent of the assigned pages. In contrast, students in these three classes reported reading on average between 90 and 100 percent of their assignments. Further investigation is needed to determine the basis for the relatively low predictions of the professors.

Psychology professor two indicated that test preparation could occur in two ways, *average* students should read the text and take class notes, and *good* students should do well by taking class notes without reading the text material. This relatively unusual recommendation warrants further study of the professor's rationale and use of reading for the course. She also indicated most students should read the text several times a week, while some need to read the text every day. Like the other professors, she predicted that students were reading approximately 60 percent of the reading assignments. Students in her class agreed that they needed to read the text and take class notes. However, when asked how much of the reading they had completed, no clear consensus was indicated. Unlike the students in the other classes, these students reported a broad range of completion of the reading assignments from 10 to 100 percent. This may indicate their confusion over the professor's communication of the role of the text for students who are achieving at different levels. Some students read the text at least once a week; however, many students indicated that they only read the text just before the test, a pattern not seen in the other classes.

When asked questions about the importance of class notes in test preparation, three of the four professors felt that the notes should be read on at least a weekly basis. In striking contrast to the perceptions of their professors, students in all classes indicated that they only read their class notes just prior to the test.

Discussion

In all of the classes, substantial amounts of reading were assigned, and in all but one of the classes, students reported that they were completing the majority of the reading assignments. In the class in which students were not completing their assignments, reading did not seem to play as important a role as in the other three classes and the professor reported that reading was only necessary for the average students. If Smith and Feathers's (1983b) and others' conclusions are correct and reading demands in high school are not extensive, this could indicate problems for freshman-level students who are suddenly required to do a substantial amount of reading for extended purposes beyond the introduction and/or review of concepts covered in class.

Although students reported they were doing the reading, faculty seemed to be more pessimistic. Possibly students were not able to demonstrate effectively to faculty that they were doing the reading. The reliance on lecture presentations and focus on lecture material in the examinations may not have given faculty the opportunity to accurately assess the amount of reading the students completed.

The results also indicated that students were able to perceive overt demands such as the number of texts, the length of assignments, and the type of tests, but were less able to perceive the more intrinsic demands such as the purposes for the reading assignments. Reading was used for different purposes by faculty, but the students were not always cognizant of all the purposes and tended to rely on the traditional introduction and review of information presented in class as their purposes. In all but one of the classes, students seemed confused as to what the purposes of reading were. The conclusion of this study, that student perceptions of the goals and expectations for learning differ from those expressed by their teachers, concurs with Smith and Feathers's (1983) results. In addition, students seemed to be focusing on recall learning while professors tended to report higher cognitive objectives such as interpretation and application, although this focus was not always borne out by the examinations.

The differences in professor communication were demonstrated in two of the subject classes. Students of history professor two were more aware of the task demands than the students in the other classes. Concurrence was established between history professor two and his students not only on the overt demands, but also on the more intrinsic demands. They knew the purpose of the reading, the level of the test questions, and demonstrated a greater understanding of the source of the test questions than the students in the other classes. Students in the class of psychology professor two knew the source and level of the test questions. They also recognized that the text was not as important and demonstrated this by reading it less. Further research on how professors communicate the expectations for reading to their students is needed.

The purposes and demands for reading a text in a freshman-level college class appear to be different than the purposes and demands students have experienced in high school. Before these results can be generalized, additional research examining these factors with classes at different types of colleges and with students at different levels would be necessary. Apparently students need to be made more aware of the varying purposes for reading, and professors need to more closely assess their use of reading material. This assessment could result in the development of examinations which more closely reflect professors' purposes for having students read, and communication strategies which more clearly direct students in their reading.

REFERENCES

Brown, A.L. (1980). Learning to learn how to read. In J. Langer & T. Smith-Burke (Eds.), *Reader meets author, bridging the gap: A psycholinguistic and social linguistic perspective*. Newark, DE: International Reading Association.

Brown, A.L. (1985). Metacognition: The development of selective attention strategies for learning from text. In H. Singer & R.B. Ruddell (Eds.), *Theoretical models and processes of reading* (3rd ed., pp. 501–526). Newark, DE: International Reading Association.

Brown, A.L., Armbruster, B.B., & Baker, L. (1986). The role of metacognition in reading and studying. In J. Orasanu (Ed.), *Reading comprehension: From research to practice*. Hillsdale, NJ: Erlbaum.

Caverly, D.C. (1984, November). *College students' metacognitive awareness of task demands*. Paper presented at the Twelfth Plains Regional Conference of the International Reading Association, St. Louis, Missouri.

Caverly, D.C., & Orlando, V.P. (1995, October). *How much do college students read their texts?* Paper presented at the annual meeting of the Western College Reading and Learning Association's Colorado State Conference, Colorado Springs.

Greenewald, M.J., & Wolf, A.E. (1979, November). *The multiple roles of reading in secondary content area instruction.* Paper presented at the National Reading Conference, San Antonio, TX.

Greenewald, M.J., & Wolf, A.E. (1980, December). *Frequency of reading in secondary content areas: A followup observational study.* Paper presented at the National Reading Conference, San Diego, CA.

Mikulecky, L. (1982). Job literacy: The relationship between school preparation and work place actuality. *Reading Research Quarterly, 17*, 400–419.

Moore, D.W., & Murphy, A.G. (1987). Reading programs. In D.E. Alvermann, D.W. Moore, & M.W. Conley (Eds.), *Research within reach of secondary school reading: A research guided response to concerns of reading educators.* Newark, DE: International Reading Association.

Schallert, D.L., & Tierney, R.S. (1982). *Learning from expository text: The interaction of text structure with reader characteristics.* Final report of the National Institute of Education Study (NIE-G-79-0167). Washington, DC: U.S. Department of Education.

Smith, F.R., & Feathers, K.M. (1983a). Teacher and student perceptions of content area reading. *Journal of Reading, 26*, 348–354.

Smith, F.R., & Feathers, K.M. (1983b.) The role of reading in the content classrooms: Assumptions vs. reality. *Journal of Reading, 27*, 262–269.

Directing Prose Learning With Analogical Study Guides

David A. Hayes

ollege teachers typically engage their students in a range of study activities that they believe will foster students' learning of course material. Sometimes the activities are structured so that they clearly indicate to students what is to be learned and how learning is to be demonstrated. More often, however, assignments are made that leave students to determine for themselves the significance of studied material and to guess how they should prepare for demonstrating learning. The present research tested the effectiveness of one kind of structured study activity to accompany assigned reading, completing an analogical study guide (Bean, Singer, & Cowan, 1985), by comparing its learning outcomes with the learning outcomes of two unstructured activities commonly assigned to accompany reading, essay writing, and self-questioning.

Research on study guides (Bean, Singer, & Cowan, 1985; Berget, 1973; Estes, 1973; Sanders, 1967) has produced mixed results, though guide material does appear to be helpful when constructed to guide thinking in ways that simulate the kind of thinking expected as an outcome of its use. Bean and colleagues (1985, 1987) have reported that the use of study guides that provided analogies resulted in increased learning for low achieving biology students. They concluded that analogical study guides offer a bridge from familiar experience to new concepts for which students lack adequate knowledge to grasp.

Among student-initiated study activities to accompany reading, none have been more widely recommended in recent years than having students compose brief essays or generate self-questions. Notwithstanding strong assertions about writing's value as an instructional aid (Beach & Bridwell, 1984; Flower 1979; Odell, 1980; Page, 1974; Wittrock, 1983), researchers (e.g., Bean & Steenwyk, 1984; Hare, 1985; Newell, 1984; Taylor & Beach, 1984) have offered no firm evidence that writing activities are any more effective than other study activities for fostering prose learning. Having students generate their own ques-

Originally published in Forum for Reading *(1989), volume 20, number 2, pages 20–24*

tions about texts under study (Robbins, 1957; Robinson, 1946; Stauffer, 1976) finds support in research showing that questioning oneself during study results in increased constructive and integrative discourse operations (Hayes, 1987) and increased learning from texts (Dansereau et al., 1974; Duell, 1978; Frase & Schwartz, 1975).

If prudent choices are to be made among these study activities teachers have to take into account the effectiveness of the activities relative to one another. The present research was an effort toward determining the relative effectiveness of these study tasks for learning factual information.

Method

Subjects

The subjects were 31 undergraduate women majoring in English education at a university. As part of their coursework, the subjects had received instruction and demonstrated competence in setting instructional objectives, formulating questions, and constructing tests and test-like instructional materials. Further, as a condition of advancement to the upper division, the students had demonstrated competence in composing a variety of expositional patterns, including compare-contrast essays. Thus the students had demonstrated the competence needed to perform satisfactorily the tasks of the experiment.

Materials

The materials of the experiment included three pairs of encyclopedia articles and a study guide to accompany each pair of articles. Each pair of articles was comprised of a passage describing an unfamiliar athletic game and a passage describing a familiar analogous game. The analogous pairs of passages were adapted so that they described in parallel fashion the games of cricket and baseball, rugby and football, and jai-alai and handball. The format was identical for each. The first section presented general information about the game by identifying the object of the game, number of players, and the way in which a winner is determined. The next section described the playing surface, equipment used, and scoring. Another section then explained turn taking and how the game begins and ends. Finally, each passage discussed the rules of the game, which included time-outs, legal and illegal procedures, and penalties.

Since the passages were intended only to introduce the games, the rules were discussed in general terms, rather than in exhaustive detail.

The study guides also followed an identical format. The first section consisted of a list of terms from the unfamiliar sport to be matched with the appropriate terms from the analogous familiar sport. An item-completion section followed asking for information concerning number of players, equipment, rules, and scoring. The next section contained a list of rules to be matched with the appropriate sport. The answers "both" and "neither" were included. The final section, in chart format, contained five general statements and asked for an explanation appropriate to each.

Procedure

One week prior to engaging students in the study tasks, students' knowledge of the familiar games was assessed. This measure was taken with a 75-item true-false test in which students indicated their level of confidence for each response. Responses for which a student indicated high confidence counted twice as much as responses for which a student indicated low confidence.

The students were randomly divided into three groups for comparison in a restrictively randomized quasi-experiment under a 3 (treatments) × 3 (texts) factorial design. Treatments and texts were both within-subjects factors. The three treatments were administered without time limits during two-hour class sessions. The order of treatments was the same for all students, but texts rotated to a different group at the second and third class sessions.

At the first session, students were assigned the study-guide task. For this task students were issued a pair of passages and an accompanying study guide, and without instruction beyond clarification of the requirements for completing the guide, the students were directed to try to learn as much as they could about the foreign game by studying the passages and working through the accompanying materials.

At the second session, the students' task was to formulate study questions. Prior to receiving the passages, students were given suggestions for studying the material through self-questioning. The suggestions were to try to identify the main points of information in each paragraph; to make up questions about this information; to include questions about how the information compares with information about the familiar game; to review the questions and try to answer them from memory; and to quickly reread to confirm the correctness and adequacy of the answers.

At the third session, the students were assigned to write a compare-contrast description of the two games presented in the passages issued to them. Before starting the task, students were given a quick refresher lecture on two basic approaches to writing compare-contrast essays. One approach was the so-called continuous approach, by which the games could be described separately on each feature compared. The other approach was the so-called discontinuous approach, by which the games could be directly compared throughout the composition.

Three days after all the treatments had been administered, the students took a 150-item recognition test. The items were equally divided among the three pairs of games studied. The tests generally followed the same sequence for questioning students about the games as the passages did for describing the games.

Results

Overall performance on the posttest ranged from 72 to 132 raw score points. Performance on the jai-alai–handball items ranged from 26 to 42 points, on the cricket-baseball items from 22 to 44 points, and on the rugby-football items from 27 to 44 points. Mean performance on these items by subjects who studied the texts by the three study tasks is shown in Table 1.

The results were compared with an analysis of covariance in which the pretest scores were the covariates. The analysis revealed no signifi-

Table 1

Mean performance on test items from texts studied by composing, self-questioning, and completing study guides.

Text	Composing	Study Task Self-Questioning	Study Guide	
Rugby	34.91 (3.81)*	33.10 (3.32)	34.00 (5.85)	102.90 (13.17)
Jai-alai	32.50 (3.07)	29.60 (2.27)	34.18 (4.58)	96.48 (11.64)
Cricket	30.00 (4.06)	29.18 (5.02)	36.00 (5.83)	94.94 (17.22)
	97.65 (12.29)	91.74 (12.15)	104.13 (15.96)	

*Standard deviations are in parentheses

cant interaction effects, nor any main effect due to text. The analysis did show main effects associated with the study tasks, $F(2,83) = 7.027$, $p < .001$. The study tasks accounted for approximately 17% of the variance, constituting a large effect size due to treatment.

Performance on test items from texts that had been studied with study guides was superior to performance on items studied by self-questioning (t, [30] = 4.63, $p < .001$, ES = .88) and by composing compare-contrast descriptions (t, [30] = 1.95, $p < .058$, ES = .46). Between the items studied by the latter two study tasks, performance on items studied by composing comparison-contrast descriptions was superior Ct, [30] = 1.79, p .081, ES = .48).

Discussion

How to have students make use of what they already know in learning new subject matter is a continuing concern among educators. Study activities for addressing this concern may be activities that are either carefully structured by the teacher or activities that have students largely determine for themselves which of the material studied is significant and how that material relates to their existing knowledge. The results of the present experiment indicate that superior prose learning can be expected with the assignment of study activities that are carefully structured for the learners.

Although the assessment of learning included no problem solving or transfer tasks, it did provide a measurement of learning factual information. In terms of learning factual information, the results are consistent with the findings of previous research. The present investigation found, as did King, Biggs, and Lipsky (1984), that a composition task results in better test performance than a self-questioning task. In the present investigation, however, a slightly larger effect size was observed in the contrast between the effects of composing and self-questioning tasks, perhaps due to the difference in the two investigations' writing tasks. The results are also consistent with other research that has found positive effects associated with providing students study objectives and having them respond to study questions (Duell, 1978, 1984; McGraw & Grotelueschen, 1972), as well as with having students complete study guides (Bean, Singer, & Cowan, 1985; Estes, 1973; Vacca, 1977) to accompany reading. A conclusion drawn from that area of research seems also to apply here: Study tasks that force inspection behavior results in improved learning of factual information. Further, guide materials inform students about what they are expected to learn as they engage students in tasks that resemble the final test. As has been reported of experiments involving similar test-like study tasks in which intentional learning of difficult material was expected (Anderson & Biddle, 1975; Hartley & Davies, 1976), the guide materials very likely alerted students to the demands of the final test of learning. The results of the study imply, then, two distinct functions served by guide materials. First, they focus on material to be learned, and second, they provide practice in demonstrating the learning of that material as the teacher would have it demonstrated. The differential advantages of these two functions remain to be sorted out through further study.

REFERENCES

Anderson, R.C., & Biddle, W.B. (1975). On asking people questions about what they are reading. In G.H. Bower (Ed.), *The psychology of learning and motivation (Vol. 9)*. New York: Academic Press.

Beach, R., & Bridwell, L. (1984). Learning through writing: A rationale for writing across the curriculum. In A.D. Pellegini & T.D. Yawkey (Eds.), *The development of oral and written language in social context*. Norwood, NJ: Ablex.

Bean, T.W., Singer, H., & Cowan, S. (1985). Acquisition of a topic schema in high school biology through an analogical study guides. In J.A. Niles & R.V. Lalik (Eds.), *Issues in literacy: A research perspective* (Thirty-fourth yearbook of the National Reading Conference, pp. 38–41). Rochester, NY: National Reading Conference.

Bean, T.W., Singer, H., Cowan, S., & Searles, D. (1987). *Acquiring concepts from biology text: A study of text-based learning aids and reader-based strategies*. Paper presented at the Thirty-seventh National Reading Conference, St. Petersburg, FL.

Bean, T.W., & Steenwyk, F.L. (1984). The effect of three forms of summarization instruction on sixth graders' summary writing and comprehension. *Journal of Reading Behavior, 16*, 297–306.

Berget, E. (1973). Two methods of guiding, the learning of a short story. In H.L. Herber & P.L. Sanders (Eds.), *Research in reading in the content areas: Second year report*. Syracuse, NY: Syracuse University Press.

Dansereau, D.G., McDonald, B.A., Long, G.L., Atkinson, T.R., Ellis, A.M., Collins, K.W., Williams, S., & Evans, S.H. (1974). *The development and assessment of an effective learning strategy training program* (Tech. Rep. No. 3). Fort Worth, TX: Texas Christian University.

Duell, O.K. (1978). Overt and covert use of objectives of different cognitive levels. *Contemporary Educational Psychology, 3*, 239–245.

Duell, O.K. (1984). The effects of test expectations based upon goals on the free recall of learning from text. *Contemporary Educational Psychology, 9*, 162–170.

Estes, T.H. (1973). Guiding reading in social studies. In H.L. Herber & R.F. Barron (Eds.), *Research in reading in the content areas: Second year report.* Syracuse, NY: Syracuse University Press.

Flower, L.S. (1979). Writer-based prose: A cognitive basis for problems in writing. *College English, 41,* 19–37.

Frase, L.T., & Schwartz, B.J. (1975). Effect on question production and answering on prose recall. *Journal of Educational Psychology, 67*(5), 628–635.

Hare, V.C., & Borchardt. K.M. (1984). Direct instruction of summarization skills. *Reading Research Quarterly, 20,* 62–78.

Hartley, G., & Davies, I.K. (1976). Preinstructional strategies: The role of pretests, behavioral objectives, overviews and advance organizers. *Review of Educational Research, 46,* 239–265.

Hayes, D.A. (1987). The potential for directing study in combined reading and writing activity. *Journal of Reading Behavior, 19,* 333–352.

King, J.R., Biggs, S., & Lipsky, S. (1984). Students' self questioning and summarizing as reading study strategies. *Journal of Reading Behavior, 16,* 205–218.

McGraw, B., & Groteleueschen, A. (1972). Direction of the effects of questions in prose materials. *Journal of Educational Psychology, 63,* 508–588.

Newell, G.E. (1984). Learning from writing in two content areas: A case study/protocol analysis. *Research in the Teaching of English, 18,* 265–287.

Odell, L. (1980). The process of writing and the process of learning. *College Composition and Communication, 31,* 42–50.

Page, W.D. (1974). The author and the reader in writing. *Research in the Teaching of English, 8,* 170–183.

Robbins, P.A. (1957). *How to make better grades: A course in systematic studying.* Los Angeles: Par Publishing Co.

Robinson, F.P. (1946). *Effective study.* New York: Harper & Bros.

Sadler, W.A., & Whimby, A. (1985). A holistic approach to improving study skills. *Phi Delta Kappan, 67,* 199–203.

Sanders, P.L. (1969). Teaching map reading skills in grade nine. *Journal of Reading, 12,* 283–286.

Stauffer, R.G. (1957). *Teaching reading as a thinking process.* New York: Harper & Row.

Taylor, B.M., & Beach, R.W. (1994). The effects of text structure instruction on middle-grade students' comprehension and production of expository text. *Reading Research Quarterly, 19,* 134–146.

Vacca, R.T. (1977). An investigation of a functional reading strategy in seventh grade social studies. In H.L. Herber & R.T. Vacca (Eds.), *Research in reading in the content areas: The third report.* Syracuse, NY: Syracuse University Press.

Wittrock, M.C. (1983). Writing and the teaching of reading. *Language Arts, 60,* 600–606.

EFL Learners: Summarizing Strategies in Academic Settings

Ana Maria Morra de de la Pena

T he ability to summarize information from a single source has always been considered to have great instrumental and educational value. Summaries have been used as measures of background
knowledge in content subjects and to test the capacity to analyze, interpret, and synthesize information from written texts. At the college level,
summary writing acquires definite importance since it promotes critical
reading and improves comprehension, recall, and learning in general
(Hill, 1991). Summarization skills constitute a necessary prerequisite to
the more complex processes of synthesis from multiple sources in academic writing. Since English has become firmly established as the language of international academic exchange, the capacity to summarize in
this language is essential to Argentine university students. With increasing frequency, they need to keep records of or incorporate material in
their research reports from the vast number of publications in English.

A number of studies in summary writing in English as a native language have shown that instruction and academic experience facilitate
summarization of expository text (Afflerbach, 1990; Brown, Campione,
& Day, 1981; Brown & Day, 1983; Brown, Day, & Jones, 1983;
Chambliss, 1995; Taylor, 1984; Taylor & Beach, 1984; Winograd,
1984). For native Spanish speakers of English as a foreign language
(EFL), relevant research is still lacking. This article first briefly reports results from an experimental study of the effects of explicit teaching of
expository text structure on summary writing by EFL college students. It
then examines the summarization strategies used by students with good
and poor knowledge of text structure.

Study One–Training

The conceptual framework of the first study is provided by schema theory (Anderson & Pearson, 1988; Barlett, 1932; Rumelhart, 1980) and

Originally published in The Journal of College Literacy and Learning *(1998–1999), volume 29,
pages 1–17*

the interactive models of second language reading developed in the last twenty years (beginning with Rumelhart, 1977). Schema theory emphasizes the role of preexisting knowledge structures on reading comprehension. Schema theory characterizes reading comprehension as responding to a bidirectional or interactive model of text processing—a combination of top-down and bottom-up processing. Efficient readers constantly change their processing mode according to the reading situation, text, and purpose, whereas less competent readers and EFL readers tend to over rely on the bottom-up mode (Eskey & Grabe, 1988). The most obvious cause of this dependence on unidirectional processing is lack of availability or lack of activation of content and formal schemata (Carrell, 1985; Kirkland & Saunders, 1991; Schellings & Van Hout-Walters, 1995).

This study is concerned with formal schematic knowledge. It deals with background knowledge of the general patterns of form that organize the content of an expository text which include conventional categories such as a collection of descriptions, comparison/contrast, cause/effect, problem/solution, and others.

Subjects and Procedures

In the study, 53 intermediate-level EFL students at National University of Cordoba were randomly assigned to an experimental group and a conventional group. The experiment lasted eight consecutive weeks with a ninety-minute class period each week. During class periods each group participated in a specific training program geared towards summary writing. Results were evaluated. The students in the experimental group (26 subjects) received instruction on three types of structure for expository text—problem/solution, cause/effect, and comparison/contrast—and on methods of using this knowledge to improve reading comprehension and summarization of the main points (basically strategies to detect and use the top-level organization of texts in their reading and summarization tasks). This methodology rests on the notion that the rhetorical organization of expository text interacts with the readers' knowledge of textual structure to guide them in processing texts.

The conventional group (27 subjects) received training with the same texts but a different procedure (the traditional methodology in our school). The emphasis in instruction was grammar, particularly sentence analysis and sentence combining, and vocabulary work. There was also a focus on content of the passages through question-answering and discussion. The approach used in training this group corresponds to a linear or bottom-up model of the reading process.

The teacher, who was in charge of both groups, followed scripted lesson plans that were produced and discussed thoroughly in meetings with the researcher before and during the experiment. The students in the experimental and the conventional group had to take tests in summary writing before and after the training period. For each test, three passages between 300 and 500 words long were selected. Each passage was organized according to one of the three text types under consideration in this study (comparison/contrast, cause/effect, and problem/solution). All of the texts selected dealt with the same topic so that the effect of previous knowledge of topic could be controlled. In these tests students were first instructed to read the passage carefully. Next, they had to answer an open question aimed at schema activation for the identification of rhetorical organization of the source text. Then, they had to write their summaries and give them a title.

Students had access to the source text while writing their summaries (see Appendix A, page 145). It was hypothesized that the explicit teaching of formal schemata for the three expository texts types mentioned above (problem/solution, cause/effect, and comparison/contrast) would facilitate the writing of summaries by EFL students. To score the summaries, two independent raters used an analytic scale devised specifically for this purpose (see Appendix B, page 148). Discrepancies between the raters were resolved through analyses and discussions with this researcher.

Results

In order to determine the effect of instruction, for each of the groups the mean and standard deviation of the addition of the three measures (completeness of content, balance, and fluency/use of English) in the pre- and posttests were calculated. A reliability of 95% was also calculated for the mean in each one of the groups. Results show that performance by both groups was very similar before training (see Table 1).

Table 1
Pretest

	Mean	Standard deviation
Experimental Group (26 subjects)	16.3846	4.2150
Conventional Group (27 subjects)	16.1481	3.9051
Total (53 subjects)	16.2642	3.9959

The same analysis was performed after training, and the results, reported in Table 2, show that the mean on the posttest for the experimental group is significantly larger than that of the conventional group. In other words, the training sessions for the experimental group appeared to produce statistically a significant increase in the quality of summaries written by students in that group.

Table 2
Posttest

	Mean	Standard deviation
Experimental group (26 subjects)	23.5385	4.3839
Conventional group (27 subjects)	18.5185	4.0036
Total (53 subjects)	20.9811	4.9655

The differences between experimental and conventional groups after intervention are shown in Table 3: whereas the former increased, in proportion, 7 points, the latter increased 2 points.

Table 3
Differences between pre- and posttests

	Mean	Standard deviation
Experimental group (26 subjects)	7.1538	3.9769
Conventional group (27 subjects)	2.3704	4.4820
Total (53 subjects)	4.7170	4.9452

Note: Each test consisted of three discourse types: comparison/contrast, cause/effect, and problem/solution. Results reported here were averaged across the three text types in spite of the fact that differences in the groups' performance on these types would justify further analysis.

Since this is an experimental study with dependent samples (i.e., the same students did pre- and posttests), an Analysis of Variance with repeated measures (ANOVA) was considered appropriate to evaluate the differences between groups. The use of this methodology made it possible to conduct this evaluation eliminating subject effect between the two tests (i.e., the suspicion that performance on the posttest might be predictable from performance on the pretest and could not really be attributed to experimental activities). This analysis yielded a statistically significant difference between the experimental and the conventional groups in the posttest ($p = .000$).

Conclusions

Results show that the explicit teaching of patterns of textual organization for the types comparison/contrast, cause/effect, and problem/solution has a positive effect on the quality of written summaries—quality measured in terms of content, balance, fluency, and use of English. In relation to experimental instruction, it is important to note the students' enthusiastic response during and after training. Most of them said that before the experience they had no special interest in reading expository material of the type used in this course because they did not know what to look for in it. The majority of participants in this group said that the techniques they learned during the course had helped them in their reading and understanding articles of general interest and in preparing content subjects for midterm examinations.

The most direct conclusion would be that these students are learning to distinguish essential from subsidiary information and to organize it accordingly. This is an important achievement for students who, as part of the academic requirements in Argentine universities, must read a great amount of material published in English and keep a record of the main points.

Study Two—Summarizing Strategies

The purpose of this second study was to determine the strategies students had used to condense ideas from the source text in their own summaries of expository texts. Basically, I followed van Dijk's macrorules of selection and substitution of information in the process of reconstruction of a text's macrostructure. According to van Dijk (1980), two basic processes (four macrorules)—deletion and construction—operate on the propositions of the source text to produce a macrostructure. Van Dijk's first and second deletion rules have to do with suppression of unnecessary or trivial information. The two construction macrorules involve the operations of superordination and of provision of a summary for each constituent textual unit (the paragraph). On these bases I identified five strategies used by the students in their summaries:

1. Copy: this includes word-for-word repetitions of the original and near copies. Near copies are quite similar to exact copies with minor rearrangements of syntax or the use of synonyms for one or two content words (Campbell, 1990).

2. Selection: reproducing parts of a text in verbatim form with juxtaposed or internal parts deleted. The information suppressed is redundant or inconsequential.

3. Reduction/generalization: combining two or more lexical items or propositions into one lexical item or proposition. This includes the operations of nominalization and of superordination.

4. Integration/fusion: transforming a sequence (joint set) of propositions into a single (macro) proposition. The information is expressed in a single sentence and expresses the global meaning of an episode.

5. Addition: including parts that are not in the source text.

The analysis of posttest summaries in terms of these five strategies reveals important differences between the two groups under study. Whereas the standard strategies of the experimental group were reduction/generalization and integration/fusion, those of the conventional group were copy and selection. Our experimental subjects resemble the high school and college students in the Brown and Day study (1983). Our conventional group subjects used similar strategies to those employed by the fifth and seventh graders in the same study.

Experimental Group

Subjects in this group systematically blended information across sentences and even paragraphs and stated the most important points in their own words. Their summaries reveal a noticeable tendency towards the use of lexical substitution, superordination, and nominalization. Devices to combine information frequently used by experimental subjects include conjunctive ties and pro-forms of reference and substitution (Halliday & Hasan, 1976). Some examples of the use of reduction and integration by this group are reproduced below with the wording, punctuation, and spelling of the original summaries.

Posttest 1 (see Appendix A)

Paragraph 2

"As robots are more efficient and economical, employers are using them in place of factory workers." (reduction/generalization)

Paragraph 3

"While industrial workers will surely suffer the number of redundant <u>office employees</u> (superordination) will increase." (integration/fusion)

Paragraph 4

"Among <u>the social advantages of automation in work</u> (nominalization) are the possibilities of freeing yourself from unpleasant jobs and retraining for more appealing ones. Also the possibility to work fewer hours a week." (integration/fusion)

Posttest 2 (see Appendix A)

Paragraph 4

"Automation is increasing and taking up not only workers' jobs but also jobs in other fields such as medicine." (reduction/generalization)

Paragraphs 5 and 6

"Solutions to the problem such as stopping automation and taking more time off would arise as people will work less and enjoy their lives more." (integration/fusion)

Paragraph 7

"The likelihood of this possibility may produce opposite feelings in future workers (reduced adjectival clause) and future unemployeds (reduced adjectival clause)." (integration/fusion)

Paragraph 8

"Finally automation will reduce some aspects of the housewife's work. If the father is jobless, some changes in their relationship can be foreseen." (reduction/generalization)

Reference and substitution pro-forms such as "this," "that," "here," "such," and others are common devices to help condense information in experimental group summaries. Also instances of use of the following types of conjunctive ties have been found: additive ("moreover," "furthermore," "in addition," "similarly," and "in the same way") and adversative/contrastive ("in contrast" and "nevertheless") either relating topic ideas in two consecutive paragraphs in the source text or articulating the discourse at higher levels as, for example, specifying contrast, cause/effect, or premise/solution relationships in the middle of the summary ("yet," "however," "on the other hand," "so," "therefore," "consequently," "as a result," "in this way"). These conjunctive ties add cohesion and fluency to the summaries written by experimental subjects.

Conventional Group

The prevailing strategies in the summaries by this group are copy and deletion. Here are some examples of deletion from posttest 1 (see Appendix A).

Paragraph 5

"Less time at work means more time for leisure and to improve your education. This may cause the service industry to expand and open more jobs. Then it will be cheaper to pay people to work less."

From posttest 2 I selected these examples of deletion:

Paragraph 5

"Things are going clearly in the direction of more production by fewer people. How shall people adjust their lives? Here are some probabilities considered by sociologists and futurologists: we can stop automation to keep the old jobs; we can invest new jobs not strictly necessary or we can take more time off."

Paragraph 6

"If we decide to take more time off some of us might work five days and others not at all."

Paragraph 7

"The high possibility of this situation must lead us to think about this: People working may regard themselves as privileged or unfortunate. People not working may consider themselves as second class citizens or as leisure gentlemen."

The grammatical structure of the summaries written by conventional group subjects is simpler than that of experimental subjects. There is almost no use of grammatical cohesive devices, which results in excessive use of coordination with "and" and juxtaposition of simple sentences. Cohesion is achieved mainly through lexical reiteration, which produces a general rudimentary effect. Subordination, a powerful device for the hierarchical structuring of ideas, is almost totally absent from these summaries. This leads to a surface structure that assigns equal status to sentences that have different semantic values. In the few summaries where strategy three is used, there is a marked tendency to apply too general reduction operations with the consequent loss and distortion of content. In general terms, we can say that the favored copy/deletion strategies resulted in lower scoring in the use-of-English measure and might explain the difficulties many students had in keeping within the word limit.

Summaries by both groups include a considerable number of elements nonexistent in the sources (the fifth strategy: addition). Some of these additions are easy to identify. Such is the case of descriptions of speech acts, new arguments, or the subjects' opinions. Following are some examples:

"Will a shorter working week necessarily be a blessing?" (at the end of summary, posttest 1).

"Automation will not only take away people's jobs but also create new jobs. So, let's not fear it." (at the end of summary, posttest 1).

"In the first part, the writer discusses the effects of automation on employment." (at the beginning of summary, posttest 1).

There are other elements that are very difficult to trace. For example, how is the following sentence in posttest 2 to be interpreted? "This probability may cause changes in the way people feel." Is it a new argument or simply an extreme case of reduction of paragraph seven that distorts information in the original text? In the same way, do the following expressions (underlined) represent misinterpretations, errors in the selection of the superordinate term, or the introduction of new arguments? The latter might be the case in the second example that follows:

Posttest 2

Paragraphs 6, 7, and 8

"These changes will affect <u>the family group and, of course, society</u> because people who have jobs may think they are..."

Paragraph 8

"Finally, although automation has negative effects, it is <u>very important not only for housewives but also for a change in family relationships</u>..."

Since these elements are difficult to trace back to the source, it may be concluded that there are certain summarization processes which resist analysis in terms of van Dijk's deletion and construction macrorules. These additions might be the result of inference, not in the sense of "automatic connections" but as "elaborative" and "evaluative" operations (Brown & Yule, 1983, pp. 262–268) resulting from the interpretive-constructive process of summarizing a text.

General Conclusions

Considering the significant differences between the quality of summaries written by the experimental and conventional groups and from the analysis of summarization strategies used by each group, we can draw two main conclusions. First, experimental subjects learned to detect and use patterns of textual organization for expository texts as they did their reading/summarizing tasks. This enabled them to organize information into hierarchical levels subsuming secondary ideas and details into a more global level of representation. This top-down approach may have facilitated the adoption of reduction and integration summarization strategies.

Second, conventional group subjects were trained with a methodology based on the premise that reading is a precise, sequential decoding process, which may have led them into using primarily suppression rather than integration strategies. The almost exclusive use of copy/deletion strategies resulted in the lower quality of the summaries written by this group (in terms of balance of content, fluency, and use of English).

It appears that additional experimental intervention studies could be useful in determining the ideal length of training and in improving criteria for data analysis. Instruction on text types is only one part of a comprehensive training program in summarization. Instruction can also include development of adequate reading and comprehension skills with metacognitive training in the process of summary writing (planning, evaluation, and revision). Differential effects in students at various proficiency levels could also be explored and determined as suggested by Carrell (1988) who argued that EFL skills are crucial to success in summary writing.

In regard to the finding of new elements that seem to be the result of inferential processes, researchers are encouraged to develop experimental techniques to determine the role of inference in summary writing. Such studies could replace simplistic metaphors and intuitive conclusions about inference.

REFERENCES

Afflerbach, P.P. (1990). The influence of prior knowledge on expert readers main idea construction strategies. *Reading Research Quarterly, 25,* 31–46.

Anderson, R.C., & Pearson, P.D. (1988). A schema-theoretic view of basic processes in reading comprehension. In. P. Carrell, J. Devine, & D. Eskey (Eds.), *Interactive approaches to second language reading* (pp. 3, 17, 55). Cambridge, UK: Cambridge University Press.

Barlett, F.C. (1932). *Remembering: A study in experimental and social psychology.* Cambridge, UK: Cambridge University Press.

Brown, A.L., Campione, J.C., & Day, J.P. (1981). Learning to learn: On training students to learn from texts. *Educational Researcher, 10,* 14–21.

Brown, A.L., & Day, J.D. (1983). Macrorules for summarizing texts: The development of expertise. *Journal of Verbal Learning and Verbal Behaviour, 22,* 1–4.

Brown, A.L., Day, J.D., & Jones, R.S. (1983).*The development of plans for summarizing texts* (Tech. Rep. No. 268). Urbana, IL: University of Illinois, Center for the Study of Reading.

Brown, G., & Yule, G. (1983). *Discourse analysis.* Cambridge, UK: Cambridge University Press.

Campbell, C. (1990). Writing with others' words: Using background reading text in academic compositions. In B. Kroll (Ed.), *Second language writing: Research insights for the classroom* (pp. 211–230). New York: Cambridge University Press.

Carrell, P. (1985). Facilitating ESL reading by teaching text structure.*TESOL Quarterly, 19*(4), 727–752.

Carrell, P. (1988). Interactive text processing: Implications for ESL second language reading classrooms. In P. Carrell, J. Devine, & D. Eskey (Eds.), *Interactive approaches to second language reading* (pp. 239–259). New York: Cambridge University Press.

Chambliss, M.J. (1995). Text cues and strategies successful readers use to construct the gist of lengthy written arguments. *Reading Research Quarterly, 30,* 778–907.

Eskey, D., & Grabe, W. (1989). Interactive models for second language reading: Perspectives on instruction. In P. Carrell, J. Devine, & D. Eskey (Eds.), *Interactive approaches to second language reading* (pp. 223–238). New York: Cambridge University Press.

Halliday, M.A.K., & Hasan, R. (1976). *Cohesion in English.* London: Longman.

Hill, M. (1991). Writing summaries promotes thinking and learning across the curriculum: But why are they so difficult to write? *Journal of Reading, 34,* 536–539.

Kirkland, M.R., & Saunders, M.A. (1991). Maximizing student performance in summary writing: Managing cognitive load. *TESOL Quarterly, 25*(1), 105–121.

Kroll, B. (1990). *Second language writing.* Cambridge, UK: Cambridge University.

Quiocho, A. (1997). The quest to comprehend expository text-applied classroom research. *Journal of Adolescent & Adult Literacy, 40,* 450–455.

Rumelhart, D. (1977). Toward an interactive model of reading. In S. Dornic (Ed.), *Attention and performance, 6* (pp. 573–603). New York: Academic Press.

Rumelhart, D. (1980). Schemata: The building blocks of language. In R. Spiro, B. Bruce, & W. Brewer (Eds.), *Theoretical issues in reading comprehension* (pp.33–58). Hillsdale, NJ: Erlbaum.

Schellings, G.L., & Van Hout-Walters, B.H. (1995). Main points in an instructional text, as identified by students and their teachers. *Reading Research Quarterly*, *30*, 742–757.

Taylor, B.M., & Beach, R.W. (1984). The effects of text structure instruction on middle grade students' comprehension and production of expository text. *Reading Research Quarterly*, *19*(2), 134–146.

Taylor, K.K. (1984). The different summary skills of inexperienced and professional writers. *Journal of Reading*, *17*, 691–699.

van Dijk, T.A. (1980). *Macrostructures*. Hillsdale, NJ: Erlbaum.

Winograd, P.N. (1984). Strategic difficulties in summarizing texts. *Reading Research Quarterly*, *19*, 404–425.

APPENDIX A

Posttest 1*

Student's name: _____   Class:_____

Instructions: Read this passage and answer the question at the bottom of the page.

1. A revolution is under way. The technology of computer science is having a dramatic effect on our lives, and the most immediate consequences of this technology is its impact on employment.

2. Robots have already joined the work force in highly industrialized countries such as the USA, West Germany, and Japan. They have taken over routine jobs on the car assembly line, and in Volkswagen, for instance, three robots can replace ten men working on a two-shift system. Since robots can carry out tedious tasks with a high degree of reliability for an hourly wage one third that of the average human worker, employers are being pushed into cutting back the labor force.

3. While workers directly employed in manufacturing will certainly suffer, the impact of automation on the information industry will be even greater. In Britain, about 40% of the working population is engaged in making telephone calls, filing invoices, and writing reports. Since secretaries, typists, clerks managers, and accountants can be replaced by microelectronic information processors, it may not be long before white-collar desk-workers join factory workers in the increasing numbers of unemployed.

4. But let us not just look at the dark side of automation. The introduction of robots and computers in factories and offices can also bring about many social advantages. To begin with, there is a lot to be said for releasing people from work that is often noisy, dirty, and even dangerous, and many workers can be retrained for more pleasant and interesting jobs. Automation has already resulted in a shorter working week in the highly industrialized countries of Northwestern Europe. And this example is rapidly being imitated by France, Canada, and the USA.

5. Less time at work means more time available to take up leisure activities such as sports, games, and hobbies, and more opportunities to improve one's education in centers for adult training, polytechnics, or the Open University. An increased demand for leisure facilities at present is likely to lead to an expansion of the service industries (like catering, travel agencies, entertainment, and sport) and more job vacancies in the near future. If we follow the example of the Scandinavian countries, a shorter working week will not mean fewer wages. On the contrary, thanks to the new technology, it might be economic to pay people not to work!

Question: What plan did the writer use to organize the passage you have just read? Answer in one or two sentences. Now write a summary of not more than 130 words. Write down the number of words you have used at the end of your summary. Give your summary a title.

---

*Adapted from Garton-Sprenger, J., & Greenall, S. (1983). *On course for First Certificate* (pp. 80–81). London: Heinemann.

Posttest 2

Student's name: _____ Class:_____

Instructions: Read this passage and answer the question at the bottom of the page.

1. For most people the biggest effect of technical change and invention during the next thirty years is likely to be on the way they spend their days from Monday to Friday. "Work" as we know it today may be virtually abolished for many people who may be paid for not working. Don't count on it! For the time being we all have to earn our living. But in the future there may be two kinds of citizens—workers and nonworkers.

2. Already many of the essentials of life are produced very efficiently. The most notable exception is housing. Apart from that, our food and drink, our clothes and furniture, our mechanical and electronic gadgets, are all produced by a rather small number of people.

3. Now machinery and automation are continually increasing the work that each worker can accomplish in a day. For example, the produce from farms is increasing even though the number of farm workers is falling; it is not easy to think of many jobs that cannot be done by machines or which cannot at least be greatly helped by machines.

4. The ways in which machines can replace men in factories and offices are usually fairly plain, but here are some less obvious cases. A British engineer has already made a robot which can clear the dirty dishes from tables in restaurants. Machines are being developed which can give a better diagnosis of what is wrong with a patient than a doctor can using ordinary techniques. Automatic delivery to homes of parcels and groceries might be accomplished through tubes running under the road.

5. The way things are going is clear enough: towards more production by fewer people. What is not so clear is how we shall adjust our lives to it. Here are just some of the possibilities that have been considered by sociologists and futurologists: We can deliberately halt automation in order to keep the old jobs going, we can invent new jobs which are not strictly necessary (for example, in entertainment and holidaymaking), or we can take more time off.

6. If we decide to take more time off, some more choices arise. We might all work very little and have a five-day weekend, or some of us might work a five-day week and others not at all. The latter group would then be receiving old-age pensions at the age of twenty-one!

7. The high possibility of this situation coming true in the near future must lead us to think about the following: The people who will be working may regard themselves as privileged or unfortunate. The people who will not be working may consider themselves as unemployed second-class citizens or as gentlemen of leisure.

8. Finally, don't forget the housewife. However much automation might help her, a certain amount of cooking and housework will remain, especially if she has young children. If at the same time the head of the family is not going out to work, can you see any changes that are likely to come about in the relationship between husband and wife, and the roles they both play in the home?

Question: What plan did the writer use to organize the passage you have just read? Answer in one or two sentences. Now write a summary of not more than 150 words. Write down the number of words you have used at the end of your summary. Give your summary a title.

APPENDIX B

Analytic scale for the evaluation of the students' summaries

A. Content

3 The summary includes all the topic ideas, does not contain additions (the subject's own ideas or opinions), and keeps within the word limit assigned.

2 One topic idea is missing and/or the subject has included one or two additions and/or the summary exceeds by 10–12% the word limit required.

1 Incompleteness: The subject has included only one topic idea from the original and several ideas or opinions of his own. The number of words exceeds 12% of the word limit.

B. Balance

3 The summary is clearly focused; it reflects the top-level ideas of the original.

2 There are one or two instances in which the subject emphasizes points which are only subsidiary in the original text.

1 The summary represents a serious disruption of the hierarchy of ideas in the source text.

C. Fluency and use of EFL (grammar, vocabulary, spelling, punctuation)

3 The summary "flows" smoothly. Good control of connection. Flexible use of simple and complex syntactic structures (sentence level). Evidence of good control of transformation, a key operation in summary writing (Kirkland & Saunders, 1991). There is good morphological control. Vocabulary is broad and appropriately used with good control of nominalization and lexical substitution, especially superordination. Spelling and punctuation errors are not distracting.

2 There are a few problems with connection. Both simple and complex structures are present and morphological control is adequate with some inconsistencies. In some summaries fluency is achieved at the expense of accuracy. Spelling and punctuation errors are sometimes distracting.

1 Connection is sometimes absent or unsuccessful. Morphology and vocabulary may sometimes be inappropriate. Spelling and punctuation errors often cause serious interference.

D. Use of rhetorical organization

1 The summary reflects the rhetorical organization of the source text.

0 The summary does not reflect the rhetorical organization of the source text.

E. Recognition of text type

1 Subject recognizes rhetorical organization of the source text.

0 Subject does not recognize rhetorical organization of the source text

F. Title

1 Title is appropriate to the macrostructure of the summary.

0 Title is inappropriate to the macrostructure of the summary.

Main Idea Clues

Michael F. O'Hear and Patrick J. Ashton

Research over the last several years has validated a variety of readability formulas with college-level material (Fry, 1977; Longo, 1982). Nonetheless, there continues to be concern about the reliability of these formulas. Unless one has a computer with formula software, selecting passages and applying formula guidelines involves much work. Formula reliance on short passages, the danger that selected samples will not be representative of the real difficulty level of a book, and the possibility that samples may vary greatly in different areas of a book (O'Hear & Ramsey, 1983) are all cited as concerns about formulas. Finally, because formulas traditionally rely on text structure rather than on content-sensitive features, there lingers a suspicion that readability scores are based on data that are not germane to the content of material. Certain complex subject matter, philosophy for example, may not be subject to simplification in ways that would be picked up by readability formulas.

A content-sensitive way to determine readability, in addition to use of the traditional formulas, would answer many of these problems. It could overcome aversion to counts of textual features; it could minimize the danger of reliance on nonrepresentative samples; it could discriminate among complex texts whose readability scores were not indicating clear differences among them. It could also be an aid in dealing with books (math texts, for example) that do not contain text sections long enough for use with readability formulas.

Recent research (Ashton, O'Hear, & Pherson, 1983; O'Hear, Ramsey, & Pherson, 1987; Popken, 1987) suggests that main idea clues might provide just such a content-sensitive link to readability in college textbooks. Main idea clues are identified as those aids present in a text to help readers identify the main idea of individual paragraphs, chapter sections, and chapters as a whole. Developmental reading texts have identified and research has validated six of these clues in college textbooks—position, examples, repetition, key words, subheadings, and highlighted words. While these involve different types of structures (placement of ideas and elabo-

Originally published in Forum for Reading *(1989), volume 21, number 1, pages 58–66*

rative devices), both types of clues have high usage frequencies in college texts, and both are used by developmental reading specialists to point students toward substantially important text material.

If a relationship does exist between these clues and readability scores for college textbooks, such clues would be easy to use as an alternative or supportant to readability scores. Specifically, their use would involve longer passages than those used in traditional readability formulas, which, in turn, would lessen the possibility of determining readability through choice of unrepresentative passages. Further, since main idea clues lead directly to important content material, use of these clues keys directly into material students typically need to know.

The present study examines the relationship of readability to usage of main idea clues in introductory texts in sociology and in English composition texts. It seeks to establish whether use of main idea clues provides a useful supplement to readability formulas. If both clues and readability formulas provide comparable means of determining readability, then examination of main idea clues adds important additional information with which instructors might evaluate textbooks.

Review of Research

While most readability formulas were originally developed to deal with primary and secondary level material, Fry (1977) and Longo (1982) have validated their effectiveness with college-level material. However, other studies have questioned formula effectiveness with certain kinds of textbooks, particularly those which relay heavily on exercise and examples (O'Hear & Ramsey, 1983; Ramsey & O'Hear, 1985). These studies found cases in which books contained insufficient amounts of text to establish readability with specific passages. Further, even Longo's study revealed some wide variation among the readability levels established for various books. Thus, there appear to be certain gaps in formula effectiveness. However, in those instances in which readability samples produce similar results, the formulas are probably accurate in determining readability.

Three recent studies have established the existence and importance of main idea clues in college textbooks and professional academic journals (Ashton, O'Hear & Pherson, 1985; O'Hear, Ramsey, & Pherson, 1987; Popken, 1987). These studies were particularly important because, until recently, main idea clues were thought to be of minimal importance.

Braddock (1974) found that few main ideas were stated in popular articles. Although he did not deal with textbook material, other writers have used his conclusions to question the value of searching for main ideas in other types of material. For example, Moore and Readence (1980) argued that main idea statements existed only in reading improvement textbooks.

The Ashton, O'Hear, and Pherson (1985) and O'Hear, Ramsey, and Pherson (1987) studies documented the frequency and relative importance of main idea clues. This research showed that clues appear with an average frequency of 2.5 or better clues per paragraph in the texts studies. It further illustrated the relative frequency of all clues commonly listed in reading improvement texts for finding main ideas. Position, repetition, and example were seen as the most frequently used clues to the main idea.

Popken's (1987) research confirmed the existence and importance of main ideas in academic writing. In a study of professional articles in a variety of fields, he found that paragraph main ideas were stated with high frequency (from 71% of paragraphs in articles written about literature to 34% in engineering articles). When he added in section main ideas, he found that main ideas existed for 60% to 80% of the paragraphs in his sample.

Research by O'Hear and Ashton (1987) demonstrated that main ideas contain substantially important material 80%–92% of the time. Since main ideas seem to be an important part of academic writing, the question is whether main idea clues bear any relation to readability.

This study poses the question of the relationship of main idea clues to readability data. Which, if any, of the main idea clues found in reading textbooks have frequencies of use which are correlated with readability as determined by use of a readability formula? The writers assume that, based on the studies by Longo (1982) and Fry (1977), formulas are accurate in determining readability if samples taken from a text offer comparable results. The question then is whether main idea clues can be used as a content-sensitive means for determining readability as an adjunct to or in place of readability formulas.

Method

For this study, the seven English writing and introductory sociology texts used in the Ashton, O'Hear, and Pherson (1985) and O'Hear, Ramsey, and Pherson (1987) studies were chosen. It seemed, in the judgment of both the original and present authors, that these books (Bridges & Lunsford, 1984; DeFleur, D'Antonio, & DeFleur, 1984; Dougherty,

1985; Kinneavy, McCleary, & Nakadate, 1985; Lauer, Montague, Lunsford, & Emig, 1985; Robertson, 1981; Tischler, Whitten, & Hunter, 1983) were representative of mainstream texts in these areas.

The Flesch formula was used to determine readability levels for the texts. This formula was chosen both because its effectiveness with college-level material was validated by Longo (1982) and because it yields an adjective description of readability as well as a grade level. Main ideas—defined as declarative statements which are general enough to include all of the information provided in a paragraph, but not so general as to be useless to those trying to understand the paragraph (Ashton, O'Hear, & Pherson, 1985)—were identified and clues to their presence tabulated for all paragraphs, excluding chapter summaries which, by their nature, tend to contain nonstandard paragraphs.

Main idea clues were expressed in terms of the percentage of total paragraphs in which they appeared. This allowed for the computation of a Pearson's r correlation between the frequency of usage of each type of main idea clue and readability scores, and interval measure (Toothaker, 1986, pp. 168–227). Multiple regression analysis was then used to see whether frequency of usage of various main idea clues could be used to predict readability. Based on this data, it is possible to make some generalizations about the relationship of main idea clues and readability formulas.

Results

Readability scores for the textbooks examined appear in Table 1.

Readability levels for the English writing texts were uniformly lower than for the sociology texts. This is not surprising due to the density of the sociology concepts and the general "how to" purpose of the English texts. Indeed, the authors of composition textbooks, since their professional specialty is effective communication, would be expected to be more sensitive to matters of readability than sociologists. One sociology text (Tischler) varied significantly in readability across the sample chapters. Chapter readability scores from this book ranged from fairly difficult, to difficult, to very difficult. Only one of the other texts varied more than one level across the sample chapters. In fact, four of the books show no variance at all.

The presence of both texts with comparable reading levels and texts with some variety of scores was important to the study. If main idea clues worked well with both types of text, it would show that main idea clues could effectively aid in determining readability even when traditional formulas were not producing consistent scores.

Table 1
Readability scores for selected English writing and sociology tests

TEXT	READABILITY
Sociology texts	
DeFleur	23 (v.d.)
Robertson	43 (d.)
Tischler	40 (d.)
English writing tests	
Bridges	65 (s.)
Dougherty	78 (f.e.)
Kinneavy	63 (s.)
Lauer	57 (f.d.)

Scale:	
0–30	Very Difficult (v.d.)
30–50	Difficult (d.)
50–60	Fairly Difficult (f.d.)
60–70	Standard (s.)
70–80	Fairly Easy (f.e.)
80–90	Easy (e.)
90–100	Very Easy (v.e.)

Table 2 reports the correlations between usage frequency of individual main idea clues and readability scores as well as the mean frequency of each main idea clue.

Strongest correlations with readability are frequency of main ideas in the first position ($r = .65$) and last position ($r = -.61$). While these are both strong correlations, their signs indicate that frequency of main idea in the first position is associated with increased readability, while placement of main idea in the last position is associated with *lowered* readability. Note, however, that an average of only 14% of paragraphs had main ideas in the last position (Frequency is a relative term. As it is used here it refers to usage of a clue with relation to the mean appearance for all clues. Thus if a clue appears in only 40% of examined paragraphs, it still may have appeared frequently in relation to other listed clues).

On average, main idea clues appeared only slightly more frequently in the second position than in the last position, and the correlation was

Table 2
Correlation matrix for all variables

	ReadEase	FirstPos	2ndPos	LastPos	Examples	Repeat	Keywords	Subhead	Highlite	QuesAns	Mean	Sc
ReadEase	1										49.7	18.8
FirstPos	.65	1									56.4	8.0
2ndPos	-.28	-.65	1								15.8	4.9
LastPro	-.61	-.64	.18	1							14.0	5.5
Examples	.10	.17	.12	.12	1						67.6	10.2
Repeat	.29	-.14	.40	-.23	-.19	1					43.1	7.9
Keywords	-.28	-.05	.05	.05	-.13	-.04	1				13.3	7.6
Subhead	-.13	-.29	-.13	.05	-.54	-.14	-.12	1			31.2	9.0
Highlight	.09	-.05	-.01	.03	-.01	.09	.08	.18	1		8.4	6.5
QuesAns	-.35	-.30	.15	.39	.49	-.29	.04	.03	12	1	3.3	2.8

N = 17 for all correlations

once again negative, though much lower than that between last position and readability. Repetition is a main idea clue that is used fairly frequently in these texts and has in this study a moderately strong positive correlation with readability. Use of key words as main idea clues has a correlation of about the same strength, but in a negative direction. Its use is fairly infrequent, however. The most frequently used main idea clue, on average, is examples, though this factor had a negligible correlation with readability. Appearance of main idea clues in questions and answers had a moderately strong negative correlation with readability, but since this technique was not used very often, its significance is questionable. Main idea clues appeared fairly frequently in subheads, but this factor had only a small negative correlation with readability. Table 3 presents the results of a multiple regression of all nine main idea clue factors on readability scores.

While a significant amount of variance in readability is explained by this equation, the reader will note that no single factor makes a statistically significant contribution to the explanation, nor is the equation as a whole statistically significant. The lack of significance is undoubtedly explained, in part, by the intercorrelations among the explanatory factors themselves (i.e., multicolinearity).

Table 3
Multiple regression analysis predicting readability from all main idea clues

	Unstandardized Coefficient	Standardized Coefficient (β)	t-value	Probability
FirstPos	1.41	60	1.00	.35
2ndPos	.07	.02	.04	.97
LastPos	-.43	-.13	.32	.76
Examples	.43	.23	.60	.57
Repeat	.84	.35	1.25	.25
Keywords	-.44	-.18	.75	.48
Subhead	.42	.20	.60	.57
Highlite	.26	.09	.39	.71
QuesAns	-.98	-.15	.47	.65

constant = -96.30
degrees of freedom = 16
R^2 = .67
p = .28

Following standard regression techniques (see, e.g., Nie, Hall, Jenkins, Steinbrenner, & Bent, 1975, pp. 334–341), the authors developed a reduced multiple regression model to avoid this problem. Criteria for inclusion of independent variables in this reduced model included (1) strong positive correlation with the dependent variable, readability; (2) lack of strong intercorrelations with the other explanatory variables; (3) frequency average use for main idea clues; and (4) demonstration of explanatory power as indicated by the variables' standardized regression coefficient (beta) in the full model.

Five variables met the majority of these criteria: first position, repetition, key words, examples, and subheads. Not only does first position have the highest correlation with readability (see Table 2), but it also has the highest partial regression coefficients, and a high frequency of use. Since second position and last position were strongly intercorrelated with first position (though, not surprisingly, in a negative direction), it was necessary to leave them out of the reduced model.

Repetition has a moderately strong correlation with readability, moderately strong partial regression coefficients, and a relatively high average frequency of use. It has moderately strong intercorrelations only with second position, which has been eliminated from the reduced model, and question and answer format, which was eliminated from the reduced model because it was used relatively infrequently (mean = 3.3%) and was intercorrelated with first position, examples, and repetition, all of which appear in the reduced model.

The key words clue has a moderately strong correlation with readability, but is not significantly intercorrelated with any other explanatory factor.

Use of examples has the highest average frequency of use as main idea clues in our sample of textbooks. Moreover, it has the third highest standardized coefficient in the full model.

The subhead clue represents a special case. Initially it appears to have a small negative correlation with readability (-.13), but this turns out to be spurious when the other independent variables are controlled in the full model. Because of this effect, and because it has a relatively high standardized coefficient and frequency of use, the variable subheads was included in the partial model, despite a moderately strong negative intercorrelation with examples and a weak negative correlation with first position.

Table 4 presents our reduced multiple regression model.

Table 4
Multiple regression analysis for major main idea clue predictors of readability scores

	Unstandardized Coefficient	Standardized Coefficient (ß)	t-value	Probability
FirstPos	1.73	.74	3.84	.003
Repeat	1.06	.44	2.24	.047
Keywords	-.45	-.18	.95	.363
Examples	.27	.15	.63	.543
Subhead	.44	.21	.87	.403

constant = -119.86
degrees of freedom = 16
R^2 = .65
p = .026

The model as a whole is statistically significant ($p < .03$) in its ability to explain about two thirds of the variance in readability scores of textbook chapters ($R^2 = .65$). Two variables emerge as statistically significant predictors of readability. The presence of main ideas in the first position in the paragraph is by far the strongest predictor of readability. When the other independent predictors are controlled, first position accounts for about three quarters of the explained variance ($p < .01$). Its unstandardized coefficient indicates that, for every one percent increase in the appearance of main idea in the first position within a paragraph, readability scores increase by 1.73 points.

The other statistically significant predictor is repetition. Controlling for the other predictors, it accounts for slightly less than half of the explained variance ($p < .05$). Its unstandardized regression coefficient indicates a nearly perfect positive linear relationship with readability.

None of the other predictors in the reduced model is statistically significant, nor does anyone make a large contribution to the explained variance. It should be noted that key words and subheads maintain their weightings and the direction of their relationship with readability almost unchanged from the full model. The impact of examples, however, is substantially lessened in the reduced model. This is consistent with the fact that this variable shows little correlation with readability in the first place (see Table 2). On the other hand, examples seem to contribute to the reduced model by helping to increase the explanatory power of first position and repetition. Logically, one would expect it to have the greatest impact on repetition (i.e., when the repetition of main idea example clues is controlled for, the other uses of repetition take on greater significance in contributing to readability).

Discussion

Main ideas and clues for finding them appear with regularity in college textbooks writing and sociology. Certain of these clues seem to relate strongly to readability scores both positively (first position, repetition) and negatively (last position, second position, key words). This relationship is not hard to account for.

Since the most common form for written academic discourse in English places main ideas first (indeed, it is a primary pattern taught by composition instructors), one would expect that use of this device indicates an awareness of the reader's familiarity with the pattern and a desire to put important ideas up front where they will easily be seen. In contrast, writers who deviate from this rubric are distancing themselves from the common pattern, thus making it more difficult for audiences to find the pattern of the writing, and consequently making passages more difficult to read. This would seem to be a particularly important problem for academic textbook authors and editors.

Repetition is seen as positively correlated to readability because the writer who takes time to say something a second time is drawing attention to the key points. In doing so, this writer is showing a concern that readers understand what is being said. It is not surprising that this concern translates into easier readability scores.

Key words, the other negative factor, may reflect a more complex section of text, which will, of necessity, be harder to read. For example, if a series of paragraphs begins with number words (first, next, another, etc.), it may indicate a section of text with a large concentration of substantive material within a short amount of space (the key elements in Marx's dialectic, for example). In such cases, the readability might be expected to be higher.

Conclusions

Although this is only a pilot study dealing with a selection of widely used textbooks in two content areas, it suggests a possible supplement to readability levels as a criterion of ease of textbook usage. Reading sections of text for main idea placement, use of repetition, and key words seems less tedious and more appropriate than counting words, syllables, and sentences. The content-sensitive process focuses on meaning as well as formal characteristics, which ties it more closely to the realities of reading than do readability formulas with their emphasis on form alone.

This study suggests that those evaluating textbooks for readability might gain a greater idea of reading ease by selecting lengthy passages from critical text chapters and focusing on main idea placement within these passages. If main idea in first position predominates, then the book has a high probability of reading ease. If main ideas frequently occur in other positions, then the book will probably be more difficult for student use.

Many subjects will never be easy for students to understand. However, this method may be the most effective way to determine that the authors are doing their best to make the text usable. While it is clear that more research needs to be done in other academic content areas, the use of main idea clues seems a promising supplement to readability formulas in determining the reading ease of college textbooks.

REFERENCES

Ashton, P.J., O'Hear, M.F., & Pherson, V.E. (1985). The value of main idea clues for use with college textbooks. *Journal of College Reading and Learning, 18,* 59–67.

Braddock, R. (1974). Frequency and placement of topic sentences in expository prose. *Research in the Teaching of English, 8,* 287–302.

Bridges, C.W., & Lunsford, R.F. (1984). *Writing: Discovering form and meaning.* Belmont, CA: Wadsworth.

DeFleur, L.B., D'Antonio, W.V., & DeFleur, L.B. (1984). *Sociology in human society* (4th ed.). New York: Random House.

Dougherty, B.N. (1985). *Composing choices for writers: A cross-disciplinary rhetoric.* New York: McGraw-Hill.

Fry, E. (1977). Fry's readability graph: Clarifications, validity, and extension to level 17. *Journal of Reading, 21,* 242–251.

Kenneavy, J.L., McCleary, W., & Nakadate, N. (1985). *Writing in the liberal arts tradition: A rhetoric with readings.* New York: Harper & Row.

Lauer, J.M., Montague, G., Lunsford, A., & Emig, J. (1985). *Four worlds of writing* (2nd ed.). New York: Harper & Row.

Longo, J.A. (1982). The Fry graph: Validation of the college levels. *Journal of Reading, 26,* 229–234.

Moore, D.W., & Readence, J.E. (1980). Processing main ideas through parallel lesson transfer. *Journal of Reading, 23,* 589–594.

Nie, N.H., Hall, C.H., Jenkins, J.G., Steinbrenner, K., & Bent, D.H. (1975). *SPSS: Statistical package for the social sciences* (2nd ed.). New York: McGraw-Hill.

O'Hear, M.F., & Ashton, P.J. (1987). The substantive value of main idea statements in sociology textbooks. *Forum for Reading, 18*(2), 46–52.

O'Hear, M.F., & Ramsey, R.N. (1983). English handbooks: A special readability problem. *Journal of Teaching Writing, 2,* 223–232.

O'Hear, M.F., Ramsey, R.N., & Pherson, V.E. (1987). Location of main ideas in English composition texts. *Research in the Teaching of English, 21,* 318–326.

Popkin, R.L. (1987). A study of topic sentence use in academic writing. *Written Communication, 4,* 209–228.

Ramsey, R.N., & O'Hear, M.F. (1995). The OR corrective: Making readability formulas work for workbooks and textbooks. *Forum for Reading, 16*(2), 62–68.

Adding In-Class Writing to the College Reading Curriculum: Problems and Plusses

Arden B. Hamer

Reading and writing share many of the same processes (Rosenblatt, 1994; Tierney & Pearson, 1993; Wittrock, 1983). In both cases, the reader must gather and organize ideas, ask and answer questions, develop hypotheses, integrate information, draw on their background knowledge, and monitor their progress (Tierney & Peterson, 1993). Also, in both cases, the reader/writer is processing language (Squire, 1983) and ideally has a sense of ownership over the material (Boutwell, 1983).

Research has shown that writing can be used as a strategy for increasing young readers' proficiency (Goodman & Goodman, 1983; Marshall, 1987). "Opportunities to write have been found to contribute knowledge of how written and oral language are related to growth in phonics, spelling, vocabulary development, and reading comprehension" (Anderson, Hiebert, Scott, & Wilkinson, 1985, p. 79). Writing about their assignments is one way for reading students to work with the content to better understand and integrate it with what they already know (Squire, 1983; Tierney & Shanahan, 1991).

Many experts have recommended that writing be added to the reading curriculum (Hayes, 1990; Schatzberg-Smith, 1987; Tierney & Shanahan, 1991). Even though the same recommendations are made for college-level reading, in practice these two areas have not usually been connected in the classroom (Huot, 1988; Schatzberg-Smith, 1987; Troyka, 1986). The purpose of this paper is twofold—first, to describe how reading-related writing exercises were added to an established developmental college reading course, and second, to make a retrospective comparison of students in the course who both read and wrote about their reading assignments (reading-writing focused) and those who mainly read (reading focused) to meet class requirements. Both groups of students read and wrote. However, the reading-writing–focused stu-

Originally published in Forum for Reading *(1996–1997), volume 27, pages 25–34*

dents wrote more extensively in response to what was read, while the primarily reading students wrote to respond to questions requiring generally brief answers.

Reading Curriculum Experienced by Both Groups

The reading course, Developmental College Reading I, was the first semester of a two-course sequence designed to help students develop college-level reading and study skills. Each class met twice a week, one hour and 40 minutes per meeting, for the 15-week semester. In the first unit of the semester, students read narratives (excerpts from autobiographies). Short stories comprised the second unit, and essays the third. The students were assigned reading guides to be done individually and were expected to be able to discuss and answer questions about the assignments in class (see Appendix, page 169). The number and complexity of the assignments in each unit increased during the semester, and the amount of teacher direction decreased. The fourth and final unit involved reading essays about a single subject with very little teacher direction. All examinations were essay and the students were required to respond to questions about individual readings. In addition, they were expected to make connections among the various readings in each unit. There was also one reading included in each examination that the students worked on independently in order to demonstrate their ability to apply the reading and study skills taught in class. Further, students were required to pass the final examination in order to proceed to Developmental College Reading II.

Description of Writing Exercises Experienced by Reading-Writing–Focused Group

The students completed 17 writing exercises (15 in class) designed to have them interact with the text they read (see Appendix). The exercises were divided into the following categories: (a) metacognitive awareness, (b) reading, (c) extending the text, (d) organizing the information in the text, and (e) relating the reading to their background knowledge and personal experiences.

The first category of exercises encouraged students to use their metacognitive abilities to evaluate their learning strategies, and consider how they could improve. One exercise in this category asked students to think about a time when they had put effort and perseverance into a task and were successful. The second category of exercises involved restating the events in a reading assignment in written form. These exercises gave the students experience with literal recall and paraphrasing. The third category had only one exercise. The students were asked to write an extension to the ending of a short story, based on information they read in the text. This exercise asked the students to recall and analyze what they learned about the characters and the events in the story and relate the information to an additional ending. The fourth category asked students to organize the information they read in a more formal manner than it had been presented in the text. The final category of exercises directed students to relate what they were reading to their own personal views, experiences, and background knowledge.

Each assignment was presented on a separate handout with the prompt printed at the top of the page. While another option would have been to use journals, individual, printed papers for each exercise were used so students could easily refer back to the prompt as they worked. For the majority of the exercises, the students wrote at the end of the class period and were permitted to leave when they had completed the writing task. The exercises done at the end of class required the students to write about information that had been covered during that class period. A few of the exercises were done at the beginning of the class in order to introduce a new topic and to engage students' interest before they began to read. All of the exercises were kept by the instructor in individual folders. Because of the addition of the writing exercises, the reading-writing–focused group spent less time discussing the assignments than the reading-focused group.

These exercises were described to the students as writing to learn. The concept of writing as a means of learning was discussed frequently during the semester. Because of this, the writing was not graded. The students were frequently reminded of this so that they would feel free to experiment and focus on their thinking and learning instead of writing what they thought would elicit a good grade.

The instructor always read the exercises and responded with handwritten notes. Her responses were in two different areas. First, the instructor responded to the ideas expressed by the students. For example, in the exercise that required the students to describe a time when they had put effort and perseverance into being successful, the instructor tried to show a parallel between that success and the success the student could find by applying the same qualities of hard work in college. In the second area of response, the instructor commented to the positive writing qualities the student used which helped the reader understand. The instructor identified good examples of organization (logical order or sequence, ideas easy to follow), focus (distinct purpose developed and maintained), and content (correct information and details sufficient to develop ideas) (Pennsylvania State Assessment System, 1992).

Students

Students involved were freshmen attending a community college located in a suburban area near a large northeastern city. They represented a mix of traditional (18 to 22) and nontraditional (over 22) ages. There were 29 students in the two sections who participated in the writing exercises (reading-writing–focused group)—15 female and 14 male, 24 traditional and 5 nontraditional students, 1 African American and 27 European American students. One student in the reading-writing–focused group spoke Spanish as her first language. Because of absences, not all students completed all exercises. Where applicable, the students' work was compared to that of 15 students in another section of the course who did not do the extensive writing exercises but participated in the same reading coursework (reading-focused group). Reading-focused participants included were 11 females and 4 males, 10 traditional and 5 nontraditional students, 1 African American and 14 European American students, and 1 ESL student who spoke Spanish as a first language.

Cautions

Because the comparison between the groups was done ex post facto, several cautions must be kept in mind. Variables were not manipulated, students were not randomly assigned to treatment groups, and causes were not attributed with certainty to specific variables (Best & Kahn, 1993). In addition, the experience of the investigator in teaching developmental students in a two-year college setting demonstrated that there were many factors that can influence students' learning. For example, they may work at full- or part-time jobs, be primary caregivers in their families, or have a history of academic failure. Such factors can limit their willingness to put extended effort into the various class activities required for the course. The time of day when classes meet also can make a difference in the enthusiasm and alertness of the students. Further, as with many students, those who participated in the extended writing exercises often hurried as they wrote and did not seem to do their best work or take seriously the exercises done at the end of the class period. Personal constraints like worries about child care, transportation, and job requirements may also play important roles in these students' participation in class.

Results and Discussion

Examination Answers and Writing Exercises

While all of the writing dealt with material that was assigned and appeared on the course examinations, the information in two of the exercises appeared again as examination questions exactly as they were presented in the writing exercises. The first case was in the first unit of the semester. Following a reading assignment, the reading-writing–focused group wrote to define two terms and restate information from the text to show why they were a problem to the success of individuals and to America. This information appeared in an examination question approximately two weeks later. The examination answers from the reading-writing–focused group were compared to those of the reading-focused group. The average answer score for the two groups was similar—eight points out of a possible 10 in the reading-writing–focused group and 7.36 points out of a possible 10 in the reading-focused group. Also, in both groups the most common error was answering only the first part of the question, which asked for a definition, and not the second part, which asked for the subsequent problems.

In the third unit of the semester, the students in the reading-writing–focused group wrote to restate and define two important terms that they read in an essay. These two terms were critical to the understanding of the author's main idea. On the examination given approximately three weeks later, the students were asked to recall the two terms and define them. This is different from the first example where the two terms were given on the examination. Again, the test scores were similar but with a slight improvement in the reading-writing–focused group. Their average score was 5.31 out of 10, and the reading-focused group's average score was 3.29 out of 10. The error patterns were similar in the two groups. Most students who received partial credit were able to partially define the terms but had trouble recalling the terms. In the reading-focused group, only 7% of the students received full credit for that question, but in the reading-writing–focused group 34.6% of the students received full credit.

This improvement in the reading-writing–focused group in the second examination question might be attributed to the fact that they answered the almost identical question three weeks apart (test/retest), or it might be that they learned and understood the information better because they thought about it and wrote about it prior to being tested.

Final Grade Comparisons

The distribution of the final course grades between the reading-writing–focused group and the reading-focused group revealed that a higher percentage of students passed in the reading-writing group, and that these students passed with higher grades. All the students took the same examinations throughout the semester. The examinations were graded by the same instructor.

In order to eliminate as much instructor bias as possible, all the examinations were read within a limited time period. Further, each question was read and graded on all the examinations before moving on to the next question. Also, there was no opportunity for bonus work or bonus points. Therefore, the final grade reflected the actual coursework completed and competency on the course assessments, and not the effort students were willing to put into extra work to improve their grade.

In the reading-writing–focused group, a smaller percentage of students failed the course, and a large percentage passed with higher grades. Ten percent of the reading-writing group failed as compared to 26.7% of the reading-focused group. Sixty-two percent of the reading-writing–focused group received "As" and "Bs" compared to 33% of the reading-focused group (see Table 1). The pattern of grades earned indicates that the reading-writing–focused group performed better in the course on required activities than the reading-focused group.

Implications

One purpose of this paper was to describe how reading-related writing exercises were added to an established developmental college reading course. The analysis of trends in this informal study suggests that while it can be problematic to include additional writing, it can be done with-

Table 1
Final grades: Reading-writing–focused group and reading-focused group

Group	n	Final Grade	%
Reading-Writing	7	A	24.1%
Reading	3	A	20%
Reading-Writing	11	B	37.9%
Reading	2	B	13%
Reading-Writing	7	C	24.1%
Reading	6	C	40%
Reading-Writing	2	D	6.9%
Reading	0	D	0
Reading-Writing	2	F	6.9%
Reading	4	F	26.7%
Reading-Writing	18	A and B	62.1%
Reading	5	A and B	33%
Reading-Writing	25	A, B, and C	86.2%
Reading	11	A, B, and C	73%

out substantially diminishing the basic coursework that must be completed. By slightly shortening the discussion time, the students in the reading-writing–focused group were able to complete the same assignments as the reading focused group and still have time to write in class.

The second purpose was to compare the performance of students who completed reading-related writing exercises to those who did not. The students who did extended reading-related writing earned better grades than the students who did not write. Higher percentages of students in the reading-writing–focused group earned passing grades and earned higher grades than those in the primarily reading-focused group. The latter group was taught by the same instructor but did not do the extended writing exercises. Even though the extended writing activity was frequently done hurriedly at the end of class, the grades earned by the reading-writing group were higher. These results suggest that it might be beneficial to conduct studies in which students are randomly selected or controlled, classroom reading and writing activities are more carefully balanced, and data analyses are employed which reveal the relationships under study with more clarity.

REFERENCES

Anderson, R.C., Hiebert, E.H., Scoll, J.A., & Wilkinson, I.A.G. (1985). *Becoming a nation of readers*. Washington, DC: The National Institute of Education.

Barnwell, T., & McCraney, L. (1997). *Instructor's manual to accompany an introduction to critical reading*. Orlando, FL: Harcourt Brace College Publishers.

Best, J.W., & Kahn, J.V. (1993). *Research in education* (7th ed.). Needham Heights, MA: Allyn & Bacon.

Boutwell, M.A. (1983). Reading and the writing process: A reciprocal agreement. *Language Arts, 60*(5), 723–730.

Goodman, K., & Goodman, Y. (1983). Reading and writing relationships: Pragmatic functions. *Language Arts, 60*(5), 590–599.

Hayes, C.G. (1990). *Using writing to promote reading to learn in college*. Paper presented at the annual convention of the International Reading Association, Atlanta, GA. (ERIC Document Reproduction Service No. ED 322 499)

Huot, B. (1988). Reading/writing connections on the college level. *Teaching English in the Two Year College, 15*, 90–98.

Marshall, J.D. (1987). The effects of whole language instruction on academically underprepared college students. In A.M. Scales & B.G. Brown (Eds.), *Innovative learning strategies: Eleventh yearbook, 1993–1994* (pp. 13–33). Pittsburgh, PA: College Reading Improvement Special Interest Group, International Reading Association.

Pennsylvania State Assessment System. (1992). *Writing assessment handbook*. Harrisburg, PA: Pennsylvania Department of Education.

Rosenblatt, L.M. (1994). The transactional theory of reading and writing. In R.B. Ruddell, M.R. Ruddell, & H. Singer (Eds.), *Theoretical models and processes of reading* (4th ed., pp. 1057–1092). Newark, DE: International Reading Association.

Schatzberg-Smith, K. (1987). The reading-writing connection I: Writing to learn from text. *Research and Teaching in Developmental Education, 3*(2), 52–54.

Squire, J.R. (1983). Composing and comprehending: Two sides of the same basic process. *Language Arts, 60*(1), 2–10.

Tierney, R.J., & Pearson, P.D. (1983). Toward a composing model of reading. *Language Arts, 60*(1), 2–10.

Tierney, R.J., & Shanahan, T. (1991). Research on the reading-writing relationship: Interactions, transactions, and outcomes. In R. Barr, M.L. Kamil, P. Mosenthal, & P.D. Pearson (Eds.), *Handbook of reading research* (Vol. 2, pp. 246–280). White Plains, NY: Longman.

Troyka, L.Q. (1986). Closeness to text: A delineation of reading processes as they affect composing. In T. Newkirk (Ed.), *Only connect: Uniting reading and writing*. Upper Montclair, NJ: Boynton/Cook.

APPENDIX

Example of reading guide and discussion questions completed by both the reading-writing–focused and the reading-focused groups:

After reading "Mother Tongue" by Amy Tan, the students answered the following questions in small groups and then shared their answers with the whole class:

1. Explain what Tan means by "different Englishes."
2. How does Tan's mother's ability to speak English differ from her ability to understand it?
3. Why is Tan uncomfortable using the words "broken" or "limited" to describe her mother's English?
4. How does the English spoken by Tan's mother affect the way she is treated by other people?
5. Why did Tan have a difficult time on standardized tests?
6. Why does Tan think there are not more Asian American writers represented in American literature? (Barnwell & McCraney, 1997, p. 98)

Example of writing exercises completed only by the reading-writing focused group:

1. After reading "Mother Tongue" by Amy Tan and "Does America Still Exist" by Richard R. Rodriquez, the students responded in writing to the following:

   In Southern Florida many signs and announcements are in both Spanish and English because of the many Spanish-speaking citizens. Some U.S. citizens feel this is wrong. They feel we should use only English and require new citizens to immediately learn to speak and read English.

   a) What is your opinion in this debate? Explain the reasons behind your views.
   b) Pick one of the authors that we have just read. What do you think their opinion would be? Why? (Be sure to use information from the essays to prove your point.)

An Examination of At-Risk College Students' Sexist Attitudes Toward Reading

Maria Valeri-Gold and Nannette E. Commander

Sexist attitudes toward reading among at-risk college student populations exist on many campuses across the United States (Baron, 1996; Green, 1994; Mazurkiewicz, 1960). These attitudes are reflected in comments like, "men generally view reading as a feminine activity," "real men don't read," "books are too girlish," and "reading is just for girls." According to Baron (1996) and Osmont (1987), gender has an effect on college students' attitudes toward reading. Social and cultural expectations also play a major role in perceiving reading as a female rather than a male activity, and students learn from an early age about their gender roles through what they observe from their adult role models, in particular, parents and teachers (Osmont, 1987).

A review of the literature indicates that a multitude of studies have been conducted that investigates students' sexist attitudes, perceptions, and stereotypes toward reading in the elementary, middle, high school, and secondary school grade levels (Colles & Ollila, 1990; Davies & Bremer, 1993; Downing & Thomson, 1997; Dwyer & Reed, 1989; Groff, 1962; Kelly, 1986; Ley, Schaer, & Dismukes, 1994; Rachal, Leonard, & Jackson, 1991; Rye, 1983; Shapiro, 1990; Tullock & Alexander, 1980). Yet a paucity of research in examining sexist attitudes toward reading with at-risk college students exists. However, the few studies that have been conducted with at-risk college-level students yield interesting results.

Mazurkiewicz (1960) used a version of his *Male-Female Attitude Activity Inventory* with college-bound students enrolled in a summer developmental reading course to test his initial hypothesis that males perceive reading as a feminine activity. The inventory contains a list of 41 activities both males and females can participate in during their lives. In this study students classified the activities by marking either "M" or

---

Originally published in The Journal of College Literacy and Learning (2000–2001), *volume 30, pages 1–9*

"F" before each activity based on a code—M equals mostly masculine activities; F equals mostly feminine activities. For example, some activities listed on the survey are sewing and mountain climbing. Students could classify sewing under mostly feminine activities, while mountain climbing could be classified under mostly masculine activities. Results revealed that both male and female students clearly stated that reading was a mostly feminine activity.

Mazurkiewicz (1960) conducted another study to investigate the extent that fathers and sons view reading as a mostly masculine or mostly feminine activity using the same survey. He noted that 81% of the sons and 72% of the fathers perceived reading as a female activity, and this attitude appears to influence reading ability. Mazurkiewicz also tested the hypothesis that a relationship existed between the father's and son's attitude when they were examined on the basis of whether the son is in an academic or vocational curriculum. He found that a relationship existed when the son was involved in a vocational curriculum.

Winchock (1995) administered the *Mazurkiewicz Male-Female Attitude Activity Inventory* to at-risk community college students and high school students in grades 9 through 12 who were enrolled in basic reading skills classes. Ninety-one surveys were completed and results were tabulated. He found that 91% of the males and 94% of the females perceived reading as a feminine activity.

Baron (1996) examined gender attitudes toward reading with college readers enrolled in six sections of a developmental reading course at Kean College of New Jersey. The *Mazurkiewicz Male-Female Attitude Activity Inventory* (Mazurkiewicz, 1960) was used with a forced choice of "mostly masculine" or "mostly feminine." Fifty-nine students (26 males and 33 females) completed the surveys. Results indicated that 87% of both male and female students responded that reading was a mostly feminine activity, with 69% of the males and 97% of the females choosing this response. Findings revealed that the percentage of males in this study who perceived reading as a mostly feminine activity was lower than that of the Mazurkiewicz study (1960), where 81% of sons and 72% of their fathers viewed reading as a female activity.

The purpose of this study is to examine the sexist attitudes of at-risk college students enrolled in a College Survival Skills for Success course at Georgia State University using the *Mazurkiewicz Male-Female Attitude Activity Inventory*.

Method

Participants

Ninety-one college students (34 males and 57 females, mean age = 21.4 years) enrolled in five sections of a College Survival Skills for Success course participated in this study. The subjects enrolled in this course are at-risk college students whose cumulative and/or semester grade point average falls below 2.0. A major component of this class includes the teaching of effective reading and study skills strategies. The participants included 39 white students (25 females and 14 males), 42 African American students (26 females and 16 males), 6 Asian American students (2 females and 4 males), and 3 Hispanic American students (2 females and 1 male), and 1 female student of Indian descent. All subjects were treated in accordance with the "Ethical Principles of Psychologists and Code of Conduct" (American Psychological Association, 1992).

Procedures

Students were administered the *Mazurkiewicz Male-Female Attitude Activity Inventory* (1960) with forced choice of "mostly masculine" and "mostly feminine" as the two responses. Students were instructed that a third option did not exist; specifically, they could not classify reading as both a male and female activity. According to Mazurkiewicz (1960), the forced choice would indicate the students' real attitudes toward reading. Students placed their responses directly on the survey, and they were instructed to mark the letter "M" beside the activity that they classified as "mostly male" or the letter "F" for a "mostly feminine" activity. The surveys were collected and the researchers of the study tabulated data.

Results

Thirty-four males and 57 females completed the *Mazurkiewicz Male-Female Attitude Activity Inventory*. Results indicated that 12 males (35.3%) and 4 females (7%) responded that reading was a "mostly masculine" activity. Twenty-two males (64.7%) and 53 females (93%) indicated that reading was a "mostly female" activity. Of the 91 students who completed the survey, 82.4% stated that reading was a "mostly feminine" activity (see Table 1).

Table 1
Numbers and percentages of all male and female students in the survey who perceived reading as a mostly masculine or mostly feminine activity

	Mostly Masculine		Mostly Feminine	
	Number	Percent	Number	Percent
Males (34)	12	35.3	22	64.7
Females (57)	4	7	53	93
TOTAL (91)	16	17.6	75	82.4

Discussion

Based upon the results of this study and earlier investigations, reading continues to be perceived as a mostly feminine activity by both males and females. Analysis of the data confirms the findings conducted by Mazurkiewicz (1960), Winchock (1995), and Baron (1996). In Mazurkiewicz's study (1960), 81% of the males and 72% of the boys' fathers viewed reading as a mostly masculine activity. Ninety-one percent of the males and 94% of the females viewed reading as a female activity in Winchock's study (1995). In Baron's study (1996), 84.7% of both male and female students responded that reading was a mostly feminine activity. In this study, 82.4% of both males and females stated that reading was a mostly feminine activity.

It appears from the finding of this study that the majority of males (65%) who viewed reading as a mostly masculine activity may have been at-risk readers throughout their earlier school years. Mazurkiewicz (1960) found that as males progress through school, they increasingly perceive reading as a female activity and that reading achievement scores were higher for males who considered reading to be a masculine activity. Groff (1962) and Rye (1983) concur with Mazurkiewicz's (1960) findings that males' attitudes were related to their reading ability.

Teachers' expectations and perceptions of reading can affect the attitudes of males and females toward reading (Davies & Bremer, 1993; Groff, 1962; Rye, 1983). The at-risk college students in this investigation may have encountered negative reading experiences in their elementary, middle, and/or high school grades. For example, Davies and Bremer (1993) administered a questionnaire to determine if differences exist between the attitudes of males and females toward reading aloud to significant adults or themselves. Participants included a random sample of 216 students ages 6–7+, 189 students ages 8–9+, and 206 students 10–11+ years of age within six primary schools in the United Kingdom. Students were asked to choose between five options (very happy, happy, neutral, unhappy, very unhappy). Findings revealed that female students felt positive (happy, very happy) about reading aloud to the teacher, and the male students felt negative (unhappy, very unhappy) about reading aloud to the teacher. Significant differences between the sexes were found in the second grade (1%) and the fourth grade (5%). Davies and Bremer (1993) also noted that both males and females felt more positive about reading at home than at school. Regardless of grade level, educators need to encourage both males and females to become engaged readers by providing a variety of reading environments that promote an interest in literacy and improve reading perceptions.

The selection of reading materials can affect reading attitudes and perception (Shapiro, 1990). Providing students with eclectic approaches to reading with a plethora of reading materials may change the attitudes of both males and females toward reading. According to Gilbert (2000), selecting books for males with engaging masculine characters or nonfiction books and magazines or sports and other subjects can improve their attitudes toward reading and reading ability.

Implications

Based upon the findings of this study, college educators need to develop a reading curriculum that meets the individual and group needs of their at-risk college students. College educators need to pay attention and scrutinize the reading objectives they create for both male and female students enrolled in their classrooms. Classroom instructors and their students can work together to develop reading objectives for the course. Students can provide input by creating reading goals that they feel are important to help them meet with success in the course. Thus, students can become active participants in assessing their reading progress, attitudes, behaviors, and interests.

College reading textbooks chosen for students in at-risk college classrooms should include a variety of literary genres that represent strong male and female role characters that appeal to both males and females. College educators can select textbooks that move away from the "drill and skill" approaches to reading that require students to read a selection and then answer questions about the passage by circling the correct option. At-risk students need a potpourri of reading materials and approaches that provide them with opportunities to interact with the text and become engaged readers regardless of gender. They also need to be exposed to reading selections that ask them to reflect on issues that affect them personally, socially, and academically. Such reading activities can help students generate a positive enthusiasm toward reading information found in their core and major college course textbooks. Students should also have input into the selection of the materials and activities that are chosen for classroom instruction in order to meet their individual needs. These reading materials and assignments should also contain selections that represent the diverse backgrounds and cultures of the students along with activities that integrate the four communicative arts—reading, speaking, listening, and writing.

Recommendations

The findings in this study offer college educators who teach developmental or at-risk students opportunities for future research. The recommendations are as follows:

1. This study was conducted with at-risk college students using the *Mazurkiewicz Male-Female Attitude Activity Inventory*. Another study can be conducted with regularly admitted students to note any similarities and/or differences between their responses and at-risk college students by administering the same survey.

2. This study can be replicated with at-risk college students and/or regularly admitted students using a different survey that assesses how students perceive reading.

3. A study can be developed that investigates the influence that a mother's attitude toward reading can have on her son's or daughter's attitude.

4. A study can be created that investigates the influence that a father's attitude toward reading can have on his daughter's attitude.

5. A study can be conducted that examines both influences of mothers' and fathers' attitudes toward reading on their sons' or daughters' attitudes.

6. A study can be created that examines the reading attitudes of both males and females enrolled in at-risk college courses or in regular-admit basic writing courses.

REFERENCES

American Psychological Association. (1992). Ethical principles of psychologists and code of conduct. *American Psychologist, 47*, 1597–1611.

Baron, J. (1996). *Sexism attitudes towards reading in the adult learner population.* Unpublished master's thesis, Kean College of New Jersey, Union.

Colles, B., & Ollila, L. (1990). The effect of computer use on grade one children's gender stereotypes about reading, writing, and computer use. *Journal of Research and Development in Education, 24*(1), 14–20.

Davies, J., & Bremer, I. (1993). Comics or stories: Differences in the reading attitudes and habits of girls and boys in years 2, 4, and 6. *Gender and Education, 5*(3), 305–320.

Downing, J., & Thomson, D. (1997). Sex role stereotypes in learning to read. *Research in the Teaching of English, 11*(2), 149–155.

Dwyer, E.J., & Reed, V. (1989). Effects of sustained silent reading on attitudes towards reading. *Reading Horizons, 29*(4), 283–293.

Gilbert, S. (2000). *A field guide to boys and girls.* New York: HarperCollins.

Green, S. (1994). Sexism in developmental education: Tackling the demon. *Research and training in developmental education, 9*(2), 13–24.

Groff, P.J. (1962). Children's attitudes towards reading and their critical reading abilities in four content-type materials. *Journal of Educational Research, 55*(7), 313–317.

Kelly, P.R. (1986). The influence of reading content on students' perceptions of the masculinity or femininity of reading. *Journal of Reading Behavior, 18*(3), 243–256.

Ley, T.C., Schaer, B.B., & Dismukes, B.W. (1994). Longitudinal study of the reading attitudes and behaviors of middle school students. *Reading Psychology: An International Quarterly, 15*, 11–38.

Mazurkiewicz, A.J. (1960). Social-cultural influences and reading. *Journal of Developmental Education, 3*(3), 254–263.

Osmont, P. (1987). Teacher inquiry in the classroom: Reading and gender set. *Language Arts, 64*(7), 758–761.

Rachal, J.R., Leonard, R., & Jackson, L.S. (1991). Reading habits of students in adult basic education and high school equivalency programs. *Reading Research and Instruction, 30*(3), 76–88.

Rye, J. (1983). The importance of attitude: Some implications. *Reading, 17*(1), 13–22.

Shapiro, J. (1990). Sex-role appropriateness of reading and reading instruction. *Reading Psychology, 11*(3), 241–269.

Tullock, R.R., & Alexander, J.E. (1980). A scale for assessing attitudes towards reading in secondary school. *Journal of Reading, 23*, 609–614.

Winchock, J.M. (1995). *Sexist attitudes towards reading and writing in the young adult and adult learner population.* Unpublished master's thesis, Kean College of New Jersey, Union.

College Students' Use of Computer Technologies

Alice Scales

Researchers have acknowledged that college students have used the computer successfully in programs aimed at improving writing skills (Hawisher & Fortune, 1989; Liou, 1993; Lowe & Bickel, 1993; Mullins, 1988; Williamson, 1993). The extent of college students' use of computer technology to aid them as they complete their assignments remains as a question for research. Reading and study skills' programs have, on occasion, introduced college students to the advantages of using computers. Additionally, these students have been instructed in procedures for using word processing and other computer-based programs (Gold, 1992; Pobywajlo, 1989; Scales, 1993–1994). College students who use computer resources would seem to have an advantage over those who do not. For example, when they use word-processing packages, they often have on-screen access to a spelling and grammar checker, and a thesaurus. Further, they can move text around as they write. As a result, they can print out assignments that have a more polished and professional appearance. Computer use offers other advantages that can include access to a variety of databases, and the ability to send and receive electronic mail which includes facsimile (fax) capabilities.

With the conversion of many college campuses to electronic communication, it seems imperative that college students know how to access and use as many computer resources as possible irrespective of their higher education institutional level. Do university and community college students use computer resources?

Method

College reading and study skills instructors were asked to administer a computer technologies inventory to students enrolled in their classes. It took about 15 minutes of each study skills' class time for one community college instructor to administer the inventory to 56 students, and

Originally published in Forum for Reading *(1994–1995), volume 25, pages 39–49*

for one university instructor to administer the inventory to 46 students. Both administered the inventory before class discussion of the uses of computers in completing college course work assignments.

Subjects. Participants were 102 undergraduates who matriculated at an urban university and an urban community college in Pennsylvania. There were 60 females, 41 males, and 1 unidentified; 92 were white, 3 African American, 3 Asian, 2 Hispanic, and 2 unidentified. Students in the community college had an age mean of 20.05 years and university students had an age mean of 21.09 years. The 75 students who reported their majors were as follows: 10 were in the natural sciences, 2 in engineering, 7 in social sciences, 13 in humanities and arts, 16 in education, 2 in business, 8 in communications, 14 other, and 3 were undecided.

The Inventory. Thirteen likert-type items made up the computer technologies inventory. Responses to the items were made using a 5-point scale (1 for never, 2 for seldom, 3 for one half the time, 4 for usually, and 5 for always). Items were focused to ask students whether they used computer technologies in the preparation of their assignments. Did they use a spell checker, thesaurus, and a grammar check computer program as they wrote their assignments? Did they submit computer-produced assignments to their professors? Did they use electronic databases, card catalogs, the Internet, internal college or university computer systems, and other electronic material (e.g., programs on disk or CD) to locate information for their assignments? Did they use fax and e-mail? And, did they like to use the computer? Additionally, such demographic data as their sex, birthdate, race, and major were requested.

Cronbach's coefficient alpha was used to measure internal consistency reliability (Alpha = .8161) for the inventory. The relevance of the inventory was surmised from my experience with teaching study skills to college students and from a computer search of the literature. For example, in my study skills' classes (Scales, 1993–1994), I teach students the advantages of using computer resources to prepare their assignments. Also, to ensure that all students in my classes use computers, I schedule a working computer laboratory session for students and require that they prepare and submit a computer-produced assignment. Responses by students to my computer laboratory sessions have been positive. Kinzie, Delcourt, and Powers (1993) designed instruments to measure attitudes and perceptions of computer technologies of students in undergraduate programs. Questions on their instruments focused on comfort/anxiety and usefulness of the computer. Questions in my inventory were focused on the usefulness of computers for preparing written assignments.

Analysis of Students' Responses

Responses of all students to the questions showed that more than one half of them always used a computer, 75.5% used a computer spell checker, and 65.7% reported that they always submitted computer-produced assignments to their professors. Fewer than 25% reported that they always used a computer thesaurus, grammar checker, database, card catalog, the Internet, fax, or e-mail (Table 1).

Community college students' response showed that almost one half of them reported that they always used a computer, more than two thirds used a spell checker, and more than one half always submitted computer-produced assignments. More than 80% reported that they never used the Internet, fax, or e-mail (Table 2).

Table 3 shows that 63% of the university students always used the computer, 82.6% used a spell checker, and 76% always submitted computer-produced assignments. Almost one half never used a grammar checker, 78% never used the Internet, and 41% never used e-mail.

Table 1
Frequency (*f*) and percentage (*P*) of responses
(*n* = 102)

	Never *f*(P)	Seldom *f*(P)	Half-Time *f*(P)	Usually *f*(P)	Always *f*(P)
1. Use Computer	7(6.9)	7(6.9)	3(2.9)	30(29.4)	55(53.9)
2. Use Spell Check	9(8.8)	5(4.9)	2(2.0)	9(8.8)	77(75.5)
3. Use Thesaurus	28(27.5)	19(18.6)	25(24.5)	12(11.8)	18(17.6)
4. Use Grammar Check	44(43.1)	20(19.6)	15(14.7)	8(7.8)	15(14.7)
5. Computer Assignments	6(5.9)	4(3.9)	9(8.8)	14(13.7)	67(65.7)
6. Use Electronic Database	36(35.3)	17(16.7)	19(18.6)	14(13.7)	15(14.7)
7. Use Electronic Material	38(37.3)	21(20.6)	10(9.8)	18(17.6)	23(22.5)
8. Use Electronic Card Catalog	33(32.4)	11(10.8)	11(10.8)	24(23.5)	8(7.8)
9. Use Internal System	45(44.1)	18(17.6)	20(19.6)	11(10.8)	1(1.0)
10. Use Internet	82(80.4)	10(9.8)	5(4.9)	4(3.9)	1(1.0)
11. Like to Use Computer	19(18.6)	18(17.6)	24(23.5)	15(14.7)	26(25.5)
12. Use Fax	83(81.4)	11(10.8)	3(2.9)	3(2.9)	2(2.0)
13. Use E-Mail	67(65.7)	14(13.7)	7(6.9)	6(5.9)	6(5.9)

Table 2
Frequency (*f*) and percentage (*P*) of responses of community college students (*n* = 56)

	Never *f*(P)	Seldom *f*(P)	Half-Time *f*(P)	Usually *f*(P)	Always *f*(P)
1. Use Computer	6(10.7)	4(7.1)	2(3.6)	18(32.1)	26(46.4)
2. Use Spell Check	8(14.3)	3(5.4)	1(1.8)	5(8.9)	39(69.6)
3. Use Thesaurus	17(30.4)	9(16.1)	11(19.6)	8(14.3)	11(19.6)
4. Use Grammar Check	22(39.3)	11(19.6)	9(16.1)	6(10.7)	8(14.3)
5. Computer Assignments	6(10.7)	3(5.4)	5(8.9)	9(16.1)	32(57.1)
6. Use Electronic Database	31(55.4)	9(16.1)	9(16.1)	3(5.4)	4(7.1)
7. Use Electronic Material	28(50.0)	12(21.4)	3(5.4)	6(10.7)	7(12.5)
8. Use Electronic Card Catalog	31(55.4)	7(12.5)	6(10.7)	8(14.3)	4(7.1)
9. Use Internal System	32(57.1)	8(14.3)	10(17.9)	3(5.4)	3(5.4)
10. Use Internet	46(82.1)	5(8.9)	2(3.6)	3(5.4)	0(0)
11. Like to Use Computer	14(25.0)	10(17.9)	10(17.9)	8(14.3)	14(25.0)
12. Use Fax	48(85.7)	5(8.9)	1(1.8)	0(0)	2(3.6)
13. Use E-Mail	48(85.7)	5(8.9)	1(1.8)	0(0)	1(1.8)

Table 3
Frequency (*f*) and percentage (*P*) of responses of university students (*n* = 56)

	Never *f*(P)	Seldom *f*(P)	Half-Time *f*(P)	Usually *f*(P)	Always *f*(P)
1. Use Computer	1(2.2)	3(6.5)	1(2.2)	12(26.1)	29(63.0)
2. Use Spell Check	1(2.2)	2(4.3)	1(2.2)	4(8.7)	38(82.6)
3. Use Thesaurus	11(23.9)	10(21.7)	14(30.4)	4(8.7)	7(15.2)
4. Use Grammar Check	22(47.8)	9(19.6)	6(13.0)	2(4.3)	7(15.2)
5. Computer Assignments	0(0)	1(2.2)	4(8.7)	5(10.9)	35(76.1)
6. Use Electronic Database	5(10.9)	8(17.4)	10(21.7)	11(23.9)	11(23.9)
7. Use Electronic Material	10(21.7)	9(19.6)	7(15.2)	12(26.1)	8(17.4)
8. Use Electronic Card Catalog	2(4.3)	4(8.7)	5(10.9)	16(34.8)	19(41.3)
9. Use Internal System	13(28.3)	10(21.7)	10(21.7)	8(17.4)	5(10.9)
10. Use Internet	36(78.3)	5(10.9)	3(6.5)	1(2.2)	1(2.2)
11. Like to Use Computer	5(10.9)	8(17.4)	14(30.4)	7(15.2)	12(26.1)
12. Use Fax	35(76.1)	6(13.0)	2(4.3)	3(6.5)	0(0)
13. Use E-Mail	19(41.3)	9(19.6)	6(13.0)	6(13.0)	5(10.9)

Significant differences were found between the community college and university students' response to all items ($p < .001$). Item differences for using the spell checker, electronic database, electronic material, electronic card catalog, internal computer systems, e-mail, and submitting computer-produced assignments to their professors were found between the groups of students. Also, higher means were reported for the university students (Table 4).

Significant differences were found between females and males responses about their using electronic material, internal systems, and the Internet to locate material. Higher means were reported for the male students (Table 5).

Table 4
t test for differences between community college (CC) and university (Un) students

Items	Groups	n	M	SD	t	df	Prob.
Total Items	CC	56	2.4704	.698	-4.53	99	.001
	Un	45	3.0712	.614			
2. Use Spell Check	CC	56	4.1429	1.495	-1.98	99	051
	Un	45	4.6444	.908			
5. Computer Assignments	CC	55	4.0545	1.380	-2.51	97	.014
	Un	44	4.6364	.750			
6. Use Electronic Database	CC	56	1.9286	1.283	-5.31	98	.001
	Un	44	3.3182	1.343			
7. Use Electronic Material	CC	56	2.1429	1.458	-2.80	99	.006
	Un	45	2.9556	1.445			
8. Use Electronic Card Catalog	CC	56	2.0536	1.381	-7.52	99	.001
	Un	45	3.9778	1.138			
9. Use Internal System	CC	56	1.8750	1.207	-3.02	99	.003
	Un	45	2.6444	1.351			
13. Use E-Mail	CC	55	1.2000	.650	-5.28	97	.001
	Un	45	2.3409	1.430			

Table 5
t test for differences between community
college and university students by sex

Items	N	M	SD	*t*	*df*	Prob
7. Use Electronic Material	61	2.2623	1.448	-2.15	100	.034
Females	41	2.9024	1.513			
Males						
9. Use Internal System	61	1.8689	1.103	-3.29	100	.001
Females	41	2.7073	1.470			
Males						
10. Use Internet	61	1.1803	.563	-2.64	100	.010
Females	41	1.6098	1.070			
Males						

Summary and Implications

Did students use computer resources for their written assignments? Most of the students in these educational institutions have used computer resources to prepare their written assignments. More of the students (three fourths) reported that they always used a spell checker more than any other computer resource, and more (two thirds) submitted computer-produced assignments than not. Only 7 of the students (6 of the 7 were community college) reported that they have never used the computer to prepare their assignments and 6 (all 6 were community college) have never submitted computer-produced assignments to their professors. Additionally, community college students reported less use of computer resources than university students.

Students in classes where computer resources for writing have been promoted have reported positive gains from their experiences (Liou, 1993; Williamson, 1993). Therefore, it is my contention that more promotion of computer resources in classes would enhance the production of college students' assignments. Particularly, in colleges where students may be unaware of the advantages of computers, and when students do not use them in the preparation of their assignments, it behooves instructors to strongly encourage students to make use of computer technologies. Moreover, classroom instructors could require that students submit only well-prepared computer-produced assignments. However, when it is known that students lack skills in computer use, then classroom instructors should ensure that students receive instruction in computer use through a student service program or study skills classes. If neither, student service program nor study skills classes are available, then the instructor could schedule an in-class working session with computers designed to familiarize students with the alternatives available to them for composing and producing written assignments.

REFERENCES

Gold, M.V. (1992). The bridge: A summer enrichment program to retain African American collegians. *Journal of the Freshman Year Experience, 4*(2), 101–117.

Hawisher, G.E., & Fortune, R. (1989, Fall). Word processing and the basic writer. *Collegiate Microcomputer, 7*(3), 275–284, 287.

Kinzie, MC., Delcourt, M.A.B., & Powers, S.M. (1993, April). *Computer technologies: Attitudes and self-efficacy.* (ERIC Document Reproduction Service No. ED 357 064)

Liou, H.C. (1993, Summer). Investigation of using text-critiquing programs in a process-oriented writing class. *CALICO Journal, 10*(4), 17–38.

Lowe, N., & Bickel, R. (1993). Computer-assisted instruction in Appalachia's post-secondary schools. *Journal of Educational Research, 8*(1), 46–52.

Mullins, C.J. (1988, Winter). Teaching technical writing with PCs. *Technical Writing Teacher, 15*(1), 64–72.

Pobywajlo, M. (1989). *The AFT program at UNHM: Reaching out to underprepared students.* (ERIC Document Reproduction Service No. ED 324 673)

Scales, A.M. (1993–1994). Enhancing the college reading study course experience with computer use. *Forum for Reading, 24*(24), 20–31.

Williamson, B.L. (1993). *Writing with a byte. Computers: An effective teaching methodology to improve freshman writing skills.* (ERIC Document Reproduction Service No. ED 362 245)

Addendum in 2002 to "College Students' Use of Computer Technologies"

The use of computer resources to fulfill college assignments is more widespread now than when this article was first published (Scales, 1994–1995). My purpose in this article was to show the results of the extent of college students' use of computer resources. At that time, of the students who participated in that study, only 53.9% reported that they always used the computer for preparing their assignments, 80.4% never used the Internet, and 65.7% never used e-mail. I used those data, my other experiences (Scales, 1993–1994), and reports of computer usage in classrooms by others (Burke, Peterson, Segura, & Johnson, 1992; Platt, 1992) to further my thinking for revising my own college reading and study skills course. For it was my contention then and still is now that "more promotion of computer resources in classes would enhance the production of college students' assignments" (Scales, 1994–1995, p. 48).

Following my advice, over the years I have steadily included more learning of skills and practice with computer resources for students in my reading and study skills' classes. More specifically, my college reading and study skills course is now computer based. I use the *Interactive Computer Based College Reading, Writing, and Study Skills Text* (Scales & Biggs) as the primary textbook. Instructional text is computer based. All assignments are computer produced. Students must access resources through the Internet, they must use e-mail, and they must write a major term paper using computer resources. When asked their views of taking the computer-based course, students reported that they were pleased to be able to learn so much about computer usage as they did their assignments. They were particularly delighted to have been able to learn to access various academic databases through the Internet. Such exposure provided resources that they used to assist them in studying for their other courses.

Finally, as stated earlier, "it behooves instructors to strongly encourage students to make use of computer technologies" (Scales, 1994–1995, p. 48) if students are not doing so. Also, to instructors who are aware of students with poor computer skills, those students should be referred to a study skills class, a student service center, or a tutor for computer instruction. Students must be computer literate. Many courses that they take in college require the retrieval and study of voluminous documents. Today, an expedient way of searching for and locating those documents is through the Internet. A use of the Internet provides access to numerous electronic databases, libraries, reference materials, journals and magazines, organizations and agencies, institutions and foundations, and a host of other genres that provide an abundance of resources for student academic consumption. Study of such documents can be enhanced with computer usage. For example, students may access numerous abstracts or whole documents through the Internet, copy and paste several into one file, read each, and organize or sequence the information for later study. Caverly and MacDonald (1998), Hawes (1998), and Lancaster (2001) have described additional ways of using the Internet and other technologies with college students.

Today, academic as well as economic survival skills appear to be linked to computer usage. Students who master such skills are better positioned to access resources and use them for advancement than those who are not. To ensure computer literacy, college reading and study skills classes must function as a catalyst that hastens the inclusion and use of computers in academic settings.

REFERENCES

Burke, M., Peterson, C., Segura, D., & Johnson, L. (1992). *Computer-assisted vs. text-based practice: Which method is more effective?* Paper presented at the annual Midwest Reading and Study Skills Conference, Kansas City, MO. (ERIC Document Reproduction Service No. ED350 046)

Caverly, D.C., & MacDonald, L. (1998). Techtalk: Distance developmental education. *Journal of Developmental Education, 21,* 36–37.

Hawes, K.S. (1998). Reading the Internet. Conducting research for the virtual classroom. *Journal of Adolescent & Adult Literacy, 41,* 563–565.

Lancaster, M.B. (2001). *Jefferson Davis Community College and developmental education: A partnership for student success.* (ERIC Document Reproduction Service No. ED454 892)

Platt, G.M. (1992). *Assessing program effectiveness. It's a tough job, but somebody's got to do it.* Annual report of the South Plains College Learning Center, Levelland, Texas, 1991–1992. (ERIC Document Reproduction Service No. ED346 916)

Scales, A.M. (1993–1994). Enhancing the college reading study course experience with computer use. *Forum for Reading, 24,* 20–31.

Scales, A.M. (1994–1995). College students' use of computer technologies. *Forum for Reading, 25,* 39–49.

Scales, A.M., & Biggs, S.A. *Interactive computer based college reading, writing, and study skills text.* Manuscript submitted for publication.

SECTION III

Program and Strategy Descriptions

eaching is a juggling act among theory, research, and the enhancement of students' metacognitive abilities. Theories and research are the underpinnings of your theoretical and pedagogical frameworks. You are confronted with other nonteaching challenges in the classroom. For example, on your class roster you have a nontraditional, single parent who works part time and is enrolled as a full-time student, or a freshman who decided not to do any work in high school, but is now away from the parental authority and enjoys a new sense of freedom. This section of articles focused on program and strategy descriptions will be a guide as you strive to enrich and validate your pedagogy to meet the needs of your students as they develop compensatory skills to ensure their academic survival.

Each student is unique and has various learning strategies and needs to find a balance among academe, work, social life, and family. Educators are in the position to challenge their students intellectually while being sensitive to students' emotional, social, and cultural needs.

The articles in this section provide the seasoned professional in the developmental reading field, as well as the apprentice, a range of options for practical application. Which article is the best for you and your program? It depends. Sometimes, educators are like some of our students: We want a quick answer to achieve our most celebrated moment in teaching—the "teachable moment." In this Program and Strategy Descriptions section, you will first read an article on a college developmental program, followed by a series of articles on strategies, and concluded with a portfolio assessment article.

Dillard provides insights into a framework of a developmental reading program's goals, administration, and organization. Next, O'Dell and Craig describe the teaching of previewing as a learning cognitive metastrategy in their action research article.

Because there are so many college students whose study strategies need further development, Hayes and Alvermann provide an active plan for studying, learning, and applying information, under a premise that students need to be taught how to learn. Educators acknowledge that there are students who study with the goal of learning just enough for them to pass a test, but strive for students to develop their cognitive and metacognitive strategies for long-term learning. Tei and Stewart inform readers of the importance of teaching components of effective studying, summary writing as metacognitive strategy, and the use of self-questioning study techniques.

As developmental educators strive to develop students' metacognitive strategies, problem-solving abilities, and critical thinking, questions always arise about the effectiveness of textbooks as instructional aids. Schumm, Leavell, and Haager guide educators with an article and valuable chart for selecting appropriate texts to meet students' thinking and learning needs.

College instructors frequently assert that students are unable to comprehend important concepts in their textbooks. Spires's article describes research about the development of comprehension strategies and provides a model of reader-generated elaborations as a comprehension strategy.

This section continues with Strode's article about reading and writing as part of the communication process. She validates the importance of annotation and its relationship to summary writing as a reading comprehension strategy.

To further students' metacognitive awareness, Chamblee demonstrates the benefits of using reader response to assist in the communicative process. She shows how reader response relates to independent and self-confident readers. Chamblee's research correlates to Soldner's article about how using learning logs in a college developmental reading class enhances metacognitive awareness. Soldner also provides a list of learning logs suggestions.

This section concludes with Casazza's thoughts on how educators can add assessment to their teaching. She succinctly provides a rationale and guide for establishing an authentic student-driven reading portfolio.

As you read the articles in this section, we encourage you to reflect on your theoretical frame and pedagogical choices. Because teaching is a worthwhile endeavor, these articles provide numerous opportunities for you to continue to develop your metacognitive awareness in your teaching of college developmental reading.

The Goals, Administration, and Organization of a College Developmental Reading Program

Mary L. Dillard

n this paper, assumptions are made that (1) not all developmental reading programs are organized or managed in the same way; (2) reading faculty learn from each other through an exchange of information; and (3) too often, articles in our professional journals are limited in scope, so much so that we often do not have a broad overview of what each other is doing. This rather broad description of the goals, administration, and organization of the Northwestern developmental reading program is being offered in an effort to exchange information with fellow reading faculty on a broader, though hopefully not superficial, basis. As in many other programs, we work with state regulations, so we are not always free to experiment with the program. Obviously, we at Northwestern do not do everything right, and even at this writing, we are undergoing healthy change. We simply want to share what we do in hopes that others may have insights into what they do better and worse than we do, and to see what is simply being done differently.

The first section of the paper deals briefly with our written program and course goals. The reader will find that the written program goals center on the more traditional components of a developmental reading program and on goals important for increasing the quality of the program. Written course goals focus on improvement in vocabulary acquisition and use, comprehension, test-taking skills, obliterating test anxiety, and the comfortable use of varied reading rates. More space is given to our unwritten course goals which reflect our concern for the whole student. They include helping students to improve their attitudes; encouraging students to attend to their physical, emotional, and academic needs; breaking barriers between faculty and students; improving students' concentration and self-discipline; helping students to develop a sense of responsibility for self, and for the faculty to support the freshman orientation program.

Originally published in Forum for Reading *(1987), volume 18, number 2, pages 63–74*

Section two briefly describes the administrative framework under which the program operates and the duties of the reading program co-ordinator. Section three describes the major components of the reading program itself—courses, conferences, testing, grading, evaluation, and support services.

I. Goals of the Reading Program

A. Program Goals

Major program goals for developmental reading include goals for our students and those goals which will help expand and improve our program. Goals for our students include the following: (1) to raise the students' reading levels to enable them to be academically successful in college; (2) to increase their literal, inferential, and evaluational comprehension levels; (3) to increase their general, and to a lesser extent, their content area technical vocabulary so that college level work is less difficult; and (4) to provide students with adequate study skills for academic success.

Goals for the expansion and improvement of the program include the following: (1) to conduct research into the innovative use of methods and materials for the improvement of teaching developmental reading students; (2) to develop minicourses in reading in the content areas as the need arises; (3) to pursue a holistic, cooperative approach across campus for improving all the academic developmental courses and for working with developmental students; (4) to involve other departmental faculty, staff, graduate assistants, and upper division education majors in the developmental reading program; (5) to provide a wide array of support services for those students who need more than whole-class instruction, including tutors, use of learning lab, and a variety of materials; and (6) to conduct an ongoing evaluation of the program and student progress.

B. Written Course Goals

According to departmental policy, traditional course goals are stated as behavioral objectives in course syllabi and include improvement in vocabulary acquisition and use, comprehension, test-taking skills, a reduction of test anxiety, and an increased use and awareness of various reading rates. Improvement in vocabulary acquisition and use is mainly developed through the use of oral and written exercises through whole and small groups and/or individually. These exercises stress (1) the use of context clues for meaning, (2) awareness of multiple meanings of words, and (3) emphasis in technical vocabulary for various content areas. Where appropriate, such strategies as semantic webbing, semantic factor analysis, and structured overviews are used. Group work includes exercises and discussions of appropriate and inappropriate word choice and a sharing of individual vocabulary acquisition strategies.

A second course goal involves improvement of comprehension at all levels through the student's increased ability to (1) state and use facts found in a selection; (2) recognize main ideas and supporting details; (3) follow a sequence of events, especially when the time sequence is convoluted; and (4) draw conclusions based on material read. Comprehension improvement also comes through the students' increased awareness of (1) the difference in reading requirements for fiction and nonfiction; (2) an author's organizational patterns, mood, tone, and style; (3) the students' own need to link what they read to what they already know (schema theory); and (4) the importance of thinking about how they know (metacognition). Comprehension tasks include vocabulary since it is used to express concepts and should not be isolated from tasks involving comprehension improvement. Other comprehension tasks include (1) increasing the length of silent sustained reading, (2) tapping into prior knowledge before reading and linking it to what is to be learned through such strategies as structured overviews and PReP, (3) discussing the right and wrong responses to reading selections, and (4) thinking about the reading process as it is experienced by the students. Writing skills, such as outlining, paraphrasing, and summarizing, are also incorporated into the course as an aid to comprehension.

A third course goal seeks the improvement of such test-taking skills as (1) following directions, (2) time awareness, (3) intelligent guessing, (4) active reading, (5) recognition of the different types of information required by various tests, and (6) test anxiety. Students work on exercises developed for increasing their awareness of the importance of following directions. Improvement in the enhancement of time awareness comes through a steady diet of timed readings and through vocabulary drills developed for students to practice choosing appropriate synonyms for as many of the 100 words as they can do in 10 minutes. The latter exercise is directly related to taking the Nelson-Denny Reading Test and is intended to help students become aware of how fast they must work on this test. Another skill is reading actively on tests. For improvement of this skill, students are taught how to read to answer questions by a modified version of the survey and question part of

SQ3R. Students are also taught to be test-wise by learning when they should guess, how to reduce the odds in guessing, and when desperate, what choices have a greater chance of being right. They are also taught to be aware of absolutes, such as always and never. As a further part of their test-taking skills, students are encouraged to ask their other professors about the types of tests given in their classes and how to prepare for them; therefore, an ongoing goal for reading faculty is to explain how reading students are tested and what the tests actually test. For example, it is often difficult for our students to understand that the vocabulary words on the Nelson-Denny Reading Test are representative of words they encounter, and that they are not being tested on the ideas or information in the comprehension reading selections but on their ability to extract meaning. Included with these test-taking skills is work on controlling test anxiety through pointing out such factors as (1) the need for being academically prepared for tests; (2) being on time for the testing session; (3) having appropriate supplies; (4) sitting in a familiar place; and (5) being physically prepared through a good night's rest, appropriate meals, and general good health. Relaxation exercises are introduced for the severely stressed student, and the college counselor's workshop on handling stress is recommended.

A final goal for the course involves increasing the students' awareness of the need for reading various materials at different rates. They are given practice in reading various kinds of content area reading and in skimming and scanning exercises. Study plans are used in conjunction with these exercises to help students become more efficient in their use of reading time.

Readers will notice a rather reduced list of study skills taught as part of the reading courses. Missing are such skills as time management, goal-setting, note-taking, or using the library. These skills are taught in the freshman orientation course.

C. Unwritten Course Goals

Unwritten goals of the reading course encompass much more than reading skills, as they are concerned with the whole student and are often difficult to measure. These goals are important because they are often part of a student's inability to be successful in an academic setting. Such unstated course goals include improved attitudes, improved general well-being, breaking barriers between faculty and students, work on concentration and self-discipline, helping students develop self-responsibility, and supporting the freshman orientation program.

1. Improved Attitudes. Many entering freshmen maintain the high school mentality of thinking someone or something is making them go to school and that they are there against their will. Many times they enter college with a teach-me-if-you-can attitude and use disruptive behavior techniques that gave them the attention they sought while in high school. Instructors work on students' attitudes by (1) having them concentrate on their short- and long-range goals through oral and written work, (2) demonstrating to students that class work is important for meeting these goals, (3) showing them that being in college is a free choice, and (4) organizing the work and setting the class tone so that disruptive techniques are obviously inappropriate and immature. Instructors, through well-planned lessons, provide opportunities for positive attention for students. Instructors also create opportunities for the freshmen to get to know each other, for example, through small-group work. Through early control and management of the class, which is linked with well-planned lessons that show the students that there is indeed something they need to learn, instructors work toward making students their partners in the responsibility for what gets done in class.

Direct talks about reasons for students being in developmental reading classes are helpful. Somehow there seems to be more of a social stigma attached to being in the developmental reading class as opposed to composition or mathematics. Many times students think that being assigned to the class means that they cannot read whereas they know they can. They have to understand that they simply need to improve. In our direct talks with them, we give them the following possibilities for their being in the class: (1) the need for improvement in acquiring and using general and technical vocabulary, (2) the need for improved comprehension on all levels, (3) the need for better test-taking skills which may simply be "rusty" at this time, (4) the need for increased awareness of using various reading rates, (5) the need for better control of test anxiety, or (6) any combination of the above. This kind of direct talk does wonders; it allows them to rationalize about their being in the class, an important ego or image protector for some, and for others, it helps them to see what their weaknesses are and to begin improving their reading.

2. Improved General Well-Being. We cannot teach reading skills in isolation to our developmental freshman students. We have to consider aspects of their lives besides the academic. Therefore, we encourage students to work on their physical and emotional needs, their social lives, and their changing self-images. We stress management of their lives so that they have time for physical exercise; leisurely, healthy meals; reflection; hobbies; and making new friends.

3. Breaking Barriers. Part of attitude and image change evolves through breaking barriers between faculty and students. Instructors early on establish the fact that they aren't the enemy or the cause for the students' being in a developmental reading class. Rather, instructors try to establish a cooperative atmosphere that suggests that they are there to help students be successful, to exit the reading program as quickly as possible, and, in the long run, to get what they want out of life. This atmosphere further suggests that poor skills, whatever the cause, are the enemy, and instructor and student fight together against it.

4. Improved Concentration and Self-Discipline. Many times in the students' past, arrested and underdeveloped concentration, along with limited self-discipline, have attended learning problems. For example, many of our students skimmed through high school classes doing surface work, finishing an assignment early, and usually not very well, and often have spent too much time just sitting out a class. To help students improve their concentration and self-discipline, our instructors plan class work so that quality counts and so that no one ever runs out of something challenging to do. Classes are held full time, and students quickly learn that they are expected to work the entire class period each class meeting. However, the class time is divided into a variety of activities so that too much isn't expected of them all at once.

5. Self-Responsibility. Because developmental students often need to work on self-responsibility, the course is designed to help them share in the responsibility for their learning. Essential requirements for the course are drafted carefully so that they are fair and enforceable, because once a requirement is made, it must be applied to everyone. Students are held responsible for knowing and meeting requirements, and they are helped to do so by the instructors giving written copies and discussing the requirements in class. We see our responsibility as holding to the requirements because many of our students need the structure and need to know that requirements must be met. If a student does not meet a requirement, he must live with the consequences, whereas the instructor, while enforcing requirements, also tries to see that the consequences do not constitute a major disaster. For example, if a student fails to meet enough course requirements so that he fails at midterm, the instructor makes every effort to see that the student does not give up hope of passing the course. In clear and concrete terms, the instructors tell the student what he must do to pass the course.

Part of a student's need to accept responsibility is tied to his ability to feel capable and worthy. Instructors try to see that students find out that they can do the work—that they don't have to be given anything because they can earn it. One way this is done is through individual work with students during class. Instructors work in a nonthreatening, student-centered way by guiding students through a series of questions which incorporate the students' strategies and lead to the students' solving the problem or reaching an acceptable answer rather than having the instructor give the answer while the student remains passive. The attitude of the instructor is to help students "see" or understand how to arrive at solutions and answers. This approach may be as old as Socrates, but it works.

6. Support of the Freshman Orientation Program We support the freshman orientation program because the instructors in that program teach many of the study skills for which we were formally responsible. Their program has freed us to concentrate on skills more directly related to reading rather than trying to be all things to all people. We support their program by encouraging students to practice the study skills learned in the orientation program and by providing out-of-class opportunities for doing so. For example, students do various time management homework exercises and are given reading class credit for them.

II. Administration of the Reading Program

The Department of Education is responsible for providing personnel, including the reading coordinator, professors, and graduate assistants assigned to teach the courses. The reading coordinator, who is an assistant professor in the Education Department, teaches four sections of developmental reading, administers the program, trains the graduate assistants, coordinates their teaching schedules with their own course schedules, attends coordinators' meetings across campus, runs training sessions for learning lab tutors, selects learning lab materials for reading, revises the course syllabi, chooses textbooks, conducts on- and off-campus testing, evaluates the program and staff, and coordinates her program with the developmental education learning lab. Other departmental duties include advising elementary education majors, working with various departmental and campus-wide committees, and teaching upper level reading courses during the summer session. She reports directly to the chairman of her department.

III. Organization of the Reading Program

A. Courses

The reading program consists of three courses. The first course, Reading 0900, is designed for students reading below the eighth-grade equivalent level as measured by the various forms of the Nelson-Denny Reading Test. Textbooks used for this course include (1) Rhonda Atkinson and Debbie Longman's *Reading Enhancement and Development*, West Publishing Company, 1985, and (2) Helen H. Gordon's *Wordforms–Context, Strategies, and Practice*, Book I, Wadsworth Publishing Company, 1985.

The second level course, Reading 0910, is designed for students reading on the eighth- and ninth-grade equivalent levels as measured by the various forms of the Nelson-Denny Reading Test. Textbooks used for this course include (1) Arthur Whimbey's *Mastering Reading Through Reasoning*, Innovative Sciences, Inc., 1985, and (2) Helen H. Gordon's *Wordforms–Context, Strategies, and Practice*, Book II, Wadsworth Publishing Company, 1985.

The third course, Reading 0920, is designed for students reading on the tenth-grade equivalent level as measured on the various forms of the Nelson-Denny Reading Test. Textbooks used for this course include (1) Arthur Whimbey's *Analytic Reading and Reasoning*, Innovative Sciences, Inc., 1983, and (2) James F. Shepherd's *College Vocabulary Skills*, Houghton Mifflin Company, 1983. The latest edition of Shepherd's book has been ordered for next semester.

It should be noted here that the two highest levels, Reading 0910 and 0920, could be combined quite easily, but for psychological reasons, we offer the three levels. In the state universities of Louisiana, students are presently given three semesters to complete their developmental courses in reading, math, and English. If they fail to do so, they may be dismissed from the university. Offering three courses psychologically helps those students who start at the lowest level, make small amounts of progress, and thus move gradually through all three courses. By rewarding a small amount of progress by having a student move up to the next course, the student is encouraged to stay in school, whereas, if only two courses were offered, greater progress would have to be made before a student could feel as though something had been accomplished. Students receive three hours credit for each reading course successfully completed. Although the credit does not count toward a degree, it does count in receiving financial aid.

B. Conferences

1. Substance. Midterm and final conferences are considered major parts of the reading program. During the conferences the students are encouraged to use self-diagnosis to gain insight into their reading problems and to share the responsibility for their improvement. Self-diagnosis is encouraged by the instructor's asking the students what areas of reading, such as vocabulary improvement or comprehension, they feel they need to work on most, and why they think so. What the instructor is really doing is assisting students to become more aware of what is going on in their heads as they read and to come to some conclusions about it. Remedies to reading problems should not be sought haphazardly. Students should be able to identify symptoms, be consulted in the diagnosis, and share in the search for cures for their problems.

Students, by means of instructor's questions, are also led to see the relationship of skills taught and tasks performed in the reading course to reading in their regular college courses, and they are encouraged to use strategies learned and practiced in reading classes in these courses.

In the midterm conferences, instructors and students review their weekly reading logs which are kept from the first day of class. The forms are divided into two sections, one for academic course textbook reading and the other for leisure reading. Places are provided for recording the amount of time and material read for each day. Students are encouraged, for example, to read a minimum of 15 minutes a day on a subject of personal interest. They are also encouraged to read magazines and journals in their college majors or possible majors. The instructors talk with students about length of reading time and consistency of reading every day. Large amounts of time recorded as spent on academic course work may be a sign of trouble, so instructors discuss whether or not reading the material is a problem. The logs are an "awareness tool" which helps students see consistency of work and emphasizes the importance of working some each day rather than letting work slide.

During both midterm and final conferences, students are led to reexamine their goals as stated during the first week of class. Instructors always hope that students will feel good about what they have accomplished, but if they don't, they are redirected and shown what they need to do in order to reach their goals. Discussion may also turn to nonacademic problems, such as poor attitude and lack of motivation, if they seem to be a problem. Lastly, one of the most important parts of the midterm conferences is the students' evaluation of the course.

2. Format. While the substance of the conference is important, so, too, is the format. As part of the format, instructors use an evaluation sheet for each student as a guide for the conference and for recording information to go in the student's folder. The recording of information is done while both instructor and student sit side by side so that the student can see what is being written. The instructor writes only what both of them agree to be true. Validation of comments or statements are frequently sought. Openness of this kind has proven to be important in the conference because it breaks barriers and emphasizes that the process is a shared venture. It helps set an atmosphere of cooperation rather than confrontation or avoidance. The instructor's interest in the student is obvious through this careful and cooperative recording of information, and the record becomes concrete proof that someone cares about the student.

C. Evaluation

1. Testing Program for Students. Entering students whose ACT composite scores fall below 16 are required to take one of the various forms of the Nelson-Denny Reading Test for placement. If they read below the eleventh-grade equivalent level, the level stated in our State Developmental Task Force Report and accepted by the Board of Regents, they are required to enroll in one of the three aforementioned courses. We do question this entry/exit score, especially since the later forms of the Nelson-Denny Reading Test are easier than forms A and B; therefore, we hope a follow-up study of students exiting our program will help us decide whether or not to change the grade equivalent level for exit.

Students are given the Nelson-Denny Reading Test at midterm and as a final exam. They may exit the program from any level course at midterm by scoring eleventh-grade equivalent or above. If they do, they are not required to attend class for the rest of the semester and receive a passing grade for the course. This midterm testing has been a great motivator for those who have difficulty accepting placement in a reading class and for those older students who are rusty from too many years' absence from the classroom.

Final exams are given during the last class period of the semester, and final conferences are scheduled during the university's final exam week. Students, whose placement is based on the Nelson-Denny grade equivalent score, may move up to the next level reading course, skip a level, or exit the program. Teacher judgment and day-to-day work are important in assigning the final grade. As stated in the course syllabi, instructors have the option of not allowing students to take either the midterm or final exams, a decision based on a student's number of absences and the quality and/or quantity of day-to-day work. A backup evaluation system of power and cloze procedure tests is also used for special cases.

The midterm grade, reported as "P" for pass and "F" for failure, is thought of as a warning to students. However, final grades are reported as letter grades. An "A" received in any course means that the student exited the reading program. A grade of "D" or "F" received in a course means that the student must repeat the course. The difference in receiving a "D" or "F" depends on the quality of class work and lab attendance. The rest of the grading scale differs according to a system that provides for tracking the reading students. For example, Reading 0900 students receiving a "B" in that course enroll in Reading 0920 the next semester. A grade of "C" in Reading 0900 shows that the student will be enrolled in Reading 0910 the next semester. The scale becomes more flexible with the two upper level courses. For example, Reading 0910 students who receive a grade of "B" or "C" enroll in Reading 0920. The difference in the grade reflects the quality of class work and lab attendance. Reading 0920 students who exit the program receive a grade of "A," "B," or "C," again depending on the quality of classwork and lab attendance.

Some problems with our testing program include fairness in giving makeup exams; maintaining the eleventh-grade equivalent level as our exit score; refusing to immediately give the test again to those students who are disappointed with their scores; criticism by students who cannot see the relationship of classwork to taking the Nelson-Denny Test, even though the courses have been streamlined to teach only those skills necessary to pass the test; and deciding how to help students who are unable to read on the eleventh-grade equivalent level after three semesters of reading courses.

2. Course and Instructor Evaluation. As previously stated, students are given two opportunities to evaluate the course and the instructor. The first, at the midterm conference, is informal and oral, with suggestions made by the students recorded in a special section on the conference evaluation sheet. At this conference, students are asked (1) what the instructor could be doing in class that isn't presently being done to help students improve their reading, (2) if instructors should be doing more or less of some class activities, and (3) what seems to be really helping or not helping very much. By using this informal, conversational method, students feel that they are not on the spot but that the instructors really want feedback while there is time in the course to make changes. Instructors usually tell students about some of the changes in the course that have come about from student suggestions. The idea is not original with the program coordinator, but was introduced to her by Milton "Bunk" Spann several years ago when he served as a developmental education consultant for Morristown Junior College in Tennessee. A reduced version of his open-ended written evaluation is used in our program for our final, formal evaluation (see Appendix, page 203). Although using an open-ended questionnaire takes more class time, pertinent information is gathered this way. Using the open-ended questionnaire, we know not only what students approve or disapprove of in our program, but why. Several changes in both the curriculum and in the textbooks used have been made, based on both the informal oral and more formal written evaluations.

D. Use of Support Services

The entire developmental education program is supported by learning labs and academic counselors. For example, our third semester reading students are required to attend the lab for 90 minutes a week. Their instructors identify and report skills for the students to practice in the lab to the academic counselor who then meets with the students and schedules them for lab work, either in self-paced programs or with a tutor who works with the student using various strategies, such as a modified version of the ReQuest method for comprehension or semantic webbing for vocabulary acquisition. Instructors also use the lab by checking out lab materials for classroom use or by scheduling whole classes for the lab during regular class time for individual- or small-group work.

Conclusion

In concluding this paper, in which an overview of the goals, administration, and organization of the Northwestern developmental reading program has been given, we realize that such an undertaking does not lend itself to an in-depth discussion of the various components of the program, but we do hope that further discussions of various aspects of such programs are forthcoming. In a further effort to exchange ideas with developmental reading faculty, we have included a list of references at the end of this paper that have been especially helpful to us as we have worked toward the improvement of our own program.

REFERENCES

Breen, E.J. (1982). *A study of the influence of previewing techniques on the reading comprehension of community college students.* Doctoral dissertation, University of Washington.

Buchanan, B.N., & Sherman, D.C. (1981). *The college reading teacher's role in higher education today.* Paper presented at the annual meeting of the European Conference on Reading, Joensuu, Finland.

Crawford, J.J. (1983). *Evaluation of a college reading program.* Paper presented at the annual meeting of the College Reading Association, Atlanta, GA.

Diddock, D.L. (1983). *A college reading program: A study of effects on grades, units completed and college retention.* Doctoral dissertation, University of the Pacific.

Gordon, B., & Flippo, R.F. (1983). An update on college reading improvement programs in the southeast United States. *Journal of Reading, 27*(2), 155–163.

Green, M.L. (1983). *An investigation of seven commercial reading materials for adults to determine if these reflect adult learning principles and adult reading needs.* Doctoral dissertation, Texas Woman's University.

Gudan, S. (1983). *The Nelson-Denny Reading Test as a predictor of academic success in selected classes in a specific community college.* Doctoral dissertation, Schoolcraft College.

Leverett, R.D. (1983). *Skilled and deficient readers: A comparison of two groups of college freshmen on auditory, language, and metacognitive abilities.* Doctoral dissertation, George Peabody College for Teachers of Vanderbilt University.

Livingston, C.L. (1973). Behavioral objectives for learning outcomes of reading and study skills programs in the community junior college. *Programs and Practices for College Reading, 2,* 62–71.

Perez, S.A. (1983). A successful developmental reading program for college freshmen. *Reading Improvement, 20*(3), 233–235.

Rosen, E. (1982). *Design, implementation, and evaluation of a criterion-referenced diagnostic/prescriptive reading course for college students.* Doctoral dissertation, University of New Mexico.

Spann, M. (1984). *Faculty evaluation form.* Unpublished evaluation form, Appalachian State University.

Starkie, G.B. (1982). A developmental reading program: How it works at one college. *Reading Improvement, 19*(4), 279–281.

APPENDIX

PLEASE READ THIS STATEMENT BEFORE YOU BEGIN

I can't begin to answer the question "How can I improve student learning?" without consulting you—the students. If I am going to improve my ability to help you learn, it is important for me to know in very *specific* ways what you see me doing and how you feel that my actions are helping you out. I'm sure that I'm doing some things that are helping you out just as I'm sure that some of my actions are not.

In order for me to "reality test" my ability to help you learn I need to look carefully at my own behavior and how I feel about that. Of equal importance to me is your willingness to look at my actions and tell me how you see them.

Please use all the time available to complete this evaluation. First of all, answer those items you find most interesting or perhaps easiest for you, then complete the more difficult or least interesting ones. Please be specific. General statements won't help me much. I won't promise to change, but I will promise to take you seriously. THANKS.

Student Feedback to Faculty

I. Please describe as specifically as possible (give examples) what the instructor is doing in the circumstances below.
1. When you find the instructor most helpful to your learning
2. When you find the instructor least helpful to your learning
3. When you feel that the instructor has made himself clearly understood
4. When you feel that the instructor has not made himself clearly understood
5. When you find the instruction most relevant to your life and prior learning
6. When you find the instruction least relevant to your life and prior learning

II. Please answer the following, questions as specifically as possible in terms of your own feelings about the course and your performance.
1. Which assignments were most helpful in helping you really learn and understand the assignments?
2. Which assignments were least helpful in helping you really learn and understand the assignments?
3. When did you feel that your grades were most accurate in terms of your performance?

4. When did you feel that your grades were least accurate in terms of your performance?
5. When did you feel that the instructor was most prepared and enthusiastic?
6. When did you feel that the instructor was least prepared and enthusiastic?

Faculty Response Sheet

1. Generally, from your students' answers, how do you think your students view the class and curriculum?

ABOVE AVERAGE   AVERAGE   BELOW AVERAGE

2. In general, based on your students' answers, how do you think your students rate you as an instructor?

ABOVE AVERAGE   AVERAGE   BELOW AVERAGE

3. In which areas do you feel your students were most accurate in their perceptions?

4. In which areas do you feel your students were least accurate in their perceptions?

5. What changes *could* you make in curriculum based on student response?

6. What changes *could* you make in method of instruction based on student response?

Previewing for a New Age

Kate O'Dell and Judith Cope Craig

t is the first day of the semester. An education instructor watches as her university students file into the classroom. They are talking, greeting classmates, and shuffling through their book bags. Inadvertently, the professor overhears a grumbler saying,

> Yeah, I just came from the bookstore. Shot a hundred bucks just on the two lousy books for *this* course. And when I go to sell them back, the bookstore will either refuse them or give me half my money back. What a waste!

The grumbler is talking about books the instructor has meticulously selected for the course. This student is already planning to sell the textbooks back to the bookstore, and has instantly formed a negative impression of the texts. The grumbler is also wondering what kind of instructor would subject a student to such economic hardship. Clearly, this student does not know the purpose of the texts or their content or relevance to the course. The instructor must help this student break through these cognitive and emotional barriers that separate student and text.

Fortunately, the instructor has a plan. As Joyce (1995) suggested, "The problem with getting inside the act of reading...is its ubiquity— there's no escaping it, and like any environment that we are overly familiar with, we no longer see it" (p. 1). To assist students in actually *seeing* their texts, this instructor facilitates formal previews of each text as part of the opening activities of class. It is a tried-and-true practice she has used for years.

In the preceding scenario, the instructor was confident that the use of a textbook previewing strategy would assist students' reading of the texts; however, she also knew that as reflective practitioners, a teacher must periodically reexamine even the givens of instruction. Recent developments in neuroscience that are uncovering the workings of the human brain are prompting educators to reexamine teaching and learning at all ages and developmental levels (e.g., Sylwester, 1995). While wholesale application of the research is premature (Bruer, 1999), over-

Originally published in The Journal of College Literacy and Learning (2000–2001), *volume 30, pages 23–33*

all findings to date suggest that educators need to reinvestigate instructional practices and scrutinize the results to answer two fundamental questions: (a) Are our practices congruent with current information about brain function and capacity? and (b) If not, what methods might be more effective in helping students gain access to written material?

Another factor that provides context for discussions about pedagogy is near-universal recognition of fundamental changes in the purposes and processes of schooling. One aspect of this paradigm shift is that the behavioral-rational model of teaching and learning, which has dominated our thinking in education, is beginning to yield to constructivist and brain-based models. Educational theory in the future will be shaped by the New Science (especially chaos and complexity theory), the rapidly changing demographics of the United States, and a sociopolitical landscape dotted with paradoxes (Brown & Moffett, 1999). Teachers of adults and college students will need to design instruction framed by principles of learning such as those suggested by Brown and Moffett:

- True learning comes from a fusion of head, heart, and body....
- Learning is strategic. (pp. 31–32)

The purpose of this paper is to present an application of information from two action research studies and a brief synthesis of some developments in neuroscience toward the reexamination of previewing as a reading strategy. The authors are teacher educators who undertook their informal research activities in order to make curricular decisions about what to recommend to future teachers as potentially useful strategies. However, they also believe that the conclusions have relevance to reading teachers of college and adult students.

A Brief History of Previewing

The 1940s wartime call for increased numbers of military fighter pilots resulted in rapid training efforts. Student pilots were required to read a large volume of very complex material in a short time. Furthermore, they needed long-term memory for content detail; in fact, their lives and the lives of their crew would depend upon it. Previewing was developed as a study tool to aid in reading comprehension. Theoretically, the previewing would provide the reader with a metaview of the reading material. The metaview would serve as a framework upon which to fix the content particulars. The study technique used by the military, PQRST, involved previewing the material first, then questioning before reading, studying, and testing. The military study strategy eventually evolved into SQ3R (Survey, Question, Read, Recite, Review) which has been widely taught as a study strategy to upper elementary through college-age students (Cochran, 1993).

Is Previewing Brain Compatible?

Returning to the questions that initiated this discussion of previewing, the authors asked themselves if currently used teaching strategies are compatible with information coming from neuroscience. In fact, a review of the literature yielded extensive support for the pedagogy that assists students in learning to make their own situational decisions about their reading strategies. Researchers address principles of learning in some of the most recent literature that applies brain research to education (e.g., Caine & Caine, 1991; Jensen, 1998; Matthews, 1997; Ornstein, 1997; Ornstein & Ehrlich, 1989; Smilkstein, 1997).

Many parallels may be drawn between principles of brain-compatible teaching and learning and the best pedagogy in previewing. Two of the more important principles of brain-based learning can be directly compared to the intended outcomes of previewing, especially if each student is making all of the decisions about strategies to be used. For example, the principle, "The search for meaning occurs through 'patterning'" (Caine & Caine, 1991, pp. 81–82), addresses the brain's need to organize and categorize incoming stimuli. All of the systems for previewing offer instruction and practice in creating patterns for the information one receives from reading texts. A corollary to the brain's need for patterning is its innate search for meaning. This preprogrammed necessity of the brain to find meaning is reflected in previewing strategies which guide readers to discover their motivation to engage the text and determine a purpose for reading.

Effective previewing pedagogy assists students in achieving command of the strategies themselves (e.g., encourages metacognition and the formation of metastrategies). Metastrategies exploit the well-established principle that every human brain has two kinds of memory systems: a rote system for acontextual memories and a cognitive map system for memories that drive the innate search for meaning. Students may learn SQ3R by practicing the steps in order with one type of text or a particular purpose. However, when they are able to create a new previewing process for a different text and/or a different purpose, they have integrated the component strategies of SQ3R into original approaches that are highly responsive to the new contexts.

A Survey: Questions About Previewing

In the summer and fall of 1997, one of the authors and an English instructor distributed a survey asking students to describe their use of previewing as a strategy. The survey included items such as, *If you preview, how much time do you usually take?* and *When you preview, what kinds of things do you look for in the text/electronic text?* Respondents were requested to circle choices from a list and/or write in other items.

Of the 133 students who completed the survey adequately enough to permit a simple tally, 86% reported that they looked through the text before they start to read. However, they generally spent only three to five minutes engaged in this activity and only sometimes had a specific goal in mind. One student commented, "If I am pressed for time, I often skim the material to get an idea of how long it will take. If I am not pressed for time, I don't look through the text."

While the number of surveys returned was limited, the students who responded represented a wide spectrum of students—from freshman to graduate study level. Our overall finding was that previewing is used and, by implication, still needs to be taught. The questionnaire did not ask if the students had ever been directly instructed in previewing. However, the skills that are most often taught appeared to correspond to the practice of how these students actually used the strategy. One important result of the survey was that no one answered the questions with reference to electronic texts. When we distributed some surveys with the specific request that the questions be answered with electronic texts in mind, the results did not differ significantly.

Student Teachers Meet Their Textbooks

An informal study of student teachers provided the authors with some useful information about previewing as a strategy. Twenty-three education majors described in the opening scenario completed a questionnaire on the first day of class. One question asked was, "Do you preview your texts before beginning your reading assignments?" The results were that ten answered that they did preview, five did not, four said that they did so sometimes, three indicated that they covered summaries only, and one did not respond. During the second class period, the instructor reminded the students that as future teachers they would be likely to have input in selecting textbooks for adoption on several occasions. They were also reminded that they would also be teaching their own students how to effectively engage with texts. Then students were shown a list of inconsiderate text features cited by Armbruster (1984). Students recognized and discussed features like cluttered page layouts and poorly organized tables of contents. In addition, the instructor led the students through a preview of one of the course textbooks. A second preview was assigned as homework. Following the homework assignment, students shared their observations about it. No additional attention was given to previewing as a strategy. Near the end of the semester, students were asked to write in response to the prompt, "Did the previewing done at the beginning of the semester have any effect on your reading of the course textbooks?" Surprisingly, two students indicated that this was the first previewing they had ever done. One said that it was the first time that previewing was assigned and not simply a suggested activity.

Among the 23 students, 20 said that text previewing had helped them read their assignments. Their claims were that previewing had shown them the layout pattern of the chapters, which resulted in more efficient reading. Students were able to predict where to find information and better insight on which parts to read and which to skim.

Three students claimed that previewing was not helpful; however, one of the three discovered features she otherwise would have missed and a second student said that she was glad to know where the chapter summaries were located. The last student said he thought previewing was a great idea, but that he had devised his own system that worked best for him.

Other comments from students in the class were that previewing had made the textbook less threatening and that the students felt more confident about using the text as a source of information. The grumbler even confessed,

> Yes, I think previewing the text was useful. At the very least, previewing the text sold me on the book as a resource. I am always leery of textbooks because of their ridiculous cost, and I usually view them with quite a bit of cynicism. [Seventy-nine dollars??!!—the cost of the textbook] With the preview I was able to see the value in the book and begin to change my perception from "money pit" to "handy reference."

Another student made a different confession. She wrote, "The preview made me realize all the wonderful things the book had to offer, and I actually read it."

Although these responses were from students in only one class, the instructor concluded that the strategy was worthwhile enough to continue using it as a class assignment. By linking previewing to job skills, the professor motivated students to pay attention. Looking at the text from a considerate [more easily read] versus inconsiderate [less easily read] perspective allowed the students to activate their prior knowledge as textbook readers. Sharing through discussion after the previewing was useful. While most of the students recognized major features of the text, the discussion allowed every student to see the texts' most salient features.

Discussion

Student comments seem to suggest that learning and using previewing skills at the college level is beneficial. In order to meet the rigors of college reading, they believe they benefited from guidance about how to use strategies to improve their study and learning.

Previewing appears to be compatible with brain research and what we now know about learning. The elements of patterning, of cueing systems, and of schema theory are at work within the context of previewing. Jensen (1998) argues that, "We are on the verge of a revolution: the application of important new brain research to teaching and learning" (p. 1); he also warns that we should proceed with caution. The collaboration between neuroscience and education is in its earliest stages, and we do not know the answers to many crucial questions. Further, Bruer (1999) warns that much of what educators know about the brain as it is related to education is actually based in cognitive and developmental psychology, the behavioral sciences, and our scientific understanding of the mind rather than in brain research.

Despite the admonitions to proceed warily, the authors are encouraged by what they learned from their review of the literature and their action research regarding previewing as an important reading skill. Nevertheless, as professionals they recognize the obligation to continue careful study. They are particularly interested in how previewing is related to what Aarseth terms "computer-mediated textuality" (in Landow, 1994, p. 51) as well as what features will be judged considerate in the texts of the new millennium. Although the body of research on electronic text is still small and not longitudinal, researchers are finding applications and ideas for future study (e.g., Blanchard, 1989; Gillingham, 1992; Homey & Anderson-Inman, 1994; Knupfer & McIsaac, 1989).

What to Do on Monday Morning

One Monday morning task is to build metacognitive skills. Specifically, it is important for students to be able to take into account their affective schema and recognize how these interact with new material they are reading. Students can read from textbooks in various disciplines and keep a running written record of their feelings as they read. They can be guided by questions such as, "What words did you react to?" "What images did you form as your read?" "What is your predominant feeling after reading this excerpt?" As each excerpt is completed, students can design a grid that classifies their feelings on the basis of the type of material they read. After reading three excerpts, students can combine their grids and do a feature analysis. This can be in the form of a grid or Venn diagram.

When members of the class have completed reading a set of excerpts and feature analyses, they can participate in a general discussion where they compare their analyses among themselves. The instructor can encourage students to reflect on what they have discovered. Students can also keep a reflective journal where they write about how they will use the information from the grids to assist them as they preview.

Other Monday morning activities include four strategies that are designed to stimulate neural growth or branching and the development of rich cognitive maps. One activity is to encourage students to think hypothetically. "Hypothetical thinking is a powerful stimulant to neural growth because it forces [an individual] to conceive of issues and consequences other than the standard and expected ones" (Cardillichio & Field, 1997, p. 34). When students have previewed, they can be guided to formulate general questions like the following (p. 35):

- What if this had happened? (something other than what the previewing seemed to indicate happened)
- What if this was not true?
- What if this had not occurred?
- What if I could do something I cannot do? [as a result of reading the text]

Another way to encourage hypothetical thinking is to "blur the picture or turn it upside down" (p. 35). After previewing, questions can take the form of reversals (from cause to effect or vice versa). Also use questions that lead to other questions. Yet another strategy is to encourage students to apply alternative symbol systems. For example, after previewing, readers can ask questions such as the following to guide reading of the text (p. 35):

- Can I make this into a word problem?
- Can I draw a picture of this?
- Can I represent this in musical terms?
- Can I act it out?

Students can also be encouraged to pose questions that lead them to analyze a text from various points of view after previewing (p. 35):

- What else could account for this?
- Who would benefit if I thought this?
- What harm might occur if _____?
- How many other ways could someone look at this?
- What would _____ (for example, my mother) say about this?

Use follow-up discussion to encourage students' understanding of the text. After students have previewed and formulated their preliminary constructions of the text, the instructor can engage them in a group discussion that includes negotiating differences, consensus building with an emphasis on the construction of knowledge. This discussion activity also provides experiences in using the social arena for examining ideas (Zahorik, 1997).

Conclusion

From research on the human brain, a rapidly expanding body of knowledge about how human beings learn is beginning to illuminate current theory and practice in every aspect of teaching and learning. This article explored pedagogy in the reading strategy of previewing. Two basic questions were addressed. First, should teachers provide instruction to their college and adult students in previewing strategies? Second, if instruction is provided, should the methods change? The authors conclude that college students do benefit from instruction when they learn previewing as a metastrategy. Since no single method is appropriate for all students in all situations, particularly with reference to electronic texts, students can be encouraged to develop a variety of ways to preview to increase their understanding of what they read.

REFERENCES

Armbruster, B. (1984). The problem of "inconsiderate text." In G.G. Duffy, L.R. Roehler, & J. Mason (Eds.), *Comprehension instruction: Perspectives and suggestions* (pp. 202–214). New York: Longman.

Blanchard, J. (1989). Hypermedia: Hypertext-implications for reading education. *Computers in the Schools, 6*(3/4), 23–29.

Brown, J., & Moffett, C. (1999). *The hero's journey: How educators can transform schools and improve learning.* Alexandria, VA: ASCD.

Bruer, J. (1999, May). *In search of...brain-based education.* Available online: http://www.pdkintl.org/kappan/kbru9905.htm.

Caine, R., & Caine, G. (1991). *Making connections: Teaching and the human brain.* Alexandria, VA: ASCD.

Cardellichio, R., & Field, M. (1997, March). Seven strategies that encourage neural branching. *Educational Leadership, 54*(6), 33–36.

Cochran, J. (1993). *Reading in the content areas for junior high and high school.* Boston: Allyn & Bacon.

Gilligham, M. (1992, April). *Goal directed reading of complex, embedded hypertexts: Effects of goal and interest on search strategies and selective attention.* Poster presented at the annual meeting of the American Educational Research Association. (ERIC Document Reproduction Service No. ED345 204)

Homey, M., & Anderson-Inman, L. (1994). The Electro Text Project: Hypertext reading patterns of middle school students. *Journal of Educational Multimedia and Hypermedia, 3*(1),71–91.

Jensen, E. (1998). *Teaching with the brain in mind.* Alexandria, VA: ASCD.

Joyce, M. (1995). *Of two minds: Hypertext pedagogy in the poetics.* Ann Arbor, MI: University of Michigan Press.

Knupfer, N., & McIsaac, M. (1989). Desktop publishing: The effects of computerized formats on reading speed and comprehension. *Journal of Research on Computing in Education, 22*(2), 127–136.

Landow, G.P. (Ed.). (1994). *Hyper/text/theory.* Baltimore: Johns Hopkins University Press.

Matthews, R. (1997). Semantic judgments as encoding operations: The effects of attention to particular semantic categories on the usefulness of interim relations in recall. *Journal of Experimental Psychology: Human Learning and Memory, 3*(8), 160–173.

Ornstein, R. (1997). *The right mind: Making sense of the hemispheres.* San Diego, CA: Harcourt Brace.

Ornstein, R., & Erlich, P. (1989). *New world, new mind.* New York: Simon & Schuster.

Smilkstein, R. (1995, April). *Transforming "below average" students into college-level readers, writers, and thinkers.* Panel presentation at the College Reading and Learning Association Convention, Tempe, AZ.

Sylwester, R. (1995). *A celebration of neurons: An educator's guide to the human brain.* Alexandria, VA: ASCD.

Zahorik, J. (1997, March). Encouraging—and challenging—students' understandings. *Educational Leadership, 54*(6), 30–32.

A Cyclical Plan for Using Study Strategies

David A. Hayes and Donna E. Alvermann

You've identified study skill needs, assessed student motivation and attitudes toward reading, written objectives for your individualized instructional program, and incorporated a variety of sound study skill strategies into your teaching repertoire. So, you ask yourself, why aren't more of the students in your Learning Skills Center applying their newly acquired skills for effective and efficient learning? Maybe your students haven't learned how to learn. Maybe they have acquired knowledge of, and a fair degree of competence in, several useful study strategies, but perhaps they lack a general plan for studying on their own.

Webster's definition of *study*, "a process of acquiring by one's own efforts knowledge of a subject," implies that one purpose for teaching study skills is to enable students to become independent learners. Trembley's (1982) advice to study skills teachers supports this definition. He advises that teachers help students take responsibility for their own learning.

Although research on the most effective ways to teach students how to study is not new (see Krumboltz & Farquhar, 1957), it is nonetheless relatively scarce. According to a survey of 213 accredited institutions in 11 southeastern states (Gordon & Flippo, 1983), postsecondary reading faculty identified the area of how to teach study skills as one of the five areas they felt most in need of further research. Based on the limited number of studies available, however, it appears that students who successfully complete a college study skills course earn significantly higher and stable grade point averages than they did before taking the course (Robyak & Downey, 1979).

Traditionally, the starting point for study skills instruction has been the indentification, isolation, and teaching of specific cognitive processes known to relate to successful studying. Thus, techniques for improving memory of what is read, such as SQ3R (Robinson, 1946) and ReQuest (Manzo, 1980), have been used. Note-taking with T-Notes (Davis & Clark, 1982) and A Note-taking System for Learning (Palmatier,

Originally published in Forum for Reading *(1984), volume 15, number 2, pages 47–52*

1973) represent the type of strategies introduced to help students integrate information from the teacher's lecture with that of the assigned text. While these information-processing strategies are valuable in their own right, there would appear to be an even better use made of them if they were to be incorporated into a larger plan for studying, one that the student takes the responsibility for managing.

Recent advances in cognitive psychology have led to a new conception of the student's role in the teaching-learning process. Weinstein (1982), for instance, asserts that

> Rather than portraying learners as passive participants who assimilate knowledge in a mechanical manner, these new conceptions characterize learners as active information processors, interpreters, and synthesizers. Students who know how to use effective strategies to organize and monitor learning, memory, and information retrieval can take greater responsibility for their own learning and become more instrumental in adapting the learning environment to fit their individual needs and goals. (p. 6)

Effective application of this theoretical notion may best be realized by helping students break down the information presented by the textbook and the instructor so that students will be able to manage their own learning. Smith (1982) suggests the following:

1. Deal with "whole" texts (for example, entire chapters or articles) as the primary unit of study.
2. Encourage students to change tasks while studying, to keep on the move.
3. Develop awareness of study as a series of decisions by which one defines and solves problems. This decision making requires trial and error behavior.
4. Emphasize synthesis of information from different sources. In every class, students have at least two vital external sources of information, the text and the lecturer. Beyond that are many others, including supplementary texts, other students, and other media. (p. 11)

In the present article, we propose a cyclical plan for studying that takes into account these information processing strategies and their effective management by students. It is a study cycle within which specific information processing strategies can be applied flexibly. Within the cycle-specific study strategies can vary from one study situation to another, and within each study situation, it can vary from one facet of study to another. But the overall study cycle itself remains invariant in its structure. Essentially, it consists of specifying study purposes, previewing the materials, proceeding through the task incrementally, and connecting the content to be learned to other knowledge about the material studied.

Setting Study Goals

Effective study requires purpose. It requires that the student know the reasons for undertaking a particular study task and set objectives to be reached when it is completed. The better the student understands the reasons for a study task, the sharper the student can focus the objectives of study and the more efficient the study activity is likely to be. A basic problem for the student is that college instructors seldom explicitly state their purposes for following a line of thinking or for adopting a particular sequence by which to present course content. The student must take the initiative to try to understand the instructor's thinking, to try to "psyche out" the instructor. If possible, the student may talk privately with the instructor to get suggestions about where to place emphasis in studying for the course and the course texts and even ask for study tips that the instructor believes helpful.

Without directly asking the instructor, the student can usually get a good idea of what the instructor deems important by sorting out what is said in class and examining it in light of introductory information given at the first meeting of the class and provided in the course syllabus. Sorting out the class discussion or lectures has the student identify the major concepts presented in class, note their supporting information, and determine how they fit together.

Typically instructors' presentations resemble textbook presentations. They introduce major concepts at the beginning of a lecture or segment of instruction, then during the lecture reiterate them with elaborative, clarifying information, and summarize them upon conclusion. Listening for points that are illustrated with anecdotes and noting information written on the chalkboard can help students identify significant course content. As soon as possible following class, the student should actively reflect on the class discussion by reviewing class notes, organizing them according to importance and relatedness, and inspecting notes for evidence of content promised either in the earliest meeting of the class or in the course syllabus. On the basis of this review of class notes, the student should come to a tentative decision—even if it means hazarding a guess—about what the instructor considers important and why it should be studied. How it can be studied successfully depends on the extent to which the student's study purposes coincide with the instructor's thinking about the content. To approximate a match between the two, the student should attempt to adopt the instructor's pattern of thinking about the material as it is revealed by emphasis and sequence in class presentations. Later, after the material is learned, this initial pattern of thinking can be discarded or reformulated to fit the student's own informed perspective. But to begin study, the student must decide upon a direction to take. The student's study direction is always indicated by the instructor's apparent instructional goals. These should be translated into the student's own study goals, formulated in terms of a purpose statement, and kept available for reference during study. Having a purpose statement written down helps the student stay on track when the frustrations of grasping abstract concepts and putting details into place tend to cloud the goals of study. Insights developed during study can be used to guide the student in amending the purpose statement. Once the student has decided upon a direction to take in studying and formulated a written statement of study goals, the student should then preview the text with an eye toward determining how it will be studied.

Preview

In previewing, the student skims the text for its gist and actively searches for clues to accomplishing the goal of the study activity. Most important of these clues are those to be found in the text's organization, its use of key terms in the headings, the kinds of information depicted in the illustrations, and the information emphasized in the end material, such as review questions and suggestions for further study. Content area texts are typically organized in such a way that major concepts are presented in the introductory portion of a text and summarized again at the end. The major concepts are often distilled into phrases that serve as headings of the text segments that develop them.

On the basis of the information gleaned during preview, the student can then make a plan for studying the text. The plan should be flexible, subject to revision, and appropriate to the goal established for studying. Flexibility cannot be overemphasized. Using incomplete data to predict the way that the study activity ought to go, the student should be aware that studying involves risk. The student may, for instance, determine that the goal of a particular study task is merely to identify specific instances of generalizations given in class and decide initially to scan parts of the text where the sought-for instances are likely to be found.

During preview, however, the student observes that instances presented in the text differ in importance, some occurring in highly specific or unusual circumstances. Given this additional information, the student will have to judge whether these differences will matter in achieving the instructional purpose intended by the instructor. If they do, revision of the study approach is in order. The study plan may even have to be scratched, time and effort may be lost, and another approach may have to be taken. Losses can be minimized, however, by incorporating into the plan allowance for unforeseen problems and provision for adjusting to them during study. Flexibility is probably best accomplished by dividing the text into parts and devising a subplan for studying each.

Intensive Incremental Study

On the basis of the preview, the student can mentally segment the text into components perhaps smaller than the text sections marked by headings or subheadings. The student can then deal with the text in parts small enough that through an appropriate active study response the student can recite content in ways relevant to the purpose of the study task. Most beginning college students can recite the essential information of as much as a page or two of a text, depending on the density of the content or ideas that bear reciting or remembering.

Once the text has been divided in this way, the student should proceed incrementally. Each segment of the text should be read at least once and, if upon first reading the material appears to warrant concentrated attention, the student should read the material again applying a study strategy that appears to best lend itself to dealing with the material. On first reading each text segment, the student should read to get its gist, note unfamiliar terms for later attention, and make a judgment about how the text segment may be important to accomplishing the student's study goal. If it lacks importance, make a mental note of it and move on to the next text segment. If it does seem important, decide how studying it might contribute to achieving the study objective and devote to it concentrated attention until the material can be recited in ways that are indicated by the purpose of the study task.

The student can respond to the text segments in a number of ways. The responses that are most likely to increase concentration and result in fuller understanding call for reacting to the text with a pencil. With a pencil the student can record the response to the text and come back to it later to check its focus, accuracy, and completeness. Among the most basic responses to a text are listing important information, paraphrasing the text, making up questions about the content, and making comparisons and contrasts in the material. Responses may take the form of formalized strategies advocated for teaching and learning from textual materials, for example, RADAR (Martin, 1983), REAP (Eanet & Manzo, 1976), SAV (Manzo, 1981), SQ3R (Robinson, 1946), and Survey Technique (Aukerman, 1972). The students may create mnemonic acronyms that arrange the first letters of key terms into word-like strings. For complex material it may help to depict graphically the relations that bind the material conceptually, particularly its sequential, chronological, and cause-effect relations. Radically new content can sometimes be initially understood by comparing it to something familiar to the student. By such comparison, unfamiliar aspects of the novel content can be conceptualized as a provisional working model for understanding while its distinguishing features are sought and used to refine understanding of the new material. The responses may be mixed and matched as the student finds most helpful. However the responses are framed, the student should observe how the textual content overlaps and supports the material provided by the course instructor. Obviously, overlapping material should be targeted for special attention. Where the text and the instructor differ, the instructor's version must for practical reasons prevail in the student's mind, but a note should be made to seek clarification from the instructor.

When the student is satisfied that the text segment has been thoroughly treated, the next text segment should be dealt with in similar fashion. If on first reading it appears irrelevant to the study purpose, the student should go on to the next text segment; if its content seems relevant to the study purpose, further study is needed. Again the student should decide on an active study response appropriate to the nature of the material and the study purpose. In each text segment considered worthy of concentrated study, the student should make a point of determining how each part of the text fits with other parts of the text.

As the student proceeds through the text, interim review of text segments studied helps pull the material together and fosters a growing sense of the significance of the content. Repetitive, cumulative reviews also provide rehearsal and "deeper processing" of the material since it enhances attention to the semantic relations in the material. The interim reviews become progressively longer as more text segments are completed, but text segments previously reviewed are likely to require less and less time and attention. Once all text segments have been addressed, the student should be ready for a global review of the material studied.

Global Review

The purpose of global review is to bring closure to the study of a text in a way that will render it memorable and useful for further study. Global review begins with the student collecting his impressions of the material studied and constructing a summarizing statement. The statement should be couched in the student's own language and should reflect any opinions or overall conclusions that have been drawn. The student should try to personalize the material. To support this statement the student should recite top-level information that has been studied, its associated propositions either implicit in the statement or capable of being compressed into generalized form. Further paring of extraneous and superfluous material takes place by eliminating from further consideration information that does not contribute to achieving the study purpose. This is the time to underline or highlight, not before. It is not until this point in the study cycle that the student can be sure that the information marked is truly relevant to the study purpose and even then whether it is worth marking. The text should be marked sparingly. Material that has been thoroughly studied ordinarily requires minimal cues for recalling it. Excessive marking of the text provides little or no help for later review and can even distract and confuse the student about what is important to remember. The student should mark only enough text to stimulate memory of its associated information.

One final consideration in the cyclical framework of studying is preparing for a unit test. It is at this point that students should augment their notes with information gained from supplementary texts, films, filmstrips, videotapes, and other media. Because few texts are in every way superior to all others, checking with additional texts offers the possibility that other authors present the material under study in more readable, more meaningful ways. As the student checks other texts, note should be made of differences in the information presented and in where the emphasis is given. This elaboration of the material, acquired perhaps by comparing and contrasting the assigned textbook author's point of view with the views of others, serves two purposes. One, it will increase the student's depth and/or breadth of understanding of a topic, and two, it may be the "frosting on the cake" in any essay or short-answer discussion question.

Ultimately, students find their own best ways of studying. As a college skills instructor, you can advance your students toward that end by providing a framework within which they can actively sift through material to be learned, translate it into their own language, and develop personalized formulas for understanding and remembering it. Through your encouragement and instruction, students can come to accept that successful study requires purpose, planning, and disciplined execution.

REFERENCES

Aukerman, R.C. (1972). *Reading in the secondary classroom*. New York: McGraw-Hill.

Davis, A., & Clark, E.G. (1982). Note-taking with T-notes. *Journal of Developmental and Remedial Education*, 5, 8–9.

Eanet, M.G., & Manzo, A.V. (1976). REAP—A strategy for improving reading/writing/study skills. *Journal of Reading*, 19, 647–652.

Gordon. B., & Flippo, R.F. (1983). An update on college reading improvement programs in the southeastern United States. *Journal of Reading*, 27, 155–163.

Krumboltz, J.D., & Farquhar, W.F. (1957). The effect of three teaching methods on achievement and motivational outcomes in a how-to-study course. *Psychological Monographs*, 71, 443.

Manzo, A. (1981). A subjective approach to vocabulary, or ...I think my brother is arboreal. *Reading Psychology*, 1, 29–36.

Martin, C.E. (1983). Using RADAR to zero-in on content area concepts. *Reading Horizons*, 23, 139–142.

Palmatier, R.A. (1973). A notetaking system for learning. *Journal of Reading*, 17, 36–39.

Robinson, F.P. (1946). *Effective study*. New York: Harper.

Robyak, J.E., & Downey, R.G. (1979). The prediction of long-term academic performance after the completion of a study skills course. *Measurement and Evaluation in Guidance*, 12, 108–111.

Smith, S. (1982). Learning strategies of mature college learners. *Journal of Reading*, 26, 5–12.

Trembley, D. (1982). Teaching study skills to the losers. *Curriculum Review*, 21, 257–258.

Weinstein, C. (1982). Learning strategies: The metacurriculum. *Journal of Developmental and Remedial Education*, 5, 6–7, 10.

Effective Studying From Text: Applying Metacognitive Strategies

Ebo Tei and Oran Stewart

To be effective learners, students should know about the state or level of their learning and the success of the strategies they are using. Students should realize when they misunderstand a concept in a chapter so that additional reading can be done or outside sources consulted. Knowing about and controlling one's learning is termed *metacognition* (Flavell & Wellman, 1977). In this article, we look at studying and learning how to study from the perspective of metacognition. The process of studying and the strategies that more successful learners have been shown to use will be examined in depth. Also, metacognitive strategies that have evolved in recent research will be briefly reviewed and instructional activities based on the strategies will be suggested. The goal of the instructional activities will be to help less successful learners develop more control over their learning.

Metacognition and Studying

The term metacognition as it has evolved in the literature implies having knowledge (cognition) and having understanding, control over, and appropriate use of that knowledge (metacognition). There are two types of metacognition (Brown, 1982). One type relates to the knowledge that successful learners have about various aspects of the learning situation, including their own capabilities and limitations as learners. The other type refers to those self-regulatory activities that successful learners engage in to produce comprehension when reading, solving a problem, or learning in general. These two forms and the activities involved in them are summarized in Table 1.

In general, the research evidence (e.g., Andre & Anderson, 1978–1979; Bransford, Stein, Shelton, & Owings, 1980; Brown, Campione, & Day, 1981; Garner & Reis, 1981; Palincsar, 1981; Paris & Lipson, 1982) indicates that when students engage in the self-

Originally published in Forum for Reading *(1985), volume 16, number 2, pages 46–55*

Table 1
Two forms of metacognition

I. Activities That Show Awareness of One's Knowledge
  A. Recognizing that one has failed to understand.
  B. Knowing the state or level of one's understanding; that is, knowing how well and how much you understand.
  C. Knowing what you need to learn in order to know or understand.
  D. Knowing the value or utility of taking corrective action to remedy failures.
  E. Knowing that different learning tasks impose different cognitive demands.
    1. Different goals for reading demand different amounts of effort.
    2. Different types of reading material demand different levels of concentration and effort.

II. Self-Regulatory Activities That Produce Understanding
  A. Analyzing the task to identify effective strategies.
  B. Monitoring the effectiveness of strategies used.
  C. Testing, revising, and evaluating strategies used.
  D. Planning the action one will take throughout the unit of reading material.
  E. Identifying the important ideas.
  F. Skimming for information.
  G. Rereading to clarify ideas.
  H. Summarizing and paraphrasing.
  I. Establishing and looking for relationships.
  J. Determining the structure of organization of information.
  K. Pausing to test one's understanding.
  L. Relating information to one's previous knowledge.
  M. Recognizing the sequence of events.
  N. Self-questioning and self-testing.
  O. Predicting the questions that will be posed after study.

regulatory activities while reading, this enables them to be aware of when they have understood, how well and how much they have understood, and what strategies to use when learning is less than satisfactory. Without this awareness of the level or state of their knowledge, students may only go through the motions of studying (perhaps skimming, taking notes, rereading, etc.) only to discover at the time of examination that the study activity was not satisfactory.

    Both effective reading and studying demand that the learner deliberately choose strategies that meet the goals and demands of the task at hand. This implies monitoring of the task demands, the learner's own capacities and limitations, and the interaction between the task demand

and the learner's abilities. Understanding and learning from texts is certainly not automatic. A text is only potentially meaningful. Only when learners deliberately use strategies can that potential be realized and effective studying achieved.

Traditionally, studying textbooks has been taught through the use of so-called formula techniques where the formula represents a step-by-step approach to studying the text. The most popular of these techniques is Robinson's (1946, 1961) SQ3R study technique. However, in terms of helping students become independent learners, these formula techniques have two major shortcomings. First, they do not train the student to *learn how to learn*. Most of them come under what Brown (1982) calls blind training. According to Brown, under blind training, students are induced to use a strategy without concurrent understanding of the significance of that activity. Thus, students are not usually taught to assess the success of using a particular strategy. Second, research shows that too many students have difficulty learning the activities formula techniques require (Andre & Anderson, 1978–1979; Baker, 1979; Brown et al., 1981; Brown & Smiley, 1977; Olshavsky, 1976–1977). Students are not usually given explicit instruction in identifying main ideas, formulating good questions, summarizing passage context, and selecting topic sentences.

In place of this blind training, students should have what Brown (1982) calls self-control training or training with cognitive awareness (metacognition). Students should not only be instructed in the use of strategy, but also *explicitly* on how to employ, monitor, check, and evaluate that strategy. One major contribution of the research on metacognition and studying is the light it sheds upon the study behavior of successful and less successful learners.

Successful and Less Successful Learners

Successful learners differ from less successful ones in important ways. The research findings (Andre & Anderson, 1978–1979; Baker, 1979; Bransford et al., 1980; Brown, 1981a, Brown et al., 1981; Brown & Smiley, 1977; Gambrell & Heathington, 1981; Garner & Reis, 1981; Paris & Myers, 1981; Olshavsky, 1976–1977) dealing with subjects across the development spectrum from children to adults show that successful learners are more knowledgeable of and use strategies during study to control and monitor their learning as it occurs. Poor learners are unaware that they must attempt to make sense out of text. They do not focus on reading and studying as meaning-getting processes. Whereas successful learners can describe their methods and strategies for reading, less successful students seem almost unaware of deliberate strategies that could be employed. Effective learners attend to more important aspects of text and also seem to seek information about the significance or relevance of facts. They take a much more active role in the learning process—relating material to previous experience or knowledge, asking questions, identifying main ideas, comparing and contrasting concepts, etc. Less successful learners on the other hand are much more passive; they fail to evaluate spontaneously whether they understand the nature of the task or whether one set of materials is more difficult to learn than another. Even more important, poor learners are less successful at using strategies effectively when attempting to learn from texts. It should be noted however, that successful learners do not necessarily use all the strategies, nor are they all equally efficient in using them. Also, adults use more of these strategies than children—there is a developmental trend.

In the light of this evidence, one can rightfully wonder whether less successful learners can be taught to gain metacognitive control over their study activity. The implications of the evidence here are that learners who are not aware of their own learning, their limitations, or the complexity of the task at hand, can hardly be expected to take preventive actions in order to anticipate and then recover from comprehension failures. Fortunately, the evidence from research also shows that with the right training, less successful learners can benefit from training in metacognitive activities (Bransford et al., 1980; Brown et al., 1981; Gambrell & Heathington, 1981; Palincsar, 1981). Also Brown (1981a, 1981b, 1982) has demonstrated that metacognition is an acquired skill whose development can be facilitated with the proper instruction. It follows from this that an effective way to help less successful learners overcome their reading and studying problems is to teach them the metacognitive strategies. However, the solution is not that simple. The major problem is that most of the self-regulatory activities in the table have not yet been translated into explicit pedagogic procedures to be used by both teachers and learners. Our task in the next two sections is first to describe the elements necessary for effective studying and then translate two of the major metacognitive strategies into explicit studying and reading strategies.

Elements of Effective Studying

The important elements that learners should incorporate in their study, or information the teacher ought to convey to students to help them learn how to learn, include the following:

1. Having specific purposes or goals for the study session
Setting the goals or purposes of study has the effect of directing attention to (a) the topic under discussion, (b) the knowledge or skill learners are supposed to have acquired at the end of the study period, (c) amount of effort required, and (d) the strategies that may be most effective in the extraction and retention of the information. Learners must understand both the explicit and implicit demands of the task before them. For example, if the learner needs to study a chapter on "The Nerve Impulse," the individual may have to state the following: "This chapter deals with the nerve impulse. By the time I finish studying it, I have to know what it is, what it does, the things that influence it, and how all this new information relates to what we have discussed in class so far. Since I don't know anything about the nerve impulse, what will I need to do in order to find out about it? Or, given what I know now, what else do I need to do to understand the nerve impulse?"

2. Recognizing the inherent structure of the reading material
Most learners, including some successful ones, fail to realize that the author of a text is conveying information in a meaningful, organized way. A learner needs to gain insight into how that author goes about conveying information about the topic. Learners who can determine the structure of reading material are better able to plan their studying activity. Such learners may ask themselves: "Is the passage broken into sections/subsections? If so, how does that explanation progress? Do headings give clues to the ideas in the material? Does this information (headings) help tie the ideas together? Can one or two sentences or questions convey the essence of the chapter?" Determining the structure of reading material is easier said than done. Learners may not be able to achieve understanding of text organization until after an initial reading of the material or until after class discussion with the teacher and classmates. On the other hand, learners who can eventually form a viable "mental outline" of a section of text have given themselves evidence of metacognition for that information and a deep level of understanding.

3. Purposefully extracting information
The effective learner strives to make sense out of the information through self-questioning, identifying important points of the text by deleting redundant and irrelevant information, and focusing attention and effort on the major ideas. In short, the effective learner makes use of the activities outlined in Table 1. Here, effective learners may ask questions like

"How do I plan to understand this material? What strategies will I use? How am I going to approach this material? What activities can I engage in to understand what I am reading? Will I need outside help from the teacher? What is the most efficient way to understand this? Do I know enough about the material that I can skip some parts? What is the best way of determining the main ideas?" Purposeful extraction of information is the heart of effective studying because the effective learner consciously tries to make use of the self-regulatory activities. In the next section, we show how some of these skills can be taught to ineffective learners.

4. Assessing the knowledge gained
While metacognition implies that the learner engage in ongoing evaluation of the level or state of his or her understanding, the final element in effective studying requires the learner to conduct some kind of self-assessment on the information covered in the reading material. Unlike reciting where the learner merely rehearses the information, metacognitive learner's self-assessment may proceed in this manner: "What do I know about the topic after my study? What are the major ideas, and how are they related to each other? Can I summarize the reading material in 50 words, in 25 words? Can I tell a friend what I just acquired from my studying?" For each question, the learner must provide a self-satisfactory answer to ensure that the material is known.

Teaching Metacognitive Strategies

In this section, we deal with two metacognitive strategies that can be easily taught to students. Unlike the formula techniques, there are no rigid rules as to how these strategies should be taught. But, we can give certain guidelines.

Of all the activities listed in Table 1 (see page 224), the two most significant and encompassing are self-questioning and summarization. Most of the other self-regulatory activities like identifying main ideas, looking for relationships between ideas, determining the structure and organization of material, determining sequence of events, and locating and skimming redundant and unimportant information, require the learner to use self-questioning and summarization rules. So, once the learner has mastered these two major strategies, all the others can easily be acquired too.

Self-Questioning. Self-questioning by the learner has been shown to be one of the most powerful metacognitive activities (e.g., Brown, 1982; Brown et al., 1981; Palincsar, 1981). Here, interest is in teaching students how to ask themselves questions about the material. Both the process and products of self-questioning are important for this strategy: (1) knowing the material and developing questions that require knowledge of the major ideas in order to answer them sufficiently; (2) knowing that one has created such good questions that direct attention to main ideas as opposed to trivial or superficial questions that direct attention to redundant or unimportant aspects of text; and (3) using these questions throughout study of the material to assess one's learning progress.

The learner should be made aware that the author is conveying information. To know what this information is will involve constant monitoring of the reading process through asking the right questions. These questions should be asked before, during, and after reading each section of text. Questions asked before or in the middle of a text can be reformulated when more information is acquired. For example, the chapter on "The Nerve Impulse" may have a section entitled "The action potential." The natural question to ask before reading that section may be "What is the action potential?" However, this may not be the best question to ask about the information in that section. Halfway through or at the end of the section, the learner may realize that the best question to ask is "How does the neuron transmit information from one part of the body to the other?" So, there is nothing permanent about the question asked. They can and should undergo constant reformulation as the learners extract more information, in contrast to traditional efforts when teaching the formula techniques. Critical to teaching this strategy is that students have the opportunity to practice formulating, evaluating, and reformulating questions as they read various content area paragraphs.

Teaching Self-Questioning. The learner must also be made aware that before any portion of text is read at all, some pertinent questions must be asked that provide context for extracting meaning. Some of the questions to be asked before reading could include the following:

> What is the nature of information being conveyed by the author?
>
> How does the author convey this information?
>
> What concepts are introduced?
>
> How are the various concepts related?
>
> How is the material organized?
>
> Can I follow the organization?
>
> Do I need to know something else in order to understand this information?

The learner must be made aware of the fact that within-section questions are different from between-section questions. The within-section questions are essentially the same as the general questions that are to be asked before reading. However, the questions are now more specific with regard to the concepts in the text. For example, whereas before one could have asked, "How are the various concepts related?" now one has to ask, "How is the nerve impulse related to the action potential?" As one moves from one subsection of text to the next, one could ask questions like,

> Did I understand the main ideas in the previous section?
>
> How are the ideas in this section related to the previous one?
>
> Did the author introduce a new concept in this section?
>
> Are the ideas in this section elaborations of the previous one?
>
> Can I make a connection between all concepts presented so far?

The learner must be made aware that postreading questions are essential for evaluating overall understanding of text. Examples of questions that could be asked after reading are

> Do I understand everything I have read?
>
> Can I give a brief summary or a gist of what I have read?
>
> Can I outline the chapter?
>
> Can I list the main points of the text?
>
> How much of this information is new and how much did I already know?
>
> Does the information here have any personal significance for me?

The net effect is that questions are asked before, during, and after reading. This provides a constant monitoring of the reading process.

Since teachers are the local "consultants" in a classroom for question-asking skill, teaching students self-questioning can be viewed as more or less showing the students what the teacher does when developing a test to create good, in-depth questions of the text. Once students know that this is what the teacher does to create their tests, and that this activity will be helpful to their study, the teacher can begin modeling questions for the students, creating questions for them about material read most recently. The teacher could say, "Looking at this material, I would ask these questions if I were designing a test." The model questions should be given a critical look by students as to their relevance to the material and to the depth of understanding required to answer them. Some criteria include the following: Why is this question better than that one? How much understanding does this question demand in order to answer it? By answering this question, will we move closer toward reaching our goals for study?

Next, the students are given the chance to make up questions about new text material, and these questions are compared to the model questions examined previously. Less able students could be paired with more able students to help them learn the process involved. Once questions are created, students can then evaluate each other's questions in terms of the above criteria and the particular passage under discussion. They should be given the opportunity to explain and defend why some questions are effective while others are not.

After much guided practice, students can then try to self-question during study on their own. Then while in class after study, students can again share their questions, discuss the merits of these questions, and describe the extent to which the process of self-questioning was helpful to their study activity.

Summarizing Text. Producing summaries of text information has a number of benefits for student learning in terms of gaining metacognition. First, summarization is a good way to estimate one's preparedness to be tested while studying is still occurring. By attempting to summarize major points, the learner is checking to see what has been gained up to that point. Second, summarization forces learners to use in-depth processing of the more important ideas in text.

Putting ideas into summary form is not a haphazard process, but one which Brown and her colleagues (Brown et al., 1981) have discovered requires the use of different rules. These general rules and strategies include (1) deletion of irrelevant or trivial information, (2) deletion of redundant information, (3) selection of topic sentences, (4) substitution of a superordinate term or event for a list of terms or actions, and (5) invention of topic sentences when none is provided by the author.

The evidence available (Brown et al., 1981) seems to indicate that there is a clear developmental trend in the awareness and use of these rules. Middle grade students are more able to learn the first two rules, while high school and college students can be taught to use all of the rules, the invention rule being the most difficult to learn. Brown et al. (1981) suggest that teaching students to use the rules during reading requires explicit instruction. Direct explanation and practice helps students to use the rules, but the researchers propose that students need to learn how to check or monitor their use of the rules to attain the most efficiency in learning. This monitoring involves students evaluating their summaries to assess the degree to which they really followed the rules, for example by asking themselves, "Did I choose a topic sentence?" and "Did I delete all trivia?" If students find that they are unable to select a topic sentence, for example, this should be a signal that comprehension is not as good as it should be and further study is needed.

Teaching Summarization. Again, only general guidelines will be given. The teacher can devise more creative ways based on the guidelines given (cf. Paris & Lipson, 1982).

1. Make students aware of the summarization rules
Most of the time, students do not use a strategy because they do not know it exists or they lack appropriate skills for using it effectively. This first step involves making students aware of the available strategies for summarizing and then explaining the relevance of these rules for effective study. Too often students are told to use a strategy based solely upon a teacher's authority and without rationale that it will actually benefit their learning or make learning easier. However, once the values for using strategies are clearly explained and demonstrated to them, students will begin and continue to use these strategies.

2. Introduce and model the use of each rule
Because rules 4 and 5 are too difficult for many middle-grade students, instruction in these should be avoided for these students. For older students, explain how each rule works, when each is applicable, and how the five rules might work together, depending upon the abilities of the students present. For each rule, direct students' attention to a piece of text and model how the rule can be used. For example, a short passage of text in history could be used to illustrate rule 1 by the teacher saying aloud what the important ideas are therein, pointing out where these are located in text, and showing students the less important information that can be left out of the summary without destroying meaning. Once students catch on to the process, as a group they can continue summarizing additional passages from that text, much as students would participate in a language experience story. Later, further condensation of these same passages could occur using the remaining summarization rules as they apply. Teacher and students can discuss how effective these rules are, their individual ease in use, and how producing summaries aids their understanding and retention of the information in the passages.

3. Give guided practice through group summary writing

Small groups of students can study text to produce a summary together, each student contributing his or her skills in locating the important ideas, in using the rules, and in composing the written summary. Later, all groups can come together to compare their summaries for the same passages and to defend what they have included or excluded in their summaries to others. This step has value in many ways. First, it helps students to get a more direct grasp of the use of summarization rules by working with peers in their application. Second, small group interaction allows students to work together upon and discuss the more or less important information in the passages at hand. This certainly is beneficial for better understanding the information for class discussion of the topic of concern. Finally, sharing summaries of different groups permits students to share the decisions they each made in the composing process. Because groups will differ in their paraphrasing of the information, groups will also be sharing their interpretations of the passages they read.

4. Direct students to summarize parts individually on their own

These summaries can then be discussed as a group much as before. The teacher can review these individual summaries as a form of assessment of student's skill in the use of the rules and then the teacher and other students can give help where needed. It is important here to have students assess and discuss the value of producing summaries for their learning to maintain their awareness of the benefits of this study activity. (For an excellent variation of this approach, see Smith-Burke, 1982.)

Summary

The point of view proposed here was that study skills and reading instruction based on the concept of metacognition are more beneficial than traditional study skills instruction. The major task remaining however is to translate the self-regulatory activities into explicit instructional formats. In this article, two major metacognitive strategies were discussed in terms of their application to classroom study skills and reading instruction.

REFERENCES

Andre, M.E.D.A., & Anderson, T.H. (1978–1979). The development and evaluation of a self-questioning study technique. *Reading Research Quarterly*, *14*, 605–623.

Baker, L. (1979). *Do I understand or do I not understand: That is the question.* Arlington, VA. (ERIC Document Reproduction Service No. ED 174 948)

Bransford, J.D., Stein, B.S., Shelton, T.S., & Owings, R.A. (1980). Cognition and adaptation: The importance of learning to learn. In J. Harvey (Ed.), *Cognition, Social Behavior and the Environment.* Hillsdale, NJ: Erlbaum.

Brown, A.L. (1981a). Metacognition development and reading. In R.J. Spiro, B.C. Bruce, & W.F. Brewer (Eds.), *Theoretical issues in reading comprehension.* Hillsdale, NJ: Erlbaum.

Brown, A.L. (1981b). Metacognition: The development of selective attention strategies for learning from texts. In *Directions in reading: Research and instruction* (30th yearbook of the National Reading Conference, pp. 21–43). Washington, DC: National Reading Conference.

Brown, A.L. (1982). Learning how to learn from reading. In J.A. Langer & M.T. Smith-Burke (Eds.), *Reader meets author: Bridging the gap.* Newark, DE: International Reading Association.

Brown, A.L., Campione, J.C., & Day, J.D. (1981). Learning to learn: On training students to learn from texts. *Educational Researcher, 10,* 14–21.

Brown, A.L., & Smiley, S.S. (1977). Rating the importance of structural units of prose passages: A problem of metacognitive development. *Child Development, 48,* 1–8.

Flavell, J.H., & Wellman, H.M. (1977). Metamemory. In R.V. Kail, Jr. & J.W. Hagen (Eds.), *Perspectives on the development of memory and cognition.* Hillsdale, NJ: Erlbaum.

Gambrell, L.B., & Heathington, B.S. (1981). Adult disabled readers' metacognitive awareness about reading tasks and strategies. *Journal of Reading Behavior, 13,* 215–222.

Garner, R., & Reis, R. (1981). Monitoring and resolving comprehension obstacles: An investigation of spontaneous text lookbacks among upper-grade good and poor comprehenders. *Reading Research Quarterly, 16,* 569–582.

Olshavsky, J.E. (1976–1977). Reading as problem solving: An investigation of strategies. *Reading Research Quarterly, 12,* 654–674.

Palincsar, A. (1981). *Corrective feedback and strategy training to improve the comprehension of poor readers.* Unpublished doctoral dissertation, University of Illinois.

Paris, S.G., & Lipson, M.Y. (1982). *Metacognition and reading comprehension.* Research colloquium presented at the Twenty-Seventh Annual Convention of the International Reading Association, Chicago, IL.

Paris, S.G., & Myers II, M. (1981). Comprehension monitoring, memory, and study strategies of good and poor readers. *Journal of Reading Behavior, 13*(1) 5–22.

Robinson, F.P. (1946). *Effective study.* New York: Harper & Bros.

Robinson, F.P. (1961). *Effective study* (Rev. Ed.). New York: Harper & Bros.

Smith-Burke, M.T. (1982). Extending concepts through language activities. In J.A. Langer & M.T. Smith-Burke (Eds.), *Reader meets author: Bridging the gap.* Newark, DE: International Reading Association.

Strategies for Considerate and Inconsiderate Text Instruction

Jeanne Shay Schumm, Alexandra G. Leavell, and Diane S. Haager

The purpose of this content analysis was to compile a list of strategies that could prove useful as an instructional aid when teaching developmental college readers how to deal with considerate and inconsiderate text. Two independent raters examined each of 46 postsecondary reading textbooks to identify strategies for (1) maximizing the use of considerate text features when they are included in content area textbooks and (2) compensating when content area textbooks do not include considerate text features. The resulting list includes a variety of strategic enablers which facilitate extraction of salient information of text. However, many of the strategies included in the sample of postsecondary reading textbooks were vague, incomplete, and lacked a real instructional component and research base. Discussion focuses on a critique of the strategies identified and offers suggestions for future research.

Strategies for Considerate and Inconsiderate Text Instruction

The importance of a good textbook to effective learning cannot be denied at any instructional level. Indeed, John Goodlad (1976) found that as grade level increases, so does dependence upon textbooks as learning tools. As students advance in school, their ability to gather meaning from text is tantamount to their success as students. Reflective of this progressive dependence upon text for information is the recent movement in postsecondary reading programs away from the traditional subskills model of reading instruction and toward a content-based approach designed to empower students to independently acquire information from different types of text (Nist & Simpson, 1987; Weinstein, 1987).

The degree to which college textbooks facilitate ease in extraction of salient information fluctuates as it does at any level (Schumm,

Originally published in Forum for Reading *(1990), volume 22, number 1, pages 31–43*

Konopak, Readence, & Baldwin, 1999; Schumm & Ross, 1990). Traditionally, quantitatively oriented readability formulas have been used to determine the appropriateness of a particular text (e.g., Dale & Chall, 1948; Fry, 1977). Of late, more qualitative evaluations are employed (particularly those based on the notion of "considerate" text) when appraising textbooks. "Considerate" or "friendly" text incorporates test-based components that facilitate information gathering (Armbruster & Anderson, 1981) such as text organization, explication of ideas, conceptual density, metadiscourse, and inclusion of any instructional devices (Singer, 1986). "Inconsiderate" text does not attend to such features and requires the reader to put forth extra effort in order to compensate (Armbruster & Anderson, 1981). For example, a complete, logically organized table of contents that provides the students with an overview of the content and structure of the book, as well as a quick way of locating specific information within the text would be a considerate feature. An inconsiderate feature of text would be the omission of a table of contents providing the reader with no overview of the book and leaving him or her to search page by page for the required information.

As Singer (1986) noted, even a considerate text presupposes a reader with the necessary resources for interacting with and constructing meaning from the text. However, Landow (1989) points out that many unskilled readers fail to use even considerate features. If this is the case, the duty of college developmental reading textbooks becomes extremely clear: (1) to develop an awareness of considerate text features and (2) to provide strategies for dealing with both considerate and inconsiderate text.

The question is, Are college developmental reading textbooks addressing these needs? Apparently not. The findings of a recent content analysis of 46 postsecondary developmental reading textbooks demonstrated that the number of strategies per book focusing on both considerate and inconsiderate text features was surprisingly low (Schumm, Haager, & Leavell, 1990). Results also indicated that significantly more strategies in these textbooks concern considerate text features than inconsiderate text features. In other words, postsecondary reading textbooks are providing a low to moderate number of strategies for reading college textbooks that are easy but little or no alternative plans of action for textbooks that are more challenging.

This paper is an extension of the line of research initiated in the quantitative content analysis described above. Although the purpose of the initial study was to compare the frequency of strategies included in postsecondary reading textbooks for considerate and inconsiderate conditions, the purpose of this more qualitative study was to identify and evaluate those strategies. It was our hope to compile a list of suggestions for students to use when their college textbooks are friendly and for when texts are more difficult. It was also our intent to detect areas of weakness (e.g., where strategies need to be augmented or indeed created) in order to provide postsecondary reading students with a suitable array of tactics to learn from text.

Method

Sample

A collection of college reading and study skills texts was developed which included titles found in *Paperbound Books in Print* (1989) and *Subject Guide to Books in Print* (1989) as well as those of other books found in our university and professional libraries. The study was limited to texts published from 1980–1989. Texts designed for international/ESL students were excluded as well as texts that were workbooks (i.e., no instructional component) or anthologies. Only one book by any particular author/publisher combination was included so that the assessment results would not misrepresent the extent to which text-friendly features are incorporated by various authors and publishers; when an author had published with more than one company, a book produced by each was included. Ultimately, the sample included 46 postsecondary reading textbooks.

Procedures

The *Postsecondary Reading Textbook Inventory* (PRTI) (Schumm, Haager, & Leavell, 1990) was used to delineate the considerate and inconsiderate features targeted for evaluation. PRTI items were derived from the Singer *Friendly Text Inventory* (FTI) (1986). While the Singer inventory was comprehensive in its inclusion of friendly text features, it was not necessarily applicable to examination of particular strategies. Therefore, alterations were warranted. Adaptations consisted primarily of collapsing related items (e.g., three items on the FTI dealt with the introduction of the book; this was reduced to one PRTI item). Thus, the 34 items on the FTI were reduced to 23 items on the PRTI. Consolidation of items led us to generate broader superordinate categories in which to organize items. The FTI consisted of five superordinate categories (organization, explication, conceptual density, metadiscourse, and instructional devices); the PRTI consisted of two: (1) textual aids, 11 items; and (2) content, 12 items. Two independent raters reviewed each of the 46 postsecondary reading textbooks included in the sample. Raters were instructed to use the table of contents and index of the book and to skim through each chapter to locate strategies. Weinstein and Mayer's definition of learning strategies (1986), "behaviors and thoughts that a learner engages in during learning and that are intended to influence the learner's encoding process," was used as a touchstone to develop operational definitions for each text feature. In order to ensure that raters would not confuse authors' attempts to simply promote student awareness of considerate text features with actual strategies for using the feature, the rating protocol included separate columns for "feature awareness" and "strategies."

After both raters completed their reviews, a list of strategies was compiled using the author's language so as not to add to or detract from his or her original meaning. The list was then revised to collapse redundant statements and to bring uniformity of strategy descriptions.

Results and Discussion

Table 1 (see page 241) exhibits the strategies identified for each of the text features included in the PRTI. The resulting list includes a variety of strategic enablers which facilitate (1) location of information, (2) orientation to content and structure of the text, (3) promotion of ongoing comprehension, and/or (4) retention of key concepts. As the table indicates, the majority of strategies were drawn from more than one postsecondary textbook.

As previously stated, our hope in conducting this content analysis was to compile a list of suggestions (typically scattered throughout postsecondary reading textbooks) for postsecondary students to use when texts are friendly and for when texts are more difficult. However, the final product, based on our in-depth perusal of "what's on the market," is riddled with a sufficient number of imperfections to raise caution about its widespread use. These shortcomings could be classified in three categories: (1) omissions; (2) vague, incomplete strategies; and (3) strategies lacking research base.

Omissions. No strategies were provided for one item in the considerate condition (metadiscourse), and six items in the inconsiderate condition (table of contents, footnotes, index, boldface/italics, cue/signal words, and rhetorical devices). Admittedly, if a textbook does not have a comprehensive table of contents, index, or footnotes, the alternatives are fairly obvious. Nonetheless, it would seem that further research in the areas of metadiscourse, text cohesion, vocabulary, and imagery would reveal alternative strategies when the text is not optimal. It should be mentioned that none of the textbooks examined even mentioned the notion of metadiscourse and its potential impact on comprehension.

Vague, incomplete strategies. For the purposes of this study, "strategy" was rather loosely defined. We were in search of "behaviors and thoughts that a learner engages in during learning and that are intended to influence the learner's encoding process." However, many of the strategies were more "loose" than we would have liked in terms of their instructional component and providing actual processes to follow. Our feeling was that most of what we found were merely 64 "suggestions" rather than "strategies." One example is, "if a definite paragraph structure is not immediately apparent, look for repeated words in the paragraph to give you some clues." We are not certain that we could model such a strategy to our students nor if we could, how useful it would prove past a certain level.

Of greater concern, some critical areas were often represented with vague or incomplete strategies. The case of main idea instruction illustrates this point. The work of Braddock (1974) and Baumann & Serra (1984) has sensitized the reading research community to the relative dearth of explicit main ideas in expository text. Nonetheless, we found strategies for finding implied main ideas to be weak (e.g., infer main idea if there is no topic sentence) or, in the case of more than 50% of the textbooks (Schumm, Haager, & Leavell, 1990), nonexistent.

Strategies lacking research base. To our knowledge, research does not exist that would support such strategies as "use the index as a study guide"; "when examining the table of contents, assess the relative importance of topics by number of pages assigned to a certain topic"; or "when you don't know the meaning/pronunciation of the word, try leaving the word out and see if you can still comprehend the text." In at least one (rather frequently cited) case, the strategy provided was inconsistent with current research (e.g., when no glossary is available, use context clues) (Schatz & Baldwin, 1985).

However, the bulk of suggestions provided were more reflective of conventional wisdom than empirical evidence (e.g., use the chapter questions, headings/subheadings, graphics, etc., as elements of chapter preview). If conventional wisdom is to be the norm, why not structure in class brainstorming activities to encourage developmental reading students to generate their own lists? Their lists would in all likelihood be equally valid and would probably foster student "ownership" of the results. On the other hand, if we feel that a knowledge base of integrated research findings is important, we should base instruction and therefore textbook content on such.

Future Directions

It is our intent to revise and embellish the strategy list with information derived from research on considerate and inconsiderate text. We have at least three reasons for pursuing this task:

1. Publishers of college-level textbooks are incorporating considerably more considerate text features than in the past (Schumm, 1984). It is our contention that we need to directly teach developmental reading students, who are often passive learners, how to use such features efficiently and effectively.

2. Any postsecondary reading instructor who has ever led students through a textbook inventory or who has taught SQ3R (Robinson, 1946) knows that somewhere, sometime, an undergraduate student will complain, "This (textbook inventory/ SQ3R routine/you fill in the blank with a teaching strategy) is nonsense. My (philosophy/literature/you fill in the blank with a discipline of choice) textbook doesn't have any (headings/subheadings/words in italics/you fill in the blank with a text feature). I can't read this book. It's just too hard!"

   These students are right! Despite author and publisher efforts, many textbooks are inconsiderate. Some aspects of inconsiderateness are quite obvious to students, while other aspects (e.g., location and clarity of context clues [Konopak, 1988]) may not be readily apparent. We feel the need to empower students with research-based coping strategies so that they can locate, comprehend, and recall information when it is presented in inconsiderate formats.

3. Finally, if developmental reading courses are going to realize credibility among university administrators, faculty, and students, then the content of such courses needs to be grounded on a sound research base. We need to continue to explore strategies in terms of their effectiveness, practicality, and flexibility across content areas in addition to investigating teacher and student perceptions of the overall merit of strategies.

Table 1
Strategies for dealing with considerate and inconsiderate text features

Feature	Included in Text (Considerate)	Not Included in Text (Inconsiderate)
1. Introduction to book	a. Use to determine overall organization plan of book.* b. Use as element of book preview.* c. Use to discern author's purpose of the thesis of the text.* d. Look for suggestions for efficient use/how to learn from text.*	a. Look for key ideas of the book in "logical places" such as the table of contents and chapter summaries. b. Read introductory anecdotes or quotations to infer author's purpose.
2. Introductions to chapters	a. Use as element of chapter review.* b. Use to gauge amount of time to spend on the chapter. c. Use to discern author's purpose. d. Use to acquire background knowledge.* e. Look up unfamiliar terms in introduction to help develop purpose for reading. f. Use to determine overall organizational pattern of chapter.*	a. Read the first and last paragraphs of chapter.* b. Read statement of purpose, if provided. c. Skim chapter for overview.* d. Read chapter summary.*
3. Chapter summaries	a. Use as element of chapter preview.* b. Use to identify key concepts.* c. Use to review for tests.* d. Relate summary back to introduction, title, and subheadings to reinforce key ideas. e. Use to promote recall of important ideas.	a. Write your own summary. b. Read first and last paragraphs of chapter.* c. Read study questions, if provided.

(continued)

Table 1 (continued)
Strategies for dealing with considerate and inconsiderate text features

Feature	Included in Text (Considerate)	Not Included in Text (Inconsiderate)
4. Heading, subheadings	a. Use as element of chapter preview.* b. Use to identify key concepts.* c. Use to determine relative importance of key concepts. d. Turn into questions to anticipate chapter content.* e. Turn into questions to predict possible test questions.* f. Use to outline chapter. g. Use to discern author's organizational pattern. h. Use to divide chapter into learning units.* i. Use to activate prior knowledge. j. Use to locate information.*	a. Use boldface, italics, repeated words to identify key concepts. b. Skim for signal words to discern author's organizational pattern. c. Read first sentence of each paragraph to detect clues about. content.*
5. Table of contents	a. Use to determine overall organizational plan of book.* b. Use as element of book preview.* c. Use to discern author's purpose or the thesis of the text.* d. Use to review for tests.* e. Use to detect relation-ships between chapters. f. Use to outline book. g. Use to assess relative importance by number of pages assigned to a certain topic.* h. Use to locate information.*	NONE

(continued)

Table 1 (continued)
Strategies for dealing with considerate
and inconsiderate text features

Feature	Included in Text (Considerate)	Not Included in Text (Inconsiderate)
6. Glossary	a. Use to define unknown/ technical terms.* b. Use to build "word bank."* c. Use to confirm your "prediction" of word's meaning based on context clues.* d. Use to review for tests.* e. Use to confirm definitions presented in class lectures.*	a. Use dictionary.* b. Use context clues.*
7. Diagrams/tables/ graphs	a. Use to clarify narrative.* b. Put graphic information into paragraph form (in your own words) to ensure that you understand it.* c. Use as element of chapter preview.* d. Use to draw conclusions. e. Use to predict test questions.* f. Use to assimilate large amounts of information at one time.*	a. Create your own diagrams/tables/graphs for study purposes.* b. Select text that has graphic aids.*
8. Marginal Annotations	a. Use as element of chapter preview.* b. Use to review for tests.*	a. Construct your own annotations.* b. Develop dialogue with author.*
9. Footnotes	a. Use to clarify ideas presented in text. b. Use to identify resources for additional reading.	NONE
10. Index	a. Use to locate specific information/terms quickly.*	NONE

(continued)

Table 1 (continued)
Strategies for dealing with considerate and inconsiderate text features

Feature	Included in Text (Considerate)	Not Included in Text (Inconsiderate)
	b. Use to identify key people in field. c. Use to review for tests.* d. Check off important items in index as they are discussed in class. This will help prepare for tests.*	
11. Boldface/italics	a. Use to determine key terms/concepts.* b. Use as element of chapter preview.*	NONE
12. Paragraph structure	a. Use to identify key concepts.* b. Use to detect author's organizational pattern.* c. Use to construct notes/semantic maps.* d. Use to enhance comprehension of text.*	a. Look for repetition of key words and phrases and transitional words to lend and coherence unity.
13. Clues/signal words	a. Use to detect organizational pattern of paragraphs.* b. Use to detect changes in course or new thought.* c. Use to find introductory or concluding statements.*	NONE
14. Rhetorical devices	a. Use to enhance comprehension of text.* b. Use to develop images.*	NONE
15. Hierarchical structure of ideas	a. Use to outline/semantic map/diagram key ideas.* b. Use to maintain focus.*	a. Use table of contents to detect purpose and organizational pattern.
16. Background information	a. Use as a foundation to learn subsequent concepts.	a. Read other sources to get background.*

(continued)

Table 1 (continued)
Strategies for dealing with considerate and inconsiderate text features

Feature	Included in Text (Considerate)	Not Included in Text (Inconsiderate)
17. Prior knowledge	a. Use to identify progression of ideas. b. Use to link concepts. from chapter to chapter. c. Use links to help you remember new information.*	a. Attempt to link new concepts with personal experience.* b. Look for similarities and differences from chapter to chapter.* c. Use heading/sub-headings/summaries, etc., to activate prior knowledge.
18. Conceptual flow	a. Adjust reading rate accordingly.*	a. Reread what you do not understand.* b. Read more slowly.* c. Divide chapters into manageable units.* d. Find another book that presents same material in more readable manner.* e. Use punctuation to aid comprehension.* f. Identify core parts of sentences.
19. Fact/opinion	a. Use clue words or phrases that indicate opinions (e.g., "I think," "I believe," etc.).*	a. Look for masked opinions or those that are stated in such a way that they appear to be true.* b. Recognize connota-tive/denotative lan-guage.* c. Become familiar with types of propaganda.*
20. Metadiscourse	NONE	a. Develop active dialogue with author.
21. Chapter questions	a. Use as element of chapter preview.* b. Use to identify key concepts.*	a. Construct questions. b. Use questions posed by instructor to guide reading.*

(continued)

Table 1 (continued)
Strategies for dealing with considerate and inconsiderate text features

Feature	Included in Text (Considerate)	Not Included in Text (Inconsiderate)
	c. Use to review for tests.*	c. Purchase a college review book or guide. d. Turn chapter summary into questions.
22. Vocabulary development	a. Make lists/flash cards as new terms are presented in text.* b. Use context clues, antonyms, synonyms, to define unknown words.* c. Use clues beyond the sentence level to detect meanings of unknown words.*	a. Try leaving word out when you don't know how to pronounce or define it. b. Use Greek and Latin roots to detect meanings of unknown words.* c. Make lists of unfamiliar terms. Use dictionary/glossary to define.* d. After defining a word, return to sentence and replace original word with definition to verify. e. Ask someone who may know the word. f. Learn word origins.*
23. Stated/unstated main ideas	a. Use to annotate text. b. Use to construct outlines/semantic maps.	a. Ask yourself, "What is the paragraph about?" or "What is the author trying to say?"* b. Infer main idea if no topic sentence.* c. Supply topic sentence if none.* d. Look for repeated terms or concepts.* e. Look at first and last sentence of paragraph.*

* Appears in more than one postsecondary developmental reading textbook.

REFERENCES

Armbruster, B.B., & Anderson, T.H. (1981). *Content area textbooks* (Reading Education Report No. 23). Champaign, IL: Center for the Study of Reading.

Baumann, J.F., & Serra, J.K. (1984). The frequency and placement of main ideas in children's social studies textbooks: A modified replication of Braddock's research on topic sentences. *Journal of Reading Behavior, 17,* 27–40.

Braddock, R. (1974). The frequency and placement of topic sentences in expository prose. *Research in the Teaching of English, 8,* 287–302.

Dale, E., & Chall, J.S. (1948). A formula for predicting readability. *Educational Research Bulletin, 27,* 37–54.

Fry, E. (1977). Fry's readability graph: Clarification, validity, and extension to level 17. *Journal of Reading, 21,* 126–130.

Goodlad, J.L. (1976). *Facing the future: Issues in education and schooling.* New York: McGraw Hill.

Konopak, B.C. (1988). Effects of inconsiderate vs. considerate text on secondary students' vocabulary learning. *Journal of Reading Behavior, 20,* 25–41.

Landow, G. (1989). Changing texts, changing readers: Hypertext in literacy education, criticism, and scholarship in reorientations. In T. Morgan & B. Hendrickson (Eds.), *Literacy theory, pedagogy and scholarship* (pp. 114–129). Urbana, IL: University of Illinois Press.

Nist, S.L., & Simpson, M.L. (1987). Facilitating transfer in college reading programs. *Journal of Reading, 30,* 620–625.

Paperbound books in print. (1989). New York: R.R. Bowker.

Robinson, F.P. (1946). *Effective study.* New York: Harper & Bros.

Schatz, E.K., & Baldwin, R.S. (1986). Context clues are unreliable predictors of word meanings. *Reading Research Quarterly, 21,* 439–453.

Schumm, J.S. (1984). *College text readability: An historical perspective.* Unpublished manuscript.

Schumm, J.S., Haager, D.S., & Leavell, A.G. (1990). *Considerate and inconsiderate text instruction in postsecondary developmental reading textbooks: A content analysis.* Manuscript submitted for publication.

Schumm, J.S., Konopak, J.P., Readence, J.E., & Baldwin, R.S. (1989). Considerate text: Do we practice what we preach? In S. McCormick & J. Zutell (Eds.), *Cognitive and social perspectives for literacy research and instruction* (Yearbook of the National Reading Conference, pp. 381–388). Chicago: National Reading Conference.

Schumm, J.S., & Ross, G. (1989, December). *Considerateness of postsecondary reading texts: A content analysis.* Paper presented at the meeting of the National Reading Conference, Austin, TX.

Singer, H. (1986). Friendly texts: Description and criteria. In E.K. Dishner, T.W. Bean, J.E. Readence, & D.W. Moore (Eds.), *Reading in the content areas: Improving classroom instruction* (pp.112–118). Dubuque, IA: Kendall/Hunt.

Subject guide to books in print. (1989). New York: R.R. Bowker.

Weinstein, C.E. (1987). Fostering learning autonomy through the use of learning strategies. *Journal of Reading, 30,* 590–595.

Weinstein, C.E., & Mayer, R.E. (1986). The teaching of learning strategies. In M.C. Wittrock (Ed.), *Handbook of research on teaching* (pp. 315–327). New York: Macmillan.

Promoting Text Engagement Through Reader-Generated Elaborations

Hiller A. Spires

One of the most difficult tasks for postsecondary reading instructors is to engage students in the textbook reading process successfully. Typically, students enrolled in college reading classes have a limited knowledge and understanding of academic discourse. As a result, they have a history of being unsuccessful with academic reading tasks and often have developed a sense of "learned helplessness" or the perception that they are unable to overcome reading failure (Mealey, 1990). Numerous research-based strategies that promote active textbook reading and learning are available for the postsecondary reading curriculum (e.g., advanced organizers, structured overviews, semantic mapping; for reviews see Caverly & Orlando, 1991; Mealey & Nist, 1989; Swafford & Alvermann, 1989). Even after students have been exposed to such strategies, however, they may still retain negative attitudes and feelings about reading.

Negative attitudes about academic reading may be in part a result of student perceptions surrounding textbooks in general. Textbooks exude authority. Textbooks can be intimidating at times for the most proficient readers and are especially overwhelming for students who have had few successful reading experiences from which to draw. The authority of the text may feed these students' sense of learned helplessness, psychologically and emotionally thwarting their attempts to interact with the text in a meaningful way. For example, students who have not been successful with academic reading are constantly reminded by the textbook that not only is their knowledge of the content area insufficient (i.e., "There is an entire book of information that I don't know."), but also their ability to access knowledge is inadequate (i.e., "I'll never understand and remember all of this."). Spiro (1980) contends that many readers give the text an autonomy that actually detracts from their engaging with the ideas that are represented. There is a metaphorical wall

Originally published in Forum for Reading *(1991–1992), volume 23, numbers 1 & 2, pages 22–32*

between the reader and the text that prohibits the student from constructing meaning and experiencing successful engagement with the author's ideas. Repeated encounters with this situation prohibit the student from experiencing self-worth in the academic context (Hull & Rose, 1989; Rose, 1989). The combination of "not knowing" and "not knowing how to know" can be devastating to the nonproficient reader and ultimately contributes to negative perceptions of the academic experience in general.

One way to make the text less intimidating and put reader and text on a more equal plane is to teach students the value of their own knowledge as it relates to a particular subject matter. This can be accomplished through the use of reader-generated elaborations. There is an ample body of research that supports the notion that reader-generated elaborations facilitate some types of comprehension as well as retention (Anderson & Pichert, 1977; Arkes & Freedman, 1984; Chiesi, Spilich, & Voss, 1979; Spires & Donley, 1992; Spires, Donley, & Penrose, 1990). In addition to assisting with the comprehension process, reader-generated elaborations can provide an immediate mechanism to help readers become emotionally involved with the text. The byproduct of generating elaborations is that students may have more of a personal investment in the reading task. Ultimately, the use of elaborations may help students make a perceptional shift in their view of academic reading and possibly contribute to breaking the cycle of learned helplessness so often associated with reading.

This article outlines an instructional strategy to be used with postsecondary reading students in order to help them actively engage with text through the use of elaborations. The strategy is based on research and theory in schema activation (Spiro, 1980) and explicit instruction (Pearson & Gallagher, 1983) and has been used successfully with postsecondary students enrolled in a reading and learning strategies course.

Explicit Instruction in the Elaboration Process

Less successful readers often do not spontaneously activate the knowledge they possess on a given topic (Bransford, Stein, Shelton, & Owings, 1981). This failure may result from a belief that information they possess is unimportant or simply a lack of awareness of the substantive role that prior knowledge plays in the comprehension process (Brown, Armbruster, & Baker, 1986).

In order to change students' perceptions about the value of their existing knowledge and ultimately their thinking processes during reading, the instructor can provide explicit instruction (see Pearson & Gallagher, 1983) in how to elaborate from text. Explicit instruction has been used successfully with a variety of age groups to teach other strategies such as reciprocal teaching (Palincsar & Brown, 1984), directed note-taking activity (Spires, in press), and metaphor interpretation (Readence, Baldwin & Head, 1987). Explicit instruction involves the following components: (a) rationale and explanation of the strategy, (b) teacher modeling of the strategy, (c) teacher and student collaboration in the use of the strategy, (d) teacher and peer feedback on the use of the strategy, and (e) student independence with the use of the strategy.

Embedded in explicit instruction is the developmental theory of Vygotsky (1978) that emphasizes the social nature of cognition and learning. Vygotsky argues that the process of expanding cognition is best achieved through social interactions or "shared meaning" between instructor and student. Over time the cognitive process is internalized and eventually reappears in the student's thinking. The distance between the point where the student initially functions with a task and the level of potential development as determined through support from an instructor or more capable peers is referred to as the "zone of proximal development." Wood, Bruner, and Ross (1976) referred to this same process as "scaffolding," by connoting the notion of the instructor providing a support (i.e., scaffold) for the learner until the learner is capable of operating at a higher cognitive level without support. The scaffold is removed and the learner functions independently at a new level of cognition. The gradual shift of responsibility from the teacher to the student for strategy completion is depicted between components (b) and (e) above and in the middle section of the model of explicit instruction (Spires & Stone, 1989) in Figure 1.

Rationale and Explanation of the Strategy

In order for the student to begin conceptualizing the importance of the strategy, it is essential to provide the student with information about why the strategy will be helpful. To accomplish this, the instructor introduces the notion of schema and prior knowledge (see Figure 2). Prior knowledge must be activated in order for the reader to comprehend text. Information already possessed is organized and stored in an existing knowledge structure or a "schema." Prior knowledge may be organized and stored in terms of general knowledge and domain-specific knowledge.

Figure 1
Shift of responsibility for task completion during instruction

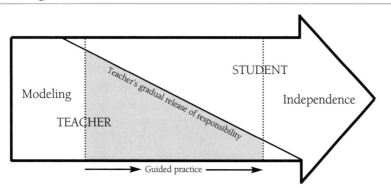

Spires & Stone (1989) after Pearson & Gallagher (1983)

Figure 2
Storage, activation, and organization of knowledge

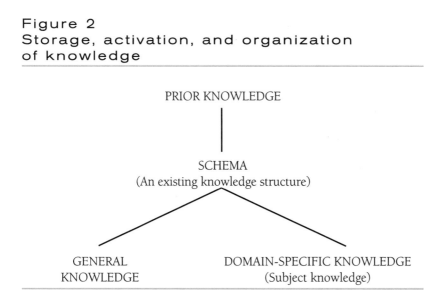

General knowledge may include information that is typically known by most people within a given cultural context as well as through personal experiences. For example, most of us have a schema for going to the movies. We know that we must pay for a ticket at the box office, enter the theater, and find a seat in the auditorium. If we trip over someone's feet we know that it is probably because our eyes have not yet adjusted to the darkness. If we step on something crunchy on the floor, we know that it is probably going to be popcorn. We know these things because we activate our schema for going to the movies and all of the experiences typically associated with going to a movie immediately come to mind.

Domain-specific knowledge is information that may be related to a specific subject domain (e.g., history, science, literature). The notion of activating schema related to a subject area can be illustrated by having the students read and generate a main concept for the following passage:

> With hocked gems financing him, our hero bravely defied all scornful laughter that tried to prevent his scheme. "Your eyes deceive. It is like an egg, not a table." Now three sturdy sisters sought truth. Forging along, sometimes through calm vastness, yet more often over turbulent peaks and valleys, days became weeks as many doubters spread fearful rumors about the edge. At last, from nowhere, winged creatures appeared, signifying momentous success. (Ellis, 1984, p. 95)

Most students will not realize that the passage is describing Columbus's voyage to America. When the students activate their "Columbus schema" and reread the passage, immediately they will make the appropriate connections with the text. The exaggerated nature of the passage demonstrates how activation of an appropriate schema helps comprehension. This is a good example to use in helping students solidify the abstract notion of schema activation.

Teacher Modeling of the Strategy

Next, the instructor reads a portion of a text that students might encounter in an academic context. The instructor generates elaborations from the text by using prompts such as

This part of the text reminds me of _____; or

When I read this section I think of _____.

The elaborations may consist of general knowledge or domain-specific knowledge. The important aspect of the modeling is that students observe how the instructor is going beyond what is literally in the text and using it as a springboard to connect his or her own realm of knowledge and experiences.

Teacher and Student Collaboration in the Use of the Strategy and Teacher and Peer Feedback on the Use of the Strategy

Next, the students and the instructor together generate elaborations. In this part of the instruction, teacher and students literally "share meaning" in order for students to move to a higher level of cognition. Guided feedback and support are given from the instructor as well as from peers. Students may work in small collaborative groups to generate elaborations. The teacher moves from group to group lending support and providing her own elaborations as necessary. The teacher encourages students to generate elaborations in both the general and domain-specific categories. As students hear the elaborations of their peers, their notions of what is acceptable broadens. Students become actively involved with the information, not simply in a literal manner but in a manner that enables them to go beyond the text.

Student Independence With the Use of the Strategy

Eventually, the instructor encourages the students to respond elaboratively to the text on their own. This can be accomplished by having students write their elaborative thoughts in the margin of the text. Students share with the group their elaborations and peers comment on the nature of the elaboration (e.g., they characterize it as general or domain specific; they comment on similarities and differences in elaborations from student to student; they tell why a particular elaboration is interesting to them; etc.). Eventually the students are operating at an independent level as they elaborate from the text.

Obviously, in an academic reading situation, the successful reader is expected to derive significant points that the author is making as well as to think beyond the text on an applicational level. The elaboration strategy can be expanded to include the generation of significant points from the text as well.

Sample Transcript

Below is a transcript of a portion of a lesson that used explicit instruction to teach reader-generated elaborations along with significant points of the text. This example includes dialogue among a teacher and five students as well as excerpts from a text that was used. The lesson begins at the point where the teacher initiates the modeling phase. Notice that the teacher first explains what she is going to do, reads the text aloud, and then attempts to verbalize her thinking processes as she generates the significant points from the text as well as her own elaborations.

T: *I am going to read a portion of this text and then model for you how I go about thinking with the text in order to comprehend. I will model how I decide what the author is saying and also how I personally connect with the text. In other words, what prior knowledge I use to relate to the text.* (Reads the first paragraph aloud.)

> "Egalitarian Relationships: The Sex-Role Revolution Begins at Home" [1]
>
> As everyone is supposed to know, there has been a sex-role revolution in this country during the past fifteen years. The typical American family with the husband at work and the wife at home with the children is no longer the typical American family. With 46 percent of all married women with children now working outside the home, the "typical" family now represents only 17 percent of all American households. The enrollment of women in the professional schools of law, medicine, and business, which used to be almost exclusively male, is now around 40 percent. And surveys show that women seniors in college have career aspirations that are virtually identical to those of the men, with both sexes now anticipating dual-career marriages.

As I read the first paragraph, and specifically, the first sentence, I see that the authors are making an assertion that there has been a sex-role revolution. In the second sentence, the authors further define what they mean by sex-role revolution by using the family as an example. As I read the rest of the paragraph, I notice that the authors are using percentages to substantiate their assertion. I also note to myself that this is a fairly typical way to support an assertion and that I have seen this method used before. I made these observations because of the frameworks that I have stored in my memory about how texts are typically put together. If one of you were to comment on what you saw as significant, you might come up with something different as a result of using a different framework.

Now let me model my thinking for you as I relate this information to what I already know. When I read this paragraph, the first thing I think about

---

1 Passage excerpts are taken from Bern, D., & Bern, S. (1988). Egalitarian relationships: The sex-role revolution begins at home. In A.B. Grinols (Ed.), Critical thinking: Reading and writing across the curriculum. Belmont, CA: Wadsworth Publishing.

is how families have changed through the years. I also think about how TV has reflected those changes. For example, when I was growing up I watched Leave it to Beaver, *which depicted a very traditional family life with the mother staying home and the father going to work. Today I think about* The Bill Cosby Show, *in which the father is a doctor and the mother is a lawyer— they both work and in equal professions. I also think about* Who's the Boss, *in which the woman has an executive level position in an advertising agency and the man manages the household. So I have some vivid images of social changes in the form of TV shows.*

I have modeled for you how I approached trying to make sense of this passage by understanding what the author is trying to say as well as by relating the information to something else I already know about. I have used an example from my own experience to help me conceptualize what the author is saying and ultimately to make the text more meaningful for me. Now I would like for us to read the next paragraph and together see if we can articulate significant points from the text and then relate it to something we know about. (Reads the second paragraph.)

> But the true nature of America's sex-role revolution was conveyed to us most clearly one night when we were dinner guests at the home of a married couple, a sociologist and a social psychologist. While dinner was being prepared and the table set, the husband, the sociologist, gave us an incisive Marxist analysis of the oppression of women throughout history, showing how societal institutions have conspired to keep them in their place. After dinner, while the dishes were being cleared and coffee prepared, he continued, explaining the steps necessary to bring about change. It was a brilliant sociological analysis. We would have liked to have heard a social-psychological perspective on the issue, too, but because of the many dinner related tasks to be attended to, his wife didn't have time to join our discussion.

What do you think the authors are doing in this paragraph?

S1: *I think the authors are using sarcasm.*

T: *Can you explain how you came up with that observation?*

S1: *Well, the husband is talking about how society has kept women in their place historically. While he is talking, his wife is doing all of the dishes. The authors are obviously poking fun at the man.*

T: *Good. So you're saying that there is a discrepancy between what the man says he believes and his actions. Does anyone else have an observation about what the authors are doing here?*

S2: *Well, the authors are being sarcastic but I think a better label to describe what the authors are doing is to say that the authors are using satire to make their point. When you use satire, you are making fun of something in order to get your point across.*

T: *Good observation. Now, what does this portion of the text remind you of?*

S3: *Well it reminds me of another T.V. show—*The Honeymooners. *Ralph was always being sarcastic to his wife and putting her in her place.*

S2: *Yeah, but the husband isn't being sarcastic here—the authors are. That's different from what you are taking about.*

S3: *Yeah, I guess so. Well it still reminds me of that show because Ralph was so sarcastic, especially sitting around the dinner table.*

S4: *It reminds me of my family because my dad is exactly like that. He tries to act like my Mom and he have this equal relationship, but she ends up doing all of the housework.*

T: *So this portion of the text reminds you of what you have seen at home. You are using prior knowledge of your family and relating it to this passage.*

S5: *Well, think how bad it use to be. We've been studying 19th century literature and back then women had to use a male name in order to get their work published. For example, George Elliot was really a women but she knew her work would not be considered for publication if she used her real name.*

Notice that Student 1 uses his own language to describe what was happening at the dinner table. Student 2 acknowledged Student 1's label, "sarcastic," but decides there is a more specific term, "satire," for describing the authors' tone. Student 3 obviously picks up on the teacher's previous cue of television shows and relates the dinner scene to *The Honeymooners*. Student 3 is associating sarcasm with Ralph's manner toward his wife, but probably does not understand fully the concept of satire that Student 2 has introduced. Student 4 quickly jumps in and relates the passage to his own home situation. Student 5 goes beyond general or personal prior knowledge and relates the passage to a subject that she is studying in English class. By allowing students to verbalize their thinking in conjunction with the text, the instructor has a clearer picture of what kinds of thinking the students are engaging in and can provide appropriate feedback or clarification.

The lesson progresses based on the model of explicit instruction until the students are working independently with the strategy. After students have responded to the text independently, the class as a whole discusses their responses to the text—both the significant points and elaborative responses. By the end of the lesson, students have processed the gist of the text and have responded through reader-generated elaborations to help them get more personally involved with the text. Students respond very favorably to this instructional process because they realize that they do have something worthwhile to contribute to what may be perceived as a formidable reading task.

Conclusion

This approach to text processing is an explicit way to teach students how to connect previous knowledge with a text. Used strategically, explicit instruction is effective in providing overt demonstrations of how readers can actively engage the text and have a voice in what they are reading. The results are that students are not alienated from the text and psychologically do not feel defeated when they are reading. Students need to understand that the more they can contribute (i.e., bring their own knowledge) to the reading process, the more likely they are to be emotionally invested in the reading task. The result of this emotional investment may be improved understanding of the text. The approach that has been illustrated here is a first step in allowing students to learn how to participate in the construction of meaning from a text by using information and images with which they are familiar. The strategy enables readers to validate their own knowledge in conjunction with a text and ultimately helps them learn to validate themselves within an academic context.

REFERENCES

Bransford, J.D., Stein, B.S., Shelton, T.S., & Owings, R.A. (1981). Cognition and adaptation: The importance of learning to learn. In J. Harvey (Ed.), *Cognition, social behavior, and the environment* (pp. 92–110). Hillsdale, NJ: Erlbaum.

Brown, Armbruster, & Baker, L. (1986). The role of metacognition in reading and studying. In J. Orasanu (Ed.), *Reading comprehension: From theory to practice* (pp. 49–75). Hillsdale, NJ: Erlbaum.

Carnine, D., & Kinder, D. (1985). Teaching low-performance students to apply generative and schema strategies to narrative and expository material. *Remedial and Special Education, 6*, 20–30.

Caverly, D., & Orlando, V. (1991). Textbook study strategies. In R. Flippo & D. Caverly (Eds.), *Teaching reading and study strategies at the college level* (pp. 86–165). Newark, DE: International Reading Association.

Chiesi, H.L., Spilich, G.J., & Voss, J.F. (1979). Acquisition of domain-related information in relation to high and low domain knowledge. *Journal of Verbal Learning and Verbal Behavior, 18*, 257–273.

Ellis, D. (1984). *Becoming a master student*. Rapid City, SD: College Survival.

Giroux, H. (1990). Reading texts, literacy, and textual authority. *Journal of Education, 172*, 84–103.

Hull, G., & Rose, M. (1989). Rethinking remediation: Toward a social-cognitive understanding of problematic reading and writing. *Written Communication, 6*, 139–154.

Mealey, D.L. (1990). Understanding the motivation problems of at-risk college students. *Journal of Reading, 33*, 598–601.

Mealey, D.L., & Nist, S.L. (1989). Postsecondary, teacher directed comprehension strategies. *Journal of Reading, 32*, 484–493.

Palincsar, A., & Brown, A. (1984). Reciprocal teaching of comprehension-fostering and comprehension-monitoring activities. *Cognition and Instruction, 1*, 117–175.

Pearson, P.D., & Gallagher, M. (1983). The instruction of reading comprehension. *Contemporary Educational Psychology, 8*, 317–333.

Readance, J.E., Baldwin, S.R., & Head, M.H. (1987). Direct instruction in processing metaphors. *Journal of Reading Behavior, 28*, 325–339.

Rose, M. (1989). *Lives on the boundary*. New York: Penguin.

Spires, H.A. (in press). Learning from a lecture: Effects of comprehension monitoring. *Reading Research and Instruction.*

Spires, H.A., & Donley, J.A. (1992, April). *Effects of reader-generated elaborations on text comprehension and attitudes toward reading.* Paper presented at the annual meeting of the American Educational Research Association, San Francisco, CA.

Spires, H.A., Donley, J.A., & Penrose, A.M. (1990, April). *Prior knowledge activation: Text engagement in reading to learn.* Paper presented at the annual meeting of the American Educational Research Association, Boston, MA.

Spires, H.A., & Stone, D. (1989). Directed reading activity: A self-questioning approach. *Journal of Reading, 33*, 36–39.

Spiro, R.J. (1980). Constructive processes in prose comprehension and recall. In R.J. Spiro, B.C. Bruce, & W.F. Brewer (Eds.), *Theoretical issues in reading comprehension* (pp. 241–278). Hillsdale, NJ: Erlbaum.

Swafford, J., & Alvermann, D. (1989). Postsecondary research base for content reading strategies. *Journal of Reading, 33*, 164–169.

Vygotsky, L.S. (1978). *Mind in society: The development of higher psychological processes.* Cambridge, MA: Harvard University Press.

Wood, D., Bruner, J., & Ross, G. (1976). The role of tutoring in problem-solving. *Journal of Child Psychology and Psychiatry, 17*, 89–100.

Teaching Annotation Writing to College Students

Susan L. Strode

A s college reading professionals search the literature in an effort to teach students to comprehend, retain, and later, recall information on their own, a proliferation of study strategies are discovered. Among the strategies that research appears to support are summary writing and text marking. Another form of writing similar to a summary and which includes aspects of text marking is an annotation. An annotation can be defined as a brief synopsis of the key ideas and information in a piece of writing. Although an annotation summarizes a piece of writing, it goes beyond a summary in requiring a comment or reaction to that writing in the annotator's own words.

This article provides detailed descriptions of how to teach annotation writing to college students. Although there are several variations on annotation and summary writing, this instruction serves as a unique illustration of the reading process as students have the opportunity to see and discuss components of this process as they occur. These instructions also may be used to combine both reading and writing in the classroom as well as speaking and listening.

Annotation Background

Research shows that summarizing in the student's own words has been found to have positive effects on reading comprehension as it, by its very nature, requires heightened attention and deeper processing (Bean & Steenwyk, 1984; Craik & Lockhart, 1972; D'Angelo, 1983; Doctorow, Wittrock, & Marks, 1978; McNeil & Donant, 1982). In terms of annotation writing, Hynd, Simpson, and Chase (1990) conclude that "It seems reasonable that annotations that paraphrase important ideas or make inferences and draw conclusions about text would be evidence of greater degrees of semantic analysis than paying attention to only the surface features of a text." Annotation writing appears to be an additional

Originally published in Forum for Reading *(1991–1992), volume 23, numbers 1 & 2, pages 33–44*

Figure 1
Relationship between the number of key ideas and the number of words

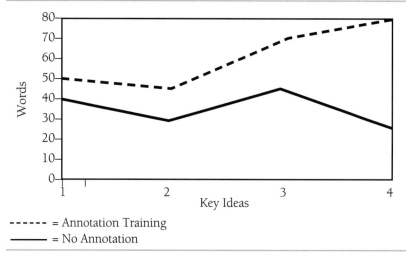

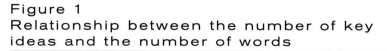

------ = Annotation Training
——— = No Annotation

aid to comprehension and retention since it better organizes thought (Eanet & Manzo, 1976; Hayes, 1987; Odell, 1980). Not surprisingly, the research literature also shows that training in annotation writing does indeed improve students' summary writing abilities (Eanet, 1976; Strode, 1989), thereby meeting a basic objective of higher literacy training.

Strode (1989) found that college students receiving annotation training used significantly fewer words to express the same amount of ideas as students not receiving annotation training. This study showed a clear trend whereby students who received annotation training used progressively fewer words to express progressively more key ideas. Figure 1 illustrates this finding.

Annotation Analogy

Another benefit of annotation writing is that its writers are not limited in terms of focus. There are many types of annotations and 10 that are used in a reading-writing study strategy called REAP (Eanet & Manzo, 1976). This strategy incorporates annotation writing as one of its components. Examples of different annotation types include summary, thesis, question, critical, heuristic, intention, motivation, probe, personal view, and inventive (descriptions of these annotation types can be found in Figure 3, pages 266–267).

A great deal of overlap occurs among these different annotation types. To illustrate this, they can be visualized as a tree. In the analogy, the summary annotation, since it is the most basic, can be represented as the trunk of the tree. The other annotation types can serve as the branches, as they do indeed branch out in different directions depending on what they ask the annotator to emphasize (see Figure 2).

Figure 2
Annotation tree

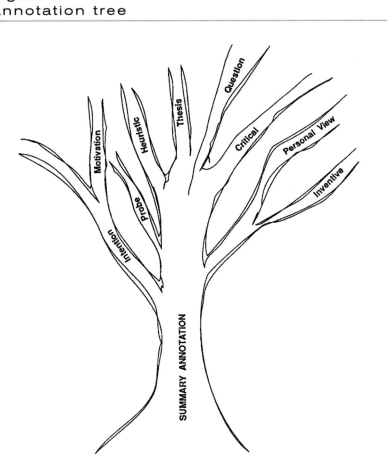

Since an annotation requires a comment or reaction to a piece of writing, I propose that reactions be built into this analogy and be visualized as a transparency. In the final stage, the "reaction transparency" lays over the annotation tree. Thus, the annotators react to the piece of writing while they address whatever the particular annotation type emphasizes.

Annotation Training

In view of the fact that this type of writing is strongly supported in the literature, it seems reasonable that annotation writing should be taught. Research in metacognition maintains that there exists a developmental trend (Ackerman, 1982; Flavell, Speer, Green, & August, 1981; Harris, Kruithof, Terwogt, & Visser, 1981; Markman, 1977; Townsend, 1983), and that many of the skills necessary for summarization are late developing (Brown & Day, 1983; Brown & Smiley, 1971). Such instruction, therefore, should be provided for the older, more mature reader who has and can utilize the necessary skills.

There are, regardless of age, some general things about teaching annotation writing that every teacher could profit from knowing. First, an annotation is brief. There is no need for a phrase such as, "This article was about...." Instead it should immediately begin with, "A woman and her son...." Second, the annotation should focus on key ideas or the gist but in terms of what the reader sees as important. In brief, annotations delete trivia, redundancies, descriptions, and conversations. They should, however, reflect the annotator's point of view or some specific purpose set out by the teacher.

Following are step-by-step instructions on how to teach annotation writing to college students in study skills classes. Here, the instructions consist of eight sessions; however, when using this procedure, the sessions do not need to be presented as separate units on eight consecutive days. The exercises on annotation writing should be intermixed with discussions on various aspects of the reading process, and are presented here separately, merely for the sake of clarity.

Session 1: An Introduction to Annotations

Directions. Explain REAP (Eanet & Manzo, 1976). Give an explanation of annotations. Ask for questions. Distribute a one-page article. Have students read the article and then write an annotation on the back. Encourage students by saying something like, "Don't worry, everyone feels awkward the first time they write about what they have read." Ask for volunteers to read their annotations. Comment on each annotation, noting (a) what is good, (b) what is not necessary, and (c) what needs to be added.

Student Annotation. *The author here is trying to express the feelings of secretaries today. She says that secretaries feel like prisoners and that they're looked down upon because of their job title.*

Comments. *This annotation does mention two key ideas in the article—secretaries feel like prisoners and are looked down on. Notice this annotation shows no bias as it clearly states that these were the feelings of secretaries. This annotation does include a few unnecessary words—"The author is trying to express...." It is obvious the author is trying to express something.*

Session 2: Noting More About Annotations

Directions. Review annotations. Ask for questions. Ask, "Do you want to revise your annotations?" (most will). Collect annotations. Read annotations aloud and comment on each. Encourage students to add their comments when they feel confident.

Student Annotation [Revision]. *The feelings of secretaries today are that they feel like they are "slaves," and are looked down upon because of their job title. They feel like prisoners.*

Comments. *This annotation is excellent. Notice how unnecessary words have been omitted and the annotation gets right to the heart of the article. It also points out that secretaries feel like prisoners.*

Session 3: Prior Knowledge and Annotations

Directions. Review annotation. Ask for questions. Distribute a one-page article. Have students read the article and then write an annotation on the back. Collect annotations. Read annotations aloud and comment on each.

Note: Point out that even though all the annotations are based on the same one-page article (not a lot of information), they are all different. The aspects of the article students consider important will depend on their previous experience with the subject. Discuss how person A may feel one way and person B may feel another, and person C still another.

This will demonstrate to students that—yes, we do take our prior knowledge with us to the printed page and that it is very important as we attempt to interpret prose.

Student Annotation. *The author feels like he was punished by the way he was treated because he is an Indian. He felt like he should be fairly treated since the Indians were here in America first. He took a look at himself and had forgotten who he was. He now is proud of what he is and is not ashamed of being an Indian, I don't think he ever was though.*

Comments. *It is a good idea to mention that the author is an Indian. Here we have a clear example of how prior knowledge can bias one from accurate comprehension. The author never said he should be fairly treated since the Indians were here in America first. The annotator was so caught up in his/her own feelings, the gist of the article was neglected.*

Student Annotation [Revision]. *A man who wants to try and prepare his daughter for what he has already been through. He is an Indian, and understands that he has to let his daughter endure the same pain and find her own inner self the way he did.*

Comments. *Excellent!*

Session 4: Benefits Become Apparent

Directions. Distribute one article to half the class and a different article to the other half. Have students read their respective articles and then write annotations on the back. Collect. Read one annotation for article A and one annotation for article B. Have each student take an article with a peer's annotation on the back so that everyone has the article that he/she has not yet read. Have students read the annotation and then the article. Have students write a second annotation and then, under that, complete the prompt, "When I read an annotation before I read the article...." Have students return the articles to their original owners. Have students respond to their peers' annotations and comments by completing the prompt, "When I read a second annotation ...."

Student Annotations and Responses.
Student A
"Nurture not nature is responsible for criminal behavior." Scientists argue back and forth whether crime is constitutional or derives from other hereditary

factors. The convincingness of the book and the new idea may just be in tune with the changing times and national mood.

Student B
The controversy roars on as to whether or not criminals are born with certain hereditary traits that make them more likely to commit crime or that criminals are a product of their environments and nurturing.

Student B
When I read an annotation before the article...I can better understand what the article is about and can therefore read it much faster.

Student A
When I read the second annotation...it seemed to be a summary of my (the first) annotation.

Comments. *Why were the articles read and annotated so much faster the second time than the first time? The annotation activated your prior knowledge, giving you a sense of the topic and a place to store the recently acquired information.*

Session 5: Annotating a Lengthy Selection

Directions. Distribute an article that is several pages long. Have students read the article. Have each student write an annotation and his/her name and class on the back.

Student annotation. *AIDS is a life threatening disease that is proving more detrimental everyday. Studies have proven that sexually promiscuous people have a greater chance of acquiring the disease, than other people.*

Session 6: Reactions to a Lengthy Selection

Directions. Distribute the article (from another class's session five) that has an annotation written on the back. Have students read the annotation and then the article. Have students write a second annotation. Collect the articles to give back to their original annotators. Return to these students their original articles from session five which now include second annotations written by students from another class.

Student Annotation. *Even though AIDS is not in danger of becoming an epidemic, it is becoming a threatening disease. Preventive methods and helping those who have contacted the disease can be helpful in controlling this fatal disease.*

Session 7: Writing Different Types of Annotations

Directions. Distribute a handout that contains brief descriptions of 10 different annotation types (see Figure 3). Assign each student a different annotation type. Have each student write an annotation, for an article previously read, which follows the format of the annotation type assigned.

Figure 3
Annotation types

An annotation is a brief digest of the ideas and informational content of a piece of writing or a short explanatory comment about it. Writing annotations can help the annotator think about and more fully understand what has been gained from reading by writing about it briefly.

The SUMMARY ANNOTATION condenses the selection into a concise form. It should be brief, clear, and to the point. It includes no more or no less than is necessary to adequately convey the development and relationship of the author's main ideas. In the case of a story, the summary annotation is a synopsis—the main events of the plot–omitting conversation, explanation, and description. With a nonfiction selection, the significant ideas are stated in such a way as to show their relationship omitting examples, elaboration, clarification, and other detail.

The THESIS ANNOTATION is an incisive statement of the author's proposition. As the word "incisive" implies, it cuts directly to the heart of the matter. With fiction, it can substitute for a statement of theme. One way to approach its writing is to ask oneself, "What is the author saying? What one idea or point is the author trying to put across to the reader?" The thesis annotation is best written in the form of a precis; unnecessary connectives are removed to produce a telegram-like, but unambiguous, statement.

The QUESTION ANNOTATION directs attention to the ideas that the annotator thinks are most important. This may or may not be the same as the author's theses. The annotator must first determine what is most significant to the issue at hand, and then express this notion in question form. This annotation answers the question, "What question(s) is the author answering with the narrative?"

(continued)

Figure 3 (continued)
Annotation types

The CRITICAL ANNOTATION is the annotator's response to the author's thesis. In general, there are three responses a reader may have—agree, disagree, or agree in part and disagree in part. The first sentence in the annotation should state the author's thesis. In the next sentence, the annotator should state his/her position, and the following sentences are devoted to defending or expanding the position which he/she takes.

The HEURISTIC ANNOTATION is a statement, usually in the author's own words, which has two purposes: to suggest the idea of the selection and to provoke a response. To write it, the annotator needs to determine the essence of the selection, and then to select a quotation that hints at that essence in a stimulating manner.

The INTENTION ANNOTATION is a statement of the author's intention, plan, or purpose in writing the selection as it is perceived by the annotator. This is particularly useful with material of a persuasive, ironic, or satirical nature. Determining intention requires that the annotator bring to bear all available clues, both intrinsic, such as tone and use of language, and extrinsic, such as knowledge of the author.

The MOTIVATION ANNOTATION is a statement which attempts to speculate about the author's likely motive(s) for having created or written certain things. It is an attempt to find the source of the author's belief system and perceptions. The motivation annotation is a high form of criticism. It often requires penetrating psychological insight.

The PROBE ANNOTATION focuses on practical points and questions which deserve further exploration before a reasoned judgment can be reached about the reading selection. The emphasis of this annotation is given to "verification," "consequences," and "alternatives." The annotator clearly and directly expresses these questions and/or the issues that require additional attention.

The PERSONAL VIEW ANNOTATION answers the question "How do personal experiences, views, and feelings stack up against the thesis or main idea?" The annotator draws upon his/her background and beliefs, comparing them with the author's central point. The relationship between these personal views and the author's is articulated in this annotation.

The INVENTIVE ANNOTATION offers an intentionally constructive point of view taken by the annotator. The annotator creates an expanded response to the author's idea(s), developing a view from another context or synthesizing it from several for this particular occasion. This perspective goes beyond the author's and enriches it by the synergistic result.

Student Annotations.

SUMMARY ANNOTATION—"War Toys on the March"
Children are watching more violent "cartoons." Some people are concerned about the behavior end and they are teaching children to love war. Some people say the "cartoons" are harmless.

THESIS ANNOTATION—"War Toys on the March"
War toys and cartoons greatly influence children's behavior in later life.

QUESTION ANNOTATION—"For My Indian Daughter"
"How can a father help his Indian daughter discover her inner-self?"

CRITICAL ANNOTATION—"Pink-Collar Worker's Blues"
I agree that the status of women (the pink collar workers), has not changed as much as people seem to think. The majority of women work as secretaries or more accurately servants to other men or women. They should not be satisfied with their position as secretaries because that lets them fit the role that men want them to keep, (beneath them).

HEURISTIC ANNOTATION—"Pink-Collar Worker's Blues"
American society has enlarged the myth of the "new woman." But does this woman really exist? In essence, most women in Americana hold "subservient" jobs; secretaries and waitresses, for example. As one secretary said, "Yes, I'll do that. I don't mind."

INTENTION ANNOTATION—"For My Indian Daughter"
The author's purpose for writing this article was to share his concern for his daughter.

MOTIVATION ANNOTATION—"Pink-Collar Worker's Blues"
In today's world, women feel cheated because of a certain status they have to achieve. Sometimes women feel rejected because of a certain way they dress. It's a shame that everyone doesn't get treated equally!

PROBE ANNOTATION—"Are Criminals Born, Not Made?"
Is crime largely the byproduct of poverty, racism, broken families, and other social disturbances? Are there differences between criminals and nonoffenders? If these differences do exist, can they be used in trial to determine an accused person's guilt or innocence?

PERSONAL VIEW ANNOTATION—"For My Indian Daughter"
One day the Indian man was at the beach when a fat white man made Indian cries with his mouth at his daughter. This is the same thing people would do

to me when I was younger. I am Hispanic and people would joke around about myself being ethnic. I don't care really what people say anymore, but I used to. I learned to live with it, just like the Indian man did, and how his daughter is going to have to. People sometimes go too far and then they wonder why there is hate in the world. Maybe there is hate because they started it.

INVENTIVE ANNOTATION—"For My Indian Daughter"
"For My Indian Daughter" relates to the essence of being an individual. The need of gaining strong character is recurrent in this story. It reinforces the saying that "strength comes from within."

Session 8: Annotating Textbooks

Directions. Have students begin annotating chapters in textbooks by selecting a chapter in a content text they must study and writing an annotation for each heading and subheading. Have students write the annotations on their own paper.

Conclusion

Experience with college-age students has shown me that the most effective way to teach annotation writing would be first to teach summary annotations very well. After a firm understanding of summary annotations (i.e., the trunk of the tree), other types of annotations (i.e., the branches of the tree) can be easily and successfully written.

In summary, writing about what was read has numerous benefits. Simply put, benefits for students are that, in addition to encoding information, they are decoding information. Furthermore, the act of writing encourages thinking which calls for deeper processing. The teacher also is able to see some of these benefits as writing about what was read demonstrates the students' level of understanding.

REFERENCES

Ackerman, B.P. (1982). Children's use of contextual expectations to detect and resolve comprehension failures. *Journal of Experimental Child Psychology, 33*, 63–73.

Anderson, R.C. (1972). How to construct achievement tests to assess comprehension. *Review of Educational Research, 42*, 145–170.

Bean, T.W., & Steenwyk, F.L. (1984). The effect of three types of summary instruction on 6th graders summary writing and comprehension. *Journal of Reading Behavior, 16*(4), 297–306.

Bromely, K.D. (1985). *Writing in the secondary school.* Urbana, IL: National Council of Teachers of English.

Brown, A.L., & Day, J.D. (1983). Macrorules for summarizing texts: The development of expertise. *Journal of Verbal Learning and Verbal Behavior, 22,* 1–14.

Brown, A.L., & Smiley, S.S. (1977). Rating the importance of structural units of prose passages: A problem of metacognitive development. *Child Development, 48,* 1–8.

Craik, F., & Lockhart, R. (1972). Levels of processing: A framework for memory research. *Journal of Verbal Learning and Verbal Behavior, 11,* 671–684.

D'Angelo, K. (1983). Precis writing: Promoting vocabulary development and comprehension. *Journal of Educational Psychology, 19,* 647–652.

Doctorow, M., Wittrock, M.C., & Marks, C. (1978). Generative processes in reading comprehension. *Journal of Educational Psychology, 70,* 109–118.

Eanet, M.G. (1977). An investigation of the REAP reading/study procedure: Its rationale and efficacy. (Doctoral dissertation, University of Missouri–Kansas City, 1976). *Dissertation Abstracts International, 37,* 3471A.

Eanet, M.G., & Manzo, A.V. (1976). REAP: A strategy for improving reading/writing study skills. *Journal of Reading, 19,* 647–652.

Flavell, J.H., Speer, J.R., Green, F.L., & August, D.L. (1981). The development of comprehension monitoring and knowledge about communication. *Monographs of the Society for Research in Child Development, 46* (Whole No. 192).

Harris, P.L., Kruithof, A., Terwogt, M.M., & Visser, P. (1981). Children's detection and awareness of textual anomaly. *Journal of Experimental Child Psychology, 31,* 212–230.

Hayes, D.A. (1987). The potential for directing study in combined reading and writing activity. *Journal of Reading Behavior, 19,* 333–352.

Hynd, C.R., Simpson, M.L., & Chase, N.D. (1990). Studying narrative text: The effects of annotating vs. journal writing on test performance. *Reading Research and Instruction, 29*(2), 44–54.

Markman, E.M. (1977). Realizing that you don't understand: Elementary school children's awareness of inconsistencies. *Child Development, 50,* 643–655.

McNeil, J., & Donant, L. (1982). Summarization strategy for improving reading comprehension. In J. Niles & L.A. Harris (Eds.), *New inquiries in reading research and instruction: Thirty-first yearbook of the National Reading Conference* (pp. 215–219). Rochester, NY: National Reading Conference. (ERIC Document Reproduction Service No. ED 264 542)

Odell, L. (1980). The process of writing and the process of learning. *College Composition and Communication, 31*(1), 42–50.

Sachs, J.S. (1967). Recognition memory for syntactic and semantic aspects of connected discourse. *Perception and Psychophysics, 2,* 437–442.

Stotsky, S. (1982). The role of writing in developmental reading. *Journal of Advanced Child Psychology, 24,* 330–339.

Strode, S.L. (1990). Re-evaluation of the effects of annotation training on the comprehension and summary writing abilities of college students. (Doctoral dissertation, University of Missouri–Kansas City, 1989). *Dissertation Abstracts International, 50,* 3196A.

Townsend, M.A.R. (1983). Schema shifting: Children's cognitive monitoring of the prose-schema interaction in comprehension. *Journal of Experimental Child Psychology, 36,* 139–149.

Reader Response
in the College Reading Class

Cynthia Chamblee

College students who possess inadequate reading and study skills are not new to American colleges and universities. These students are often referred to as underprepared, high risk, or at risk. They typically are enrolled in a reading class as a result of the perception that their reading skills are not adequate for reading and learning at the college level. Many of the students have experienced limited success in high school, and regard reading as negative and stressful. Other characteristics associated with them include the following: They (a) avoid reading when possible, even though they have developed sufficient cognitive skills; (b) feel that they lack control over their reading and have little metacognitive awareness of it; (c) have little sense of the reader's role and how to use reading; (d) do not consider themselves to be competent readers and do not expect to be successful in their efforts to improve their reading; and (e) lack interest in reading and see little practical value in it (Vacca & Padak, 1990).

Instruction for these readers when they were high school students typically ignored opportunities for socializing as a way of developing literacy and emphasized individual effort. They were often expected to read and interpret text on their own in their regular classes. Any special reading instruction they may have received in high school was most likely offered in a reading laboratory where they worked independently to overcome reading deficiencies or to develop other skills (Radebaugh & Kazemek, 1989). Later college reading instruction followed this same format with students working individually in workbooks or on study skill sheets. The value of such exercises is questionable. Unlike students considered to be more able, at-risk students seldom receive literacy instruction that emphasizes problem solving and critical thinking designed to help learners better achieve their life goals (Biggs, 1992).

Is there a better way to approach the remediation of reading skills for at-risk students than to emphasize the individual development of skills and strategies? Is there a way to motivate them and help them feel suc-

Originally published in Forum for Reading *(1993–1994), volume 24, pages 43–54*

cessful with their reading? Is there a way to foster enjoyment of reading and help them see reading as personally rewarding? One possible answer to these questions is to restructure the college reading classes to incorporate more instruction that is based on the theory of reader response.

Reader-Response Theory

Like college reading classes, reader response has a long history. Rosenblatt (1983) first introduced this theory in 1938. However, it has only been in the last few years that instructional methods based on this theory have gained wide acceptance. Rosenblatt describes reading as either efferent or aesthetic. Efferent reading refers to the reading of factual information and then responding with a specific answer. Many college reading classes have taken this stance toward reading. In this skills-type approach, vocabulary is pretaught and then comprehension questions are asked. Aesthetic reading refers to a different type of response to reading. Rosenblatt describes this type of reading as one in which the readers "acquire not so much additional information as additional experience. New understanding is conveyed to them dynamically and personally. Literature provides a living-through, not simply knowledge about" (p. 38).

Rosenblatt's theory also explains how a reader's personal schema influences interpretation of text. According to her theory, each reader's schema generates an interpretation that creates the text anew for each reader. Rosenblatt calls this act of creating meaning a transaction between reader and text. The readers' experiences and prior knowledge interact with the content and structure of the text to create meaning (Chase & Hynd, 1987).

On the other hand, critics of reader response say this approach views reading as a free association, an anything goes approach. Some teachers are uncomfortable with the approach because they want their students to know what the author really intends (Chase & Hynd, 1987; Hynd et al., 1985). But at the heart of reader response is the idea that readers are part of an interpretative community (Fish, 1980), and that through open, free discussions of personal reactions to the text, students are helped to clarify and broaden their own reactions and interpretations. Reader response, therefore, does not imply that reading is simply a personal interpretation of text. The reader starts at the personal level, but then is led to identify, evaluate, assimilate, and accommodate other interpretations (Chase & Hynd, 1987). With reader response, the reader comes to view reading as purposeful, social, and personal, not simply a process for obtaining information (Sheridan, 1991).

Reader-Response Research

Are reader-response approaches effective? More research in this area is needed, but several studies do demonstrate its effectiveness. Webb (1980) found that while the response-based approach did not have a significant effect on literature achievement or cognitive maturity, there was a positive significant effect on the students' attitudes toward literature. Also, Price (1986) reported that college freshmen receiving response-based instruction gave higher quality interpretations of poetry than did students who received more traditional instruction. Further, Hynd et al. (1985) found that the use of reader response in the college developmental classroom proved at least as successful as more traditional methods in developing comprehension and accurate recall of ideas. There is also evidence that a response-based approach can affect positive change in students' reading and writing (Chase, 1985). Other studies that involve writing resulted in higher levels of understanding (e.g., Wiseman & Many, 1992) and increased writing fluency (e.g., Newel, Suszynski, & Weingart, 1989).

Thus, although limited in the quantity of studies, research does suggest that instruction based on reader response is as effective as traditional approaches and that this approach can have a positive effect on the students' attitudes toward reading.

Reader-Response in the College Reading Class

Why is reader response appropriate for at-risk students in the college reading class? These students may have problems with reading, but they also have a lifetime of personal knowledge and experiences. Reader response allows them to bring their experiences and background knowledge to their reading and learning in meaningful ways. As a result of their ideas being validated within an academic context, they are more motivated to read. Probst (1988) points out that all students are interested in themselves, and when they are allowed to bring their own knowledge and experiences to their reading, they often become the focus of attention. They then have reason to read.

At-risk students often lack self-esteem, and the teaching of reading and writing skills may even produce a loss of self-esteem in these students (Gentile & McMillan, 1992). Reader-response approaches, which do not require students to produce correct answers but which require them to interact with the reading to produce their own meaning, result in more successful reading experiences and enhanced self-esteem.

College reading students often have little understanding of the reading process and thus lack confidence in their ability to read accurately. Reader-response instruction helps these students view reading as a process, not as a one-stage activity. Students first react to their reading by relating new information to their prior experiences and knowledge. Next, through a free exchange of responses, students are led to accept or reconsider their initial reactions. As students refer back to the text, they are able to see errors they may have made and learn more about how and why the errors occurred. Reader-response instruction guides students *toward* viewing reading as an opportunity to generate and refine ideas and *away from* an emphasis on accuracy and the recall of details. Thus, students are helped to view their errors as a natural part of the reading process (Probst, 1988).

By making students aware of alternative thoughts and behaviors and by helping them make sound choices, reader-response instruction also encourages students to solve their problems independently. This independence can build self-confidence. The building of self-confidence based on legitimate achievement is an ingredient often missing in instruction for at-risk students. In addition, self-confidence is enhanced when instructors make "comments that acknowledge students' productive efforts, [provide] opportunities for students to demonstrate newly acquired skill and knowledge, and [assist] students when they experience difficulty as they struggle to learn" (Biggs, 1992, p. 626).

Instruction Based on Reader-Response

Implementing reader-response instruction is enhanced when the following areas of concern are addressed: conditions, prereading, text reading, journal writing, discussion, and follow-up. Consideration should be given to each area before instruction begins.

Conditions. Probst (1988) cites five conditions which are necessary for response-based teaching. The first is receptivity. Teachers must create a classroom atmosphere in which students feel secure enough to freely respond. Teacher and students can use each others' ideas, building on them instead of disputing them. The second condition is tentativeness. Students must be willing to change their minds about ideas they express. They must be encouraged to add to, modify, or even reject their first responses. Rigor is the third condition; this is required of both the students and the teacher. Students must be willing to think. The teacher must be actively involved in the entire process. The fourth condition is cooperation. The class must be able to work together as a group. Suitable literature is the final condition. The literature should be worthy of reflection and have strong potential interest for the students. Probst suggests that while all five conditions may not be fully achieved in the classroom, they do represent elements of the desired classroom atmosphere for response-based teaching.

Prereading. The value of helping students access personal beliefs and subject knowledge prior to reading is well recognized (e.g., Anderson & Pearson, 1984; Spiro, 1980). When designing instruction based on reader response, traditional prereading activities should continue to precede the reading of most texts (e.g., Vacca & Vacca, 1993). Some teachers also find that prior to instruction it is helpful to discuss reader response theory and the reader's role in the meaning-making process. Reader response is new to most students, and the discussion can help make them feel more secure in responding honestly to the text (Willey, 1992).

Text Reading. The text can be read inside and/or outside the classroom. The length of the reading will often dictate the approach the teacher takes. At times it is good for the teacher to read an unfamiliar text along with the students in order to model the reading process. Some texts should be read only in the class with reading and discussion taking place alternately. The discussions can also incorporate expectations and predictions. A longer text could be started in class with the remainder of the text assigned for the next class period. Since many students have never learned what it means to read for more than information, they need to be shown how to struggle with a text to make meaning from it (Sheridan, 1991).

Journal Writing. Most reader-response lessons incorporate the use of writing in reading journals or logs. After reading, students use the journals to respond to the text read. These are usually five- to ten-minute writings that are informal, free-form responses that could be used for a variety of purposes. The journals allow students to ask questions, admit confusion, make predictions and/or associations, or react to anything they think is significant (Rogers, 1990). They can also write about their thoughts, feelings, and experiences. One strategy that can be used to help them make personal connections with the text is to have them respond to unfinished sentences such as "I notice," or "I can't understand" (Wilson, 1989). Another strategy is to ask questions like "How does this poem make you feel?" or "What aspect of the text excited or interested you most?" or "What experiences have you had that help others understand why you feel the way you do?" (Brozo, 1988). Still another strategy is looped writing (Bodmer, 1991). After reading, students are asked to free write about their reading and to write a summation sentence that contains the most interesting or predominant idea. After discussion, the summation sentence becomes the starting place for the second response. Again, they summarize and discuss and write a final summation. They conclude by discussing what the writing process has revealed. Students can further be asked to read and write three loops on their own. This process stimulates thinking about text that prepares students for substantive class discussion. A final strategy is to have students bring to class questions that they cannot answer (Muldoon, 1990). As the teacher and students share their questions, modeling occurs and students learn to construct better and more critical questions. Muldoon found that students who come to class with questions (rather than answers) are often less threatened and better prepared for learning.

Discussion. Critical to the success of any reader-response lesson are the discussions. It is through the discussions that the community of learners work together to create meaning. It is reassuring for some students to find that others have made the same connections with the text that they had, but most important is that the students get to see the varied viewpoints as these are shared, questioned, and debated (Aker, 1992; Brozo, 1988; Willey, 1992). It is at this point that students will take a closer look at the text and use it to explain or justify how they derived their meanings (Rosenblatt, 1983; Willey, 1992). They are then led to see that their own interpretations may not be the only ones justified by the text (Moffett & Wagner, 1991). As they are exposed to beliefs, opinions, and knowledge of others, they may revise or reject their own interpretations (Aker, 1992; Rosenblatt, 1983; Willey, 1992). During discussion, the teacher refrains from evaluating and correcting but does offer guidance through questions that ask students why, how, and what they mean. The teacher can also point out differences in the responses and reasons for those differences as they relate to students' varying prior knowledge and experiences (Willey, 1992). At this point, the teacher can also introduce the sociohistorical context of the text in order to help students understand the author's point of view (Chase, 1985). Opinions of critics and other academic interpretations can be shared so that students can begin to appreciate the participants in interpretative community. Discussion can be whole class or small group. Chase and

Hynd (1987) recommend that students work together in small groups using outlines or other graphic organizers to structure their reactions and ideas. To involve shy students, the teacher can ask that each student respond initially and then move to a free flowing discussion.

Follow-Up. An after-discussion essay is also a valuable component of a reader-response lesson because it allows students to integrate their ideas and interpretations with others they have heard in the classroom. In their essays, students can focus on their own interpretations of the text, note how one interpretation relates to another, or argue for one interpretation over another (Chase & Hynd, 1987). Further, they can cite quotes and specific examples from the text, as well as incorporate their own personal experiences and knowledge into their writing (Chase, 1985). Essays written may take a variety of forms (e.g., letters to authors, character or critical analyses). However, to be consistent with reader-response theory, students make their own choice of topics (Danis, 1992). If prereading activities centered around hypothetical issues and/or problems, follow up should encourage students to (a) evaluate their previous beliefs, (b) discuss any changes that took place, and (c) consider how the author or others in differing interpretive communities would react to the same issues (Chase, 1985; Chase & Hynd, 1987).

Conclusion

Educators have recognized for some time that academic assistance programs are necessary since many students enter college with inadequate reading and study skills. This need continues to exist and appears to be growing (Wyatt, 1992). When at-risk, underprepared students enter our colleges and universities, it is our responsibility to do our best to enable them to reach their potential. To achieve this goal we can look at them as reservoirs of knowledge—building on what they know instead of what they lack.

It is important, therefore, that we meet the challenge by changing the curriculum and instructional approaches to better meet the needs of this population. Students are benefited when they read and write and then share their ideas and opinions with others. They need to experience success with reading and learn that reading like writing is a process. As students are encouraged to bring themselves to their reading, to feel and think about the author's ideas (rather than focusing exclusively on finding "correct" answers), they begin to see reading as less threatening. The more they read and respond, the more fluent their reading becomes and the more useful strategies they develop. They start to take control of their own learning.

Many teachers and professors who are incorporating reader-response instruction into their classrooms are observing these positive changes in their students. Of course, no single approach can meet all the needs of this diverse population. However, a reader-response–based curriculum has the potential to convince students that they can (a) think for themselves, (b) construct meaning as they read, (c) modify their thinking to accommodate the ideas of others, and (d) function as legitimate members of the community of learners.

REFERENCES

Aker, D. (1992). From runned to ran: One journey toward a critical literacy. *Journal of Reading, 36,* 104–112.

Anderson, R.D., & Pearson, P.D. (1984). A schema-theoretic view of basic processes in reading comprehension. In P.D. Pearson (Ed.), *Handbook of reading research* (pp. 255–293). New York: Longman.

Beach, R., & Hynds, S. (1991). Research on response to literature. In R. Barr, M.L. Kamil, P. Mosenthal, & P.D. Pearson (Eds.), *Handbook of reading research* (Vol. 2, pp. 453–489). White Plains, NY: Longman.

Biggs, S. (1992). Building on strengths: Closing the literacy gap for African Americans. *Journal of Reading, 35,* 624–628.

Brozo, W. (1988). Applying a reader response heuristic to expository text. *Journal of Reading, 31,* 140–145.

Chase, N. (1985). *Reader response techniques for teaching secondary and postsecondary reading* (College Reading and Learning Assistance Technical Report 85-07).

Chase, N., & Hynd, C. (1987). Reader response: An alternative way to teach students to think about text. *Journal of Reading, 30,* 530–540.

Danis, F. (1992). Sitting swimmers and stuffed armadillos in sundresses: Reader response and classroom creativity. *CEA Forum, 22,* 1–2.

Fish, S. (1980). Is there a text in this class? In C. Kaplan (Ed.), *Criticism: The major statement.* New York: St. Martin's Press.

Hynd, C., Chase, N., Stahl, N., & Smith, B. (1985). *Reader response in the college developmental classroom.* Paper presented at the 35th National Reading Conference, San Diego, CA.

Moffett, J., & Wagner, B. (1991). Student-centered reading activities. *English Journal, 80,* 70–73.

Muldoon, P. (1990). Challenging students to think: Shaping questions, building community. *English Journal, 79,* 34–40.

Newel, G., Suszynski, K. & Weingart, R. (1989). The effects of writing in a reader-based and text-based mode on students' understanding of two short stories. *Journal of Reading Behavior, 21,* 37–55.

Newton, E. (1991). Developing metacognitive awareness: The response journal in college composition. *Journal of Reading, 34,* 476–478.

Price, M. (1986). Reader-response criticism: A test of usefulness in a first-year college course in writing about literature (Doctoral dissertation, Florida State University, 1986). *Dissertation Abstracts International, 47,* 1637A.

Probst, R. (1988). *Response and analysis: Teaching literature in junior and senior high school.* Portsmouth, NH: Heinemann.

Radebaugh, M., & Kazemek, F. (1989). Cooperative learning in college reading and study skills classes. *Journal of Reading, 32,* 414–418.

Rogers, T. (1990). A point, counterpoint response strategy for complex short stories. *Journal of Reading, 34,* 278–281.

Rosenblatt, L. (1983). *Literature as exploration.* New York: Modern Language Association.

Sheridan, D. (1991). Changing business as usual: Reader response in the classroom. *College English, 53,* 804–813.

Spiro, R. (1980). Constructive processes in prose comprehension and recall. In R. Spiro, B. Bruce, & W. Brewer (Eds.), *Theoretical issues in reading comprehension.* Hillsdale, NJ: Erlbaum.

Vacca, R., & Padak, N. (1990). Who's at risk in reading. *Journal of Reading, 33,* 486–488.

Vacca, R.T., & Vacca, J.L. (1993). *Content area reading: Literacy and learning across the curriculum.* New York: HarperCollins.

Webb, A.J. (1980). Introducing the transitive paradigm for literary response into the high school literature program: A study of effects on curriculum, teaching, and students (Doctoral dissertation, State University of New York at Buffalo, 1980). *Dissertation Abstracts International, 41,* 929A.

Willey, R.J. (1992). Fostering audience awareness through interpretive communities. *Teaching in English in the Two-Year College, 19,* 148–155.

Wilson, N. (1989). Learning from confusion: Questions and change in reading logs. *English Journal, 78,* 62–69.

Wiseman, D., & Many, J. (1992). The effects of aesthetic and efferent teaching approaches on undergraduate students' responses to literature. *Reading Research and Instruction, 31,* 66–83.

Wyatt, M. (1992). The past, present, and future need for college reading courses in the U.S. *Journal of Reading, 36,* 10–20.

Reflection and Developmental Readers: Facilitating Metacognition With Learning Logs

Laura B. Soldner

> Learning logs were more like my trial time. It encouraged me to read in a way that I could enjoy reading and understand the content. I applied various methods I learned in class to find out what I felt comfortable with. Now I know how I can enjoy reading, and I don't feel pushed to read. I realized that understanding of reading depends on my own attitude towards reading. If I'm conscious of what I'm reading, and if I have a clear purpose, reading is more enjoyable. Now I know that reading is not only for tests, but also it is for myself to gain knowledge. (Sachiko, age 21, sophomore)

Increasing numbers of postsecondary learners, like the young woman whose reflection begins this article, come to school with weak reading skills; they also come with very little awareness of their limitations and what to do about them (Soldner, 1997). As developmental educators, we are challenged to find the means to have students spend more time thinking about their reading and thinking abilities. Andrews (1997) suggests that learning logs provide an excellent means of introducing students to the importance of metacognitive awareness as well as helping them unlock their own strategies and skills to improve reading comprehension and retention. Andrews also argues that this is particularly important as students approach content area reading. This paper provides a brief examination of some recent literature on learning logs and metacognition. It also addresses how learning logs can be used in classrooms and concludes with verbatim excerpts from students' logs to illustrate the usefulness of these written records.

Note: The reflections cited were written by students whose names are replaced with pseudonyms. Original spelling, grammar, and punctuation are retained.

Originally published in The Journal of College Literacy and Learning *(1998–1999), volume 29, pages 18–24*

Learning Logs and Metacognition

College textbooks are often more difficult to read and learn from than many college students expect them to be. Some student readers come to places of higher learning with neither the awareness of, nor control over, their own reading processes (Soldner, 1997). These students lack the requisite metacognitive awareness necessary to monitor, direct, and regulate their learning of text. They are inexperienced with comprehension monitoring, and this becomes most apparent when developmental college learners attempt to tackle college textbook material.

One means that can be used to assist students with developing the needed reflective and metacognitive skills for reading is a learning log. Harris and Hodges (1995) defines a learning log as "an ongoing record of learning activity kept by students to help them evaluate their progress, think about new learning, and plan further learning" (p. 137). Learning logs allow students to become actively engaged with their reading, especially with their content area texts, and according to Andrews (1997), this writing to learn provides a format for students to demonstrate their personal understanding of the course content.

Learning logs can take a variety of forms. Most often they are notebooks dedicated to informal writing, note-taking, and musings on subjects (Alvermann & Phelps, 1994). Regular log entries give students opportunities for risk-free reflection. They become a place where students can try out ideas, put their thoughts down on paper to discover what they are thinking, and record what they have learned while reading.

The use of learning logs is not limited to postsecondary students, as illustrated by Collins (1997) in his writings on learning in adulthood. He describes learning logs as an "explicit learning mechanism" (p. 36). He discusses the importance of setting time aside to "discuss or reflect on events and extract the maximum knowledge or understanding from them" (p. 36). He finds learning logs to be powerful mechanisms to help adults to determine not only what they are learning but under what circumstances they learn or are unable to learn.

Classroom Implementation

Entries in learning logs can be specified by the instructor or can be left entirely open-ended to be determined by the students themselves. Entries are normally of two types: process and reaction (Alvermann & Phelps, 1994). Process entries generally ask students to reflect on how they have learned; reaction entries focus more on what they have learned. Both types of entries are useful and should be encouraged with college learners. Examples of process-entry prompts include such questions as the following:

- What do I know about the topic I am about to begin to read about?
- What do I want or need to know about this topic?
- What did I do while I was reading to check if I was paying attention and/or comprehending what I was reading?
- What did I understand about the material I just read?
- What didn't I understand? What was confusing? Why might this have been confusing to me?
- What vocabulary terms did I learn or didn't I understand? Why?
- What part of the reading was clear to me? Which parts did I understand easily? Why?
- What specific problems did I have reading this assignment?
- At what point did I become tired, confused, discouraged? Why?
- What did I do after I finished my reading?

Sample reaction entry prompts include directives like those listed below:

- Connect what you have read with your prior knowledge of the topic or personal experiences you have had.
- Summarize what you have read so that you could explain it to a classmate.
- Explain a theory, concept, vocabulary term, or the like in writing so you have it for later review.
- Generate questions about this reading assignment that your teacher might ask.
- Imagine that you are corresponding with the author of this text. What questions, comments, or reactions would you share with him or her?

My Experience With Learning Logs

After many years of classroom experience, I have learned how critically important it is to encourage students to write about what they have learned or how they go about learning. Their log entries can influence not only my students' cognitive knowledge but also their affective response to reading and the reading process. Writing allows students to examine whether what they are doing is working; this process allows them to build on their successes or to reflect on the difficulties they are experiencing so they can determine, for themselves, what steps to take to resolve their struggles.

As a natural outgrowth of my interests in metacognition and reflection, I have used learning logs in my course in Personal Reading Improvement. This two-credit, graded elective is recommended but not required for entering students who earn a reading subscore below 18 on the American College Test (ACT) or those with less than a 2.0 high school grade-point average. At the beginning of the semester, I introduce the concept of learning logs to students. Through modeling and guided and independent practice, I teach students the various forms their learning logs can take. To facilitate this, I distribute a list of the process and reaction prompts listed above to encourage more personalized responses in the logs. However, I admit that I encourage students to try more process than reaction prompts to get them to focus more on why they know something and how they know it.

I am particularly interested in students' transfer and application of the concepts and strategies that they learn in class to the content area courses they take in the humanities, sciences, fine arts, vocational subjects, and other disciplines. Students are required to complete an average of five learning-log sheets during each three-week period. These sheets are relatively unstructured and simply ask the students to record the date and subject, as well as their narrative log entry.

At first, some students balk at doing these because they see them as unnecessary busywork that distracts them from completing other necessary reading or homework. Normally, their attitude changes when the first logs are returned after I review them. They are surprised to find that I comment actively on their learning logs. They are shocked to find out that I read each log carefully. I circle points in their narratives to reconsider, encourage them to try strategies learned in class, or offer advice about how other students approached similar problems. I am most excited while reviewing the logs when I uncover something the student has written that actually shows him or her self-reporting what was learned or what has worked. I normally mark those reflections with a "Look what you told yourself!" remark.

Managing the Paper Load

In order to handle the paper load that comes with teaching 80 students a semester in four sections of this course, I do several things. First, I stagger the due dates so that only two classes turn their logs in at the same time. Second, I do not correct the logs for grammar, misspellings, or other technical errors. Instead, I focus on the ideas and concepts they are trying out and focus more on their thoughts than the accuracy of their writing. Third, and perhaps, most important, I use a two-color system of grading. I begin by simply highlighting those "Look what you told yourself" thoughts with a colored highlighter. Then, I use a colored pen to write any reactions, advice, or words of encouragement. I find that there are some log sheets that will go without any markings whatsoever, whereas on other pages, I'll concentrate on the points students make and add ideas of my own for them to try.

Generally, after the first set of logs is returned, most students, though not all, express greater interest in completing the logs to find out what they are teaching themselves and what I have to say about it. Besides providing students with metacognitive knowledge about themselves and their reading tasks, learning logs provide me as a teacher with important information about how my students are feeling about reading, learning, life in general, and what, if anything, I can do to assist them during classroom instructional activities.

Student Reflections

At the end of the term, as part of their final examinations, students are asked to comment on the value of writing in their learning logs throughout the semester. Following is a sample of these comments.

> These learning logs helped me a lot. They especially helped me in sociology. They helped me because I would read a little and then I would go back and write about what I had just read. It helped me comprehend what I was reading. (Trina, age 18, TRIO Program Student)

> The main value of the learning logs for me was that they gave me a source of reflective release and this is very important for my well-being. (John, age 21, Army veteran, probationary admit)

> I think learning logs helped me a lot. It's a way to put your feelings about your reading and personal ailments down on paper. This helps to clear your head. Also, if you don't understand something, you can express the frustration you feel. Your comments help also. They help me because I wouldn't normally do some of the things that you picked upon in my learning logs. You told me to try to make a chart for something I read and I did. This was much easier than trying to memorize it. (Lisa, age 18, regular admit)

Conclusion

As an educator, I am excited to have found a tool that students can use throughout their lives to increase what they learn and to feel better about their efforts. Learning logs have enormous potential for helping students develop the metacognitive awareness and strategies necessary to improve their understanding and retention of what they read. They also can improve their affective responses to these tasks.

REFERENCES

Alvermann, D.E., & Phelps, S.E. (1994). *Content reading and literacy: Succeeding in today's diverse classrooms.* Boston: Allyn & Bacon.

Andrews, S.E. (1997). Writing to learn in content area reading class. *Journal of Adolescent & Adult Literacy, 41,* 141–142.

Collins, J. (1997). The learning executive. *Inc., 19*(8), 35–36.

Harris, T.L., & Hodges, R.E. (Eds.). (1995). *The literacy dictionary: The vocabulary of reading and writing.* Newark, DE: International Reading Association.

Soldner, L.B. (1997). Self-assessment and the reflective reader. *Journal of College Reading and Learning, 28*(1), 5–11.

Enriching the Developmental Teaching and Learning Environment With Portfolio Assessment

Martha E. Casazza

The purpose of this paper is to describe a developmental literacy program that includes portfolio assessment as one of its critical components. Benefits as well as problems of program conceptualization and change are addressed. In addition, the potential impact of portfolios on faculty evaluation practices is discussed.

Background

Traditionally, portfolios in higher education have been viewed through the narrow lens of having students assemble their best work in order to be evaluated either for employment or for exit from a program of study, usually in the area of fine arts. Gradually, they have come to have broader application. They are now used increasingly to assess many areas of school learning. Currently, one third of the colleges and universities in the United States use portfolios (Aitken, 1993). As portfolios have been implemented across the curriculum, the definition has been elaborated to describe a process with specific criteria. One such definition has been proposed by Paulson, Paulson, and Meyer (1991):

> A portfolio is a purposeful collection of student work that exhibits the student's efforts, progress, and achievements in one or more areas. The collection must include student participation in selecting contents, the criteria for selection, the criteria for judging merit, and evidence of student self-reflection. (p. 60)

From this definition, it is evident that portfolios are no longer simply end products that represent the final stages of student achievement. They can include work that represents the final stages of student achievement. They can include work that represents effort and progress

Originally published in Forum for Reading *(1995–1996), volume 26, pages 1–24*

throughout the academic term. They also allow instruction and assessment to intersect (Paulson, Paulson, & Meyer). Through the self-reflection that the process requires from students, it provides the opportunity for them to become more independent and self-directed. These features of portfolio assessment can help to facilitate the significant instructional goals in most developmental studies programs.

Wulfhorst (1992) reinforces this notion by suggesting that portfolio assessment is much more than a file; she describes it as a whole learning environment. Compared to standardized tests that attempt to measure achievement in a single performance, portfolios provide an overview of the entire learning process. Students see the purpose, and they learn how to learn as they critically reflect on their development through the construction of a portfolio. Indeed, the portfolio is done *by* the student rather than *to* the student as in traditional assessment. Through this process, the students learn to value themselves as learners (Paulson, Paulson, & Meyer, 1991).

Aitken (1993) contends that by engaging in a portfolio process, students increase their level of self-esteem as well as their level of skill development. Since the process requires ongoing reflection and self-evaluation, students become more aware of where their skills are weak and where they need to improve. They become capable of assessing both their cognitive and metacognitive areas of development (Zhang, 1993). By asking the students to decide what to include in their portfolios, the responsibility for learning is clearly theirs.

In addition to placing much of the responsibility on the learner, portfolios also foster a sense of collaboration. Students and instructors collaborate to assess progress. Elbow suggests (in Belanoff & Dickson, 1991) that portfolios serve as an invitation for students and teachers to become allies and thus reduce the traditional adversarial dimension of evaluation. Also, teachers within a department can collaborate with one another to discuss criteria for content and to evaluate the final work. This process of developing the portfolio itself requires the faculty to discuss its goals and philosophy (Black, 1993). Furthermore, Belanoff (in Belanoff & Dickson) argues that when portfolios are graded collaboratively by instructors, each one becomes more aware of the community standards and as a consequence awards grades more fairly.

Simpson and Nist (1992) argue that college reading programs are enhanced when assessment models are adopted which reflect the goals and philosophy of the program. They suggest that a comprehensive model of assessment should be an integral part of the instructional process and one that empowers both the students and the instructors. In addition, the model should include measures for evaluation that apply across texts and tasks and represent various types of processing. They offer two other recommendations—that students be involved in their own evaluation, and that testing for the sake of testing should be avoided. These general suggestions from Simpson and Nist provide the very foundations of portfolio assessment: (a) Involve the students; (b) provide an intersection with instruction; (c) include a range of activities; and (d) avoid assessment that is simply tacked on to the end of coursework.

If reading is defined as an interactive and constructive process, then standardized tests that are objective and timed must be refuted (Valeri-Gold, Osson, & Deming, 1992). With traditional standardized reading tests, students respond with short answers which require lower level cognitive thinking; this leaves little opportunity to develop higher order thinking skills (Zhang, 1993). The determination of which model of assessment to use must be based on its relevance to the instructional goals and objectives. The assessment tool must be a good model for instruction rather than simply an indicator of final achievement (Reckase, 1993).

Zhang, who contends that portfolios bridge the gap between teacher-centered assessment and the actual student learning, suggests four steps for instructors to keep in mind when using portfolios: (a) state goals clearly at the beginning of the process; (b) model and participate throughout the entire process; (c) encourage regular self-evaluation; and (d) invite students to provide a self-evaluation at the end of the term.

As a result of a survey of reading professionals, Johns and Van Leirsburg (1992) discovered that even though the respondents felt that there were practical problems associated with portfolio management, the integrity and validity of this approach to assessment outweighed those problems. Survey data indicated that 70% of those responding believed that authenticity should be the anchor of reading assessment; 96% of the respondents felt that assessment should be continuous and ongoing; and 84% thought assessment should represent an active and collaborative reflection of student progress by both the instructor and the student.

Our Reading Program

Our university with its many campus locations serves an extremely diverse student population. Its students range from recent high school graduates to returning adults who have not been in school for many years to nonnative speakers who are receiving intensive English language training at the university. Students come from both suburban and urban backgrounds. They also represent a multitude of ethnic, cultural, and economic groups.

The reading program must meet the needs of this wide range of learners. Students are placed into the two-term curriculum on the basis of scores earned at or below a score of 70 on the Degrees of Reading Power (DRP) Test. This test is administered to all new students. Placement into our program courses on the basis of scores earned on this test is mandatory. Students attend classes once a week for two hours over two ten-week terms. At our institution, all developmental classes are kept small by limiting enrollment to a maximum of 15 students. The reading coursework has been divided into two terms. All students are expected to complete both terms. The grading options include P (pass), X (continue), and N (not pass). The X grade is used at the end of the first term to indicate successful completion of that component and to signal the need to continue into the second term.

The curriculum is based on Rosenblatt's transactional theory of reading (Rosenblatt, 1994) which emphasizes the active role of the reader. The primary goals are to promote critical thinking, comprehension monitoring, and the integration of reading with writing. To these ends, the instruction is not built around mastering a sequence of discrete skills, but rather around developing a repertoire of strategies that will transfer across the curriculum. These strategies include outlining, mapping, summarizing, and writing critiques of expository text.

The course is periodical based with students and instructors building the text as the terms proceed. Students are required to find articles each week in news periodicals during the first term and in discipline-related periodicals during the second term. This is intended, in part, to increase overall comprehension by building and organizing student schemata in current events and their major field of study.

Why We Changed Our Assessment Process

Several years ago, our faculty adopted the following statement as the foundation for its philosophy of assessment:

> We view assessment as an integral part of our instruction, providing a process for teachers and students to use to guide learning. It is an expanded definition of assessment in which a wide variety of indicators of learning are gathered across many situations before, during, and

after instruction. It is a philosophy that honors both the process and the products of learning as well as the active participation of the teacher and the students in their own evaluation and growth.

Even though this description was adapted from an article on portfolio assessment by Valencia (1990), it did not occur to us at the time to change our process. The assessment process that we had in place reflected the perspective expressed in this statement. We had always viewed student assessment as an integral part of our instruction; indeed, from the initial placement test to the preassessment administered during the first class session, we had always shared the results with students. In class, the preassessment became the first learning activity as the instructor facilitated a process of reviewing with the class their responses and how they might be revised.

We had also built into the curriculum a variety of indicators by which to measure student learning. Not only did we evaluate performance with informal pre- and postassessment measures, but we also administered another form of the standardized placement test at the end of the reading coursework. We continuously reflected on student progress and shared our thoughts with the students. Extensive comments were returned on assignments at every class session. In addition, midquarter conferencing with each student was built into the curriculum.

By adhering to the methods described above, the faculty felt certain that it was honoring both the process and the products of learning. It was only when the last phase of the statement caught our attention that we decided there was something missing. We wondered if we were really facilitating "the active participation of the teacher and the students in their own evaluation and growth." We acknowledged that the teachers were clearly actively involved in the process, but the students were not.

Many of the components of a portfolio approach were already in place in our reading program. What we needed to do was to involve the students more formally in the process and to clearly articulate to them what it was all about. They would have to change their own understanding of what assessment meant; their previous experiences most likely reflected a top-down, teacher-in-control method. Murname (1993) suggests that portfolio development includes a significant metacognitive component; in order to construct a portfolio, students must monitor their learning and ask themselves questions such as, "What do I know?" and "What do I need to know?" We determined that we would have to train our students to ask these questions and to assume more of the responsibility for the answers.

Student monitoring had always been one of our goals in the reading program. Our developmental reading curriculum had been designed to teach students that reading is a transactional process, and that in order to be successful readers they would need to learn to monitor their own comprehension. Two of the most significant learning objectives for the course included strategies for self-evaluation and self-regulation of comprehension. We were already providing direct instruction to students about how to take charge of their reading comprehension. We concluded that the use of portfolios would enrich student reading and enable them to apply the strategies learned in this whole learning process framework.

Valencia (1990) reinforced the fit we saw between the principles underlying our reading curriculum and those defining portfolio assessment. She suggested four guiding principles which support the portfolio approach. First, there is the issue of *authenticity*. She argued that we should assess students as they read in meaningful and variable situations. Authentic assessment provides the opportunity to truly integrate assessment with instruction. Valencia's second principle relates to emphasizing *assessment as a continuous, ongoing process*. When students are required to collect samples of their work during the quarter, the process of collection forces them to reflect on their progress, regularly and over a period of time.

The third principle underlying portfolios reminded us that since reading is a multifaceted process any attempt to measure it must also be *multidimensional*. No assessment tool, no matter how authentic it is, can provide an accurate gauge of what a student has achieved over the duration of an academic term. A single test is not likely to reveal a student's range of development in areas such as motivation, metacognitive strategies, or choice of reading materials. The fourth principle emphasized the significance of the *collaborative reflection* that is so integral to the portfolio process. Both the instructor and the student are able to use the process to assess themselves. The instructor is able to see the effectiveness of instruction at various stages, and the student can assess personal strengths and take responsibility for the learning that is still needed.

As instructors begin to reflect on the effectiveness of instruction through the portfolio, they may become aware of the values on which the curriculum is built. This type of reflection not only creates more thoughtful teaching, but it can build a stronger sense of community among teachers as they meet each term to read and discuss the student portfolios (Hamp-Lyons & Condon, 1993). This process of shared reflection and discussion leads to a greater involvement from everyone responsible for teaching as full-time and part-time faculty engage in dialogue in order to review the work of the students.

This increase in collaboration between all members of the instructional team brought benefits that we had not anticipated. Our department had always been frustrated by the lack of time we could devote to curriculum discussions; professional dialogue was always on the agenda, but was discussed after the more routine, administrative concerns. In addition, we wanted to involve the part-time instructors in a more meaningful way. With the portfolio approach to assessment, we suddenly had the forum that had been missing. At the end of each academic quarter, the entire staff of reading instructors met to read and discuss the portfolios of each student. During these half-day meetings, instructors became advocates for students and for various components of the reading curriculum. It became necessary to articulate those parts of the instruction which were the most important and why. This need to articulate points of view and to provide backup data from classroom experiences promoted a constant review of curricular assumptions and also increased the sense of ownership and commitment to the program on the part of all instructors.

In addition to the instructors' heightened sense of responsibility to the reading curriculum, we wanted to ensure that the students were assuming more responsibility for learning. To further this idea, we considered the benefits of different types of portfolios. Murname (1993) suggests that there are two types of portfolios: developmental and representational. A developmental portfolio, most likely to be found in a writing classroom, contains drafts of work as well as the final products. On the other hand, a representational portfolio contains work that exemplifies the best of a student's work.

We developed a portfolio that combines elements from both the developmental and representational approach. Our reading students are asked to include in the portfolio assignments that demonstrate progress in a particular area. For example, if a student has difficulty at the beginning of the term distinguishing the main idea from supporting details, that student should review the assignments and include those that show progress being made in this area. Thus, both works in progress and final best products are included. By directing this kind of self-evaluation, the portfolio provides the opportunity for students to "reflect upon and celebrate their effort, progress and improvement" (Murname, 1993, p. 2).

How Our Program Works

To begin, we decided to pilot the portfolio process in only two sections of our developmental reading course. By limiting the number of classes involved, we thought that we could more easily see the problems and refine the process. It was important to involve two sections rather than one in order to have two instructors for the team review process at the end of the quarter. Also, two instructors were needed to document the benefits brought on by the new dialogue regarding the reading program and its students.

The first step was to clearly articulate the portfolio concept in the syllabus that the students would receive during the first class meeting. To do this, we added one sentence to the basic course goal that had always appeared on the first page of the syllabus. The new sentence is underlined in the text below:

> The students will develop reading and study skills that will enable them to learn more efficiently and more effectively across the college curriculum. They will also monitor and confirm their progress by organizing a selected collection of their work. In addition, students will become familiar with and seek a solution to a contemporary problem through weekly periodical readings.

As students review the syllabus, the instructor points out the course goal and asks that they put it into their own words for the class. This leads to a discussion of the course content as well as the method of assessment. From the start then, students see assessment as an integral part of the course, closely linked to instruction and learning.

On page two of the syllabus we added a section describing the course assessment. The description is as follows:

> Students will choose which pieces of work will be submitted for the final reading grade. The work should be representative of the progress the student has made during the quarter. Student work should be organized in a folder that will be turned in at the end of the quarter. The folder will include a cover sheet in which the students describe their progress in reading.

The following categories of work must be included in the final folder:

Quizzes—at least one weekly quiz

Periodical Readings—at least three completed forms and the end-of-term paper

Class Assignments—at least one assignment

Application Outside of Class—at least one from another content course or interest area

Vocabulary—at least five new words

The course assessment section serves as an outline of how the process will work. It sets the stage for a continuous dialogue with the students during the entire term. There may not even be too many questions during the first class. Portfolio assessment is such a new concept to students that they do not know what questions to ask. Initially, the responsibility lies with the instructor to regularly point out assignments that students might want to include in their folders. A written note on a returned assignment or a comment made in class often serves as a reminder to the students that they should be continuously reviewing their work for possible inclusion in their portfolio folder. Gradually, students assume the responsibility for choosing appropriate work.

While the syllabus description of the process may not seem clear initially to students, it does contain several important elements. First, it asks students to decide which assignments best represent their progress. This forces them to acknowledge their weaknesses and to monitor their development in these areas. Second, it gives students a choice, but within a framework. The instructor sets the categories and the amount of work from each area that is required. This increases the student's awareness of the major components in the course and helps them to set priorities for their learning. Last, it requires the students to articulate the achievements they have made by asking for a cover sheet in which they describe their progress.

One final section on the syllabus is labeled "Final Grade" and reads as follows: The final grade will be determined from the final "portfolio" of work that is turned in by the student in addition to the instructor's assessment of the student's participation and attendance. This acknowledges the collaborative nature of the assessment process, and provides the instructor with an opportunity to include additional criteria not easily represented in a portfolio.

The Portfolio Review Process

At the second to the last class session of the academic term, students submit their portfolio folders. An emphasis is placed on organization and neatness. The students take pride in designing a title page and a typed cover sheet that describes their overall progress. The required representative assignments are organized by category and are submitted exactly as they were initially completed.

When the instructor receives the portfolios, a Review and Evaluation Sheet is attached to the front of each one. This sheet remains with the portfolio, which is filed in the reading coordinator's office, until the student completes both of the required reading courses. The sheet outlines the criteria for evaluation and provides a rating scale from one to five for each of the four components.

The first three components are identical for the Reading I and Reading II courses. The components are content, format, and basic comprehension. **Content** itemizes the assignments that must be included in the portfolio and serves as a checklist for the instructor in a preliminary overview. It is evaluated on the basis of completeness. Even though each assignment is listed separately, one overall score is given for this category. For example, if a student has provided all the assignments, a total score of 5 is given; if only half of the work has been provided, a 3 may be awarded.

Format measures how well the contents have been organized. Here, the instructor looks for various organizational aids such as a title page, cover sheet, and table of contents. In addition, neatness and clarity are important. The title page and cover sheet should be typed, and the contents should be clearly arranged in a folder that is easy to read. These expectations are communicated to the students before the end of the quarter. They are significant since many of our developmental students have problems with organization. This becomes an instructional component in itself as students may be hearing for the first time that clarity and neatness may be important for their success in other courses. Frequently, they are confused by the requirement for typed introductory pages. However, in a class that incorporates strategies for success in other courses, this is important.

The third component, **basic comprehension**, is included for both reading courses but measured using different types of text. The descriptor for Reading I, news periodicals, indicates that the instructor will be evaluating the student's development of basic comprehension through the outlines they have provided for articles found in sources such as *Newsweek*, *Time*, and *U.S. News and World Report*. For Reading II, basic comprehension is evaluated through summaries and critiques included for articles found in more focused journals such as *Journal of Reading* or

Journal of Adolescent & Adult Literacy, *Psychology Today*, and *Database* depending on the student's program of study.

The fourth category provides the opportunity to evaluate the component that provides the major focus for each reading course. For Reading I that focus is **study strategies**. For Reading II, **critical analysis** of text. To determine a score for this category, the instructor reviews the student's work for overall development in these two areas. For example, in Reading I a score of 5 would be given to the student who has developed a strategy of outlining or mapping an article to the point where it is apparent that the student can distinguish major ideas from details, organize them clearly, and recognize the author's organizational pattern. In Reading II, the ultimate goal shifts from this literal organization of text to a critical analysis of more difficult material. To achieve a score of 5, the students must demonstrate through summaries and critiques that they comprehend text. In addition, they must demonstrate that they can comment appropriately on the author's background, any apparent bias, the adequacy of supporting material, and the author's purpose.

After completing the initial review, the instructor records the number of points out of the possible score of 20 that the student has earned. Additional comments that may be appropriate are also recorded. These are frequently useful when the review team meets to discuss the portfolios.

This initial instructor evaluation must be completed in a timely manner to ensure that the portfolios are ready for the review team meeting. The whole team needs to meet before the final class sessions so that the results can be tabulated and shared with the students individually at their end-of-quarter conferences. To ensure that this will happen, the team meeting is usually scheduled at the start of the quarter so everyone knows exactly when their initial reviews must be completed and when they will have their half-day session(s).

The team review process differs for the two reading courses. This is due to the nature of the overall reading program. For those students required to take reading, both Reading I and Reading II must be completed. The grade most frequently given following Reading I is "X"—which means that the student is progressing satisfactorily but has not yet completed the reading curriculum. It is not until they have completed Reading II with a passing grade that the reading team feels confident that the students have a strong repertoire of comprehension strategies that will enable them to succeed in more advanced college coursework.

This reading curriculum design provides the rationale for the composition of the review teams at the end of the quarter. Following Reading I, team members include all reading instructors, full time and part time, from all campuses. The decision to be made at this point is to determine if a student is to move on to Reading II or to continue work in Reading I. This decision is best made by the developmental studies professionals who have knowledge and experience in the area of reading instruction. However, at the end of Reading II, a different kind of decision is made. The team determines if a student is ready to successfully engage in the reading activities of courses outside the developmental studies department. At this point, a faculty member from outside the department is included in the process. Outside involvement is helpful for several reasons. First, it keeps the reading staff in touch with the requirements of the coursework for which it is preparing the developmental students. Second, it informs the faculty outside the department of the strategies and rigorous requirements of the reading coursework.

Although the composition of the review teams differs, the process remains nearly the same. The team meets for half a day noting the initial individual portfolio reviews conducted by each instructor. Each portfolio is reviewed individually by all team members who are assembled together and provided with a listing of all the students. For each student on the list, the team member indicates a plus (+) sign for satisfactory progress or a minus (-) sign for unsatisfactory progress. In addition, comments may be added for subsequent discussion.

When everyone has had the opportunity to review all portfolios and make notations on their list of students, the discussion begins. The reading coordinator facilitates the process as each portfolio is orally reviewed. The students' instructors often serve to clarify any confusions or to add information that may be appropriate to the individual student. The discussion continues until a consensus is reached for each student. At this point, the instructor is responsible for completing a final review and evaluation sheet, attaching it to the student portfolio, and sharing the results with the student at the final conference. Following the student-instructor conference, the portfolios are copied and filed alphabetically in the reading coordinator's office. The original folder is returned to the student.

Reliability, Validity, and Other Factors

Enthusiasts for the portfolio process frequently do not discuss its technical foundations. Indeed, they are often reacting against traditional, standardized measures and simply assume that the portfolio has validity due to its authentic foundation (Calfee & Perfumo, 1993). When criteria that have been traditionally used to evaluate assessment measures are applied to the portfolio assessment process, the process appears to rank highly.

The first criterion, reliability, is associated with consistency of results. It raises questions about whether or not the results of an assessment are predictable, dependable, stable, and accurate. Reliability is most often compromised in assessment situations by factors such as insufficient length, embedded ambiguities, or careless administration (Guba & Lincoln, 1989). Since portfolio assessment does not rely on a one-time administration process, growth and development are measured over a period of time. Reliability of the process may not be in serious question as in more traditional assessment processes. Reliability is controlled in our program through the standardization of the process and content across classes. Each term, all students work within the same portfolio framework regardless of instructor or class section. In addition, the team review enhances the consistency of results and reduces individual instructor bias. Even though the instructor makes the final decision regarding a student's grade, each portfolio is evaluated and discussed by the entire faculty in the department. This tends to distance the instructor from individual students and, consequently, increase objectivity.

Another important criterion generally applied to assessment measures is validity. This refers to whether or not an assessment is measuring what it purports to measure. In our case, we want to measure reading comprehension. If we consider construct validity, the fit between the measure and the conceptual base of what is being measured, we find that the portfolio is very effective. The work assigned in the reading classes reflects our department's concept of what reading comprehension is. It is the work itself, not a representation of it, that is evaluated through the portfolio. Thus, the portfolio fits well when viewed through this lens.

Content validity is also important. Since the portfolio contains a range of authentic work from the course, and since the course itself relies on real text which mirrors what students are likely to read in advanced college classes rather than artificial text written only for instructional purposes, our process reflects content validity. The fact that construction of meaning from a wide range of meaningful material is also a part of the process strengthens its content validity.

Another type of validity is that which addresses the ability of assessment to predict success in future performance. A major goal of the reading curriculum is to provide strategies that will transfer to other courses and facilitate student success. The assignments are all based on the integration of skills using relevant text. Few assignments focus on discrete skills or artificial readings. Consequently, when students complete the reading assignments, they are using the strategies that are required for success in the more advanced courses. Success with these assignments should facilitate success in future courses. By reviewing the students' progress in such assignments and by listening to an outside faculty member comment on probable success beyond the reading course, the criterion of predictive validity seems to be well met by the portfolio process.

Other criteria are also addressed. Test fairness is one that is often considered when evaluating assessments. In the case of our reading program, students select their own articles based on interest and often prior knowledge. Thus, the issue of item or test bias has been virtually eliminated. Finally, student anxiety and motivation are also controlled in the portfolio process due to the self-selection of material to be included for review.

Summary

The use of portfolio assessment in our reading program has enriched our teaching and learning environment. It has increased the amount of professional discussion among all our reading instructors. As a consequence, the level of collegiality has grown with materials and methods being shared more regularly. The goals and specific objectives of the reading curriculum have come under regular scrutiny. This scrutiny has led to a greater understanding of its overall purpose.

In addition, the review process has provided an excellent staff development opportunity for part-time instructors. Before implementation of the portfolio process, the interaction between the full-time and part-time staff had been limited to one meeting per term where logistical concerns always had priority over discussions related to the philosophy of reading. With a better understanding of the philosophy that guides the program, part-time instructors become more involved in the entire instructional process and are more willing to develop their own materials and strategies.

Students have become more capable of evaluating their own work. This increased ability to evaluate their own learning has led them into a partnership with the instructor. Not only do they become more interested in understanding the instructor's comments on their work, but they ask more questions related to their work. As they begin to take responsibility for their learning, they have an immediate need for this feedback which leads to a genuinely active learning environment in the classroom.

Another benefit of the process is that faculty from outside the department are gaining a new perspective on the reading faculty and the students they will teach. They see firsthand that the requirements for developmental reading reflect their own high standards. They also begin to understand that reading is a multifaceted, cognitive process. We hope that this new understanding will lead to a rethinking of their reading assignments and an integration of reading instruction within their own coursework.

Department faculty will continue to refine its portfolio approach to assessment. The end of the term review is a component that needs additional scrutiny. More training for all instructors in the evaluation of student work may be scheduled. The criteria will be examined to ensure that they are defined clearly for both students and faculty. Perhaps the development of a written rubric that describes specifically the quality of work expected for each score would be helpful. However, any refinements made to the assessment process will be within the framework of portfolios. For a reading curriculum based on the construction of meaning through individually relevant text, it seems to be the most authentic measure of achievement.

REFERENCES

Aitken, J.E. (1993). *Empowering students and faculty through portfolio assessment.* Paper presented at the annual meeting of the Central States Communication Association, Lexington, KY. (ERIC Document Reproduction Service No. ED 355 599)

Belanoff, P., & Dickson, M. (Eds.). (1991). *Portfolios: Process and product.* Portsmouth, NH: Boynton/Cook Heinmann.

Black, L.C. (1993). Portfolio assessment. In T.W. Banta & Associates (Eds.), *Making a difference* (pp. 139–150). San Francisco: Jossey-Bass.

Calfee, R.C., & Perfumo, P. (1993). Student portfolios: Opportunities for a revolution in assessment. *Journal of Reading, 36*(7), 532–537.

Guba, E.G., & Lincoln, Y. (1989). *Fourth generation evaluation.* Newbury Park, CA: Sage.

Hamp-Lyons, L., & Condon, W. (1993). Questioning assumptions about portfolio-based assessment. *College Composition and Communication, 44*(2), 176–190.

Johns, J.L., & Van Leirsburg, P. (1992). How professionals view portfolio assessment. *Reading Research and Instruction, 32*(1), 1–10.

Murname, Y. (1993). Good grading student portfolios: A primer. *The National Teaching and Learning Forum, 3*(2), 1–4.

Paulson, L.F., Paulson, P.R., & Meyer, C.A. (1991). What makes a portfolio a portfolio? *Educational Leadership, 48*(5), 60–63.

Reckase, M.D. (1993). *Portfolio assessment A theoretical prediction of measurement properties.* Paper presented at the annual meeting of the American Educational Research Association, Atlanta, GA. (ERIC Document Reproduction Service No. ED358138)

Rosenblatt, L. (1994). The transactional model of reading. In R.B. Ruddell, M.R. Ruddell, & H. Singer (Eds.), *Theoretical models and processes of reading* (4th ed., pp. 1057–1092). Newark, DE: International Reading Association.

Simpson, M.L., & Nist, S.L. (1992). Toward defining a comprehensive assessment model for college reading. *Journal of Reading, 35*(6), 452–458.

Valencia, S. (1990). A portfolio approach to classroom reading assessment: The whys, whats and hows. *The Reading Teacher, 43,* 338–340.

Valeri-Gold, M., Osson, J.R., & Deming, M.P. (1992). Portfolios: Collaborative authentic assessment opportunities for college developmental learners. *Journal of Reading, 35*(4), 298–305.

Wulfhorst, C. (1992). Portfolio assessment as an evaluation tool. *Journal of the Ohio Association of Two-Year Colleges, 18*(1), 14–16.

Zhang, J. (1993). *Portfolio assessment as a reflection of transactive learning: The college developmental reading classes* (1993 collection of articles on academic and administrative issues facing SUNY's community colleges). (ERIC Document Reproduction Service No. ED 355 986)

Afterword

As current editor of *The Journal of College Literacy and Learning*, this opportunity to look back at articles from *Forum for Reading* and those under the present journal title have helped me to appreciate the variety of perspectives reflected in the work done by contributors to this volume. Each area (theoretical issues, research, and programs and strategy descriptions) addresses these perspectives. From Kingston's history of the field, to Valeri-Gold and Commander's sexism research, to O'Dell and Craig's multidisciplinary-based strategy for previewing text, I note varied perspectives. Each scholarly contribution presented here has added to the richness of the volume and to the profession's growing body of work, for those who are experienced or new to the field. The writers of the articles function in varied roles, such as English teachers, reading or writing specialists, learning skills counselors, language instructors, and psychologists. However, even with the diversity of roles and perspectives represented here, contributors to this volume share a key characteristic: They have played a part in addressing the needs of students who struggle to read, write, and learn in college.

Readers of an afterword are likely to expect some discussion about future trends. As I reread the articles included here, I was reminded of a point that Bruce (2001) makes in an article about the history of learning technologies. He argues that we create our ideas about the future from our "present realities" (p. 730). My own present realities are shaped by my experience as a scholar and reading specialist who has responsibility for preparing teachers at all levels as well as a strong interest in how challenged readers and writers survive the academic rigors of college course requirements. Participation in the preparation of this volume led me to reexamine my present realities and to make the following speculations about future trends in college literacy and learning.

• *Increasing acknowledgment of the contribution of various disciplines to better inform theory, research, and practice*—A cursory review of scholarly journals reveals a growing number of studies done by scholars who collaborate across disciplines to address problems and questions. For example, neuroscience has contributed brain research that holds promise for understanding comprehension; studies in artificial intelligence and cognitive psychology have helped us to link metacognitive behavior and study skills; and psycho- and sociolinguistics have made it easier to provide sensitive and effective instruction to language and culturally different learners. Theorists, researchers, and practitioners who situate the problems they study in a context that reaches across disciplines will bring increased understanding to the issues important to the field.

• *Increasingly closer relationships between research and practice by combining the most effective qualitative and quantitative methods to address key questions and problems*—There appears to be an increasing awareness that phenomena worth the effort of systematic study are so complex that responsible investigation requires the use of both qualitative and quantitative methods. One present reality is the emergence of self-reflective inquiry that takes the context of the questions under study into account. Classrooms and other settings where literacy instruction takes place are richly described in addition to relevant characteristics of each stake-holding group. Studies that exemplify the most disciplined, systematic study of issues while providing the fullest information needed to understand reading, writing, and learning can be conducted in light of what is currently known. Described by some as action research, this marriage of two traditions can enhance our efforts to address the problems in the field of literacy.

• *Increased and broader use of technology to embrace new and emerging literacies*—Rapidly changing refinements in computer technology is another present reality that has significant implications for the future. Currently, to be minimally prepared to function in an academic setting, students, faculty, and staff at educational institutions must be able to use word processors, e-mail, and the Internet. In addition, the most productive people in educational settings use computers and related technology for academic and other informational purposes to accomplish more of their objectives. This trend is likely to continue. Further, technological advances have made (and will continue to make) more information available than ever before. The efficient management of vast networks of information will require an increased effort to teach students to be selective and critical readers. Computer capability has already made it possible to hold discussions across space and time, offer a single instructional session for participants anywhere in the world, provide skill and practice with feedback, simulate experiences for learning through problem solving, and assess levels of achievement. Each of these capabilities can play a role in helping students become more literate. Online literacy development courses, CD-ROM and disk-based textbooks, and increasingly sophisticated distance learning options are changing the face of what we now know as college instruction. Face-to-face teaching and learning opportunities are likely to decrease but not totally disappear. Learning through some form of electronic means is likely to increase.

• *Rethinking of the purposes of higher education in view of the impact of technology*—The tension between an education-for-education's-sake approach and an education-for-pragmatic-purposes approach is not a new reality in higher education. Institutional self-studies almost always reflect a reexamination of purpose or mission. In an age of change and restructuring fueled by technological advances, faculty and administrators have been challenged to revisit traditional assumptions made about their institution's role. Many have closed or severely limited programs that address needs of underprepared students. Encouraged by arguments that those needs can be effectively managed in secondary schools, they turn their attention to those students whose academic acumen bring their colleges and universities attention for attracting the most capable students. Decision makers in universities who only recruit high-achieving students and assume that they need no academic assistance may miss out on opportunities to keep developmental programs close and available for study by collaborative teams of researchers from related fields and those experienced in literacy development. The extent to which this collaboration becomes a present reality will likely predict a future of increased understanding and acceptance of programs that assist students at all levels of achievement in college literacy and learning.

In conclusion, articles in this volume reflect the thinking and work of individuals who represent diverse points of view, roles, and disciplines as they address the literacy requirements and needs of college students. Future trends in the field are likely to involve theorists, researchers, and practitioners whose work increase in rigor as they benefit from (a) the collaborative efforts of multidisciplinary teams, (b) studies that use methods to provide increasingly greater depth and breadth of information to enhance student learning, (c) increased and more varied use of emerging technology, and (d) the rethinking of the purpose of higher education and the place of literacy instruction and learning in postsecondary institutions.

Shirley A. Biggs
University of Pittsburgh
Pittsburgh, Pennsylvania, USA

REFERENCE

Bruce, B.C. (2001). Constructing a once-and-future history of learning technologies. *Journal of Adolescent & Adult Literacy*, 44, 730–736.

Author Index

A

ACKERMAN, B.P., 262
AFFLERBACH, P.P., 133
AITKEN, J.E., 286, 287
AKER, D., 276
ALEXANDER, J.E., 170
ALEXANDER, P., 25, 66
ALLEY, G.R., 26
ALVERMANN, D.E., 248, 281
AMERICAN PSYCHOLOGICAL
   ASSOCIATION, 172
ANDERSON, J., 24
ANDERSON, R.C., 24, 88, 111,
   112, 131, 133, 161, 275
ANDERSON, T.H., 20, 25, 68, 69,
   77, 102, 103, 113, 114,
   115, 223, 225, 236
ANDERSON-INMAN, L., 211
ANDRE, M.E., 25, 223, 225
ANDREWS, S.E., 280
ANGELOU, M., 94
ANNIS, L., 68
APPLEYARD, J.A., 32
ARMBRUSTER, B.B., 68, 69, 102,
   103, 113, 114, 115, 118,
   209, 236, 249
ASHTON, P.J., 149, 150, 151, 152
ATKINSON, R., 197
ATKINSON, T.R., 127
ATWELL, N., 90, 96
AUGUST, D.L., 262
AUGUST, G.J., 69
AUKERMAN, R.C., 220

B

BAKER, L., 19, 20, 23, 24, 69, 118,
   225, 249
BALDWIN, R.S., 235, 239
BALDWIN, S.R., 250
BARKER, A.S., 68
BARLETT, F.C., 133
BARNETT, J.E., 69
BARON, J., 170, 171, 173
BARR, J.E., 88
BARTHOLOMAE, D., 88, 89
BARTLETT, B.J., 72
BARTLETT, S., 68
BARTON, W.A., 113
BAUMANN, J.F., 70, 239
BEACH, R.W., 69, 126, 133
BEAN, T.W., 126, 130, 259
BELANOFF, P., 287
BENT, D.H., 156
BERN, D., 254
BERN, S., 254
BEST, J.W., 164
BICKEL, R., 177
BIDDLE, W.B., 131
BIGGS, J.B., 60, 61, 64, 274
BIGGS, S.A., 16, 71, 130, 184, 271
BLACK, L.C., 287
BLANCHARD, J., 211
BOOKER, I.A., 7
BOROWSKI, T., 35
BOUTWELL, M.A., 161
BOYLAN, H.R., 13
BRADDOCK, R., 70, 150, 239
BRANSFORD, J.D., 223, 226, 249
BRANTHWAITE, A., 68

BREMER, I., 170, 173, 174
BRENEMAN, D.W., 13
BRIDGE, C., 71
BRIDGES, C.W., 151
BRIDWELL, L., 126
BRITTON, B.K., 70
BRITTON, J., 96, 97
BROWN, A.L., 19, 20, 23, 24, 25, 26, 68, 69, 77, 118, 133, 138, 223, 225, 226, 228, 231, 249, 250, 262
BROWN, G., 142
BROWN, J., 23, 78, 206
BROZO, W., 276
BRUER, J., 205, 210
BRUFFEE, K.A., 48
BRUGGEN J.V. VAN, 113
BRUNER, J., 250
BURGESS, T., 96, 97
BURKE, C., 77, 79
BURKE, M., 184
BUSCEMI, S.V., 90, 94
BUSWELL, G.T., 7

C

CAINE, G., 207
CAINE, R., 207
CALFEE, R.C., 298
CAMPBELL, C., 137
CAMPIONE, J., 19, 24, 133, 223, 225, 228, 231
CAMSTRA, B., 113
CANNEY, G., 21
CARDILLICHIO, R., 211
CARRELL, P., 134, 142
CARRIULO, N., 14, 15
CASALE, U.,102, 115
CASAZZA, M.E., 13, 15

CAVERLY, D.C., 120, 124, 185, 248
CERA, J.J., 71
CHALL, E., 103, 236
CHAMBLISS, M.J., 133
CHASE, N.D., 259, 272, 273, 276, 277
CHIESI, H.L., 249
CHIPMAN, S.F., 60
CHIPPENDALE, E., 77
CLARK, E.G., 215
CLAY, M.M, 23
COCHRAN, J., 207
COLLES, B., 170
COLLINS, A., 23, 78
COLLINS, J., 281
COLLINS, K.W., 127
CONDON, W., 291
COWAN, S., 126, 130
CRAIK, F.I.M., 111, 112, 259
CRAIK, R.M., 61
CROSS, D., 19, 20, 26

D

DALE, E., 103, 236
D'ANGELO, K., 259
DANIS, F., 277
DANSAREAU, D.F., 113, 127
D'ANTONIO, W.V., 151
DAVIES, I.K., 131
DAVIES, J., 170, 173, 174
DAVIS, A., 215
DAVIS, F.B., 8
DAVIS, J.K., 68
DAVYDOV, V.V., 89
DAY, J., 19, 24, 25, 26, 77, 133, 138, 223, 225, 228, 231, 262
DEBRITTO, A.M., 19, 20, 26

DeFleur, L.B., 151
Delcourt, M.A.B., 178
Deming, M.P., 288
Dewey, J., 19
Dickson, M., 287
Dijk, T.A. van, 69, 70, 137
Dismukes, B.W., 170
DiVesta, F.J., 23, 68
Doctorow, M., 259
Donant, L., 259
Donley, J.A., 249
Dougherty, B.N., 151
Downey, R.G., 215
Downing, J., 170
Dudley-Marling, C., 89
Duell, O.K., 127, 130
Duignan, W.L., 15
Dwyer, E.J., 170

E

Eanet, M.G., 220, 260, 262
Ehrlich, P., 207
Elbow, P., 88, 287
Ellis, A.M., 127
Ellis, D., 252
Emig, J., 152
Entwhistle, N., 58, 59
Erickson, L.G., 26
Eskey, D., 134
Estes, T.H., 126, 130
Evans, S.H., 127

F

Farquhar, W.F., 215
Feathers, K.M., 118, 123
Field, M., 211
Fish, S., 272
Flavell, J.H., 20, 21, 77, 78, 223, 262

Fleischauer, J.P., 14
Flippo, R.F., 215
Flower, L.S., 126
Forrest, D., 21, 23
Fortune, R., 177
Fowler, R.L., 68
Frase, L.T., 127
Freedman, D.P., 36
Fry, E., 149, 150, 151, 236

G

Gagne, E.D., 115
Gallagher, M., 249, 250
Gambrell, L.B., 22, 226
Garner, R., 20, 21, 24, 25, 223
Gibbs, G., 60, 62, 63, 65, 66
Gilbert, S., 174
Gillingham, M., 211
Glaser, R., 60
Glover, J., 77
Glynn, S.M., 68, 70
Goetz, E.T., 66
Gold, M.V., 177
Golinkoff, R., 21
Goodlad, J., 235
Goodman, K., 77, 79, 89, 161
Goodman, Y., 161
Gordon, B., 215
Gordon, C.J., 69
Gordon, H., 197
Grabe, W., 134
Gray, W., 75
Green, F.L., 262
Green, S., 170
Greenewald, M.J., 118
Grinols, A.B., 254
Groff, P.J., 170, 173
Grotelueschen, A., 130

GUBA, E.G., 298
GULLETTE, M.M., 94

H

HAAGER, D.S., 236, 237, 239
HAARLOW, W.N., 13
HALL, C.H., 156
HALLIDAY, M.A.K., 138
HAMP-LYONS, L., 291
HARE, V.C., 23, 126
HARRIS, P.L., 262
HARRIS, T.L., 281
HARTLEY, G., 131
HARTLEY, J., 68
HASAN, R., 138
HAWES, K.S., 185
HAWISHER, G.E., 177
HAYES, C.G., 161
HAYES, D.A., 127, 260
HAYWARD, K.G., 23
HEAD, M.H., 250
HEATHINGTON, B.S., 22, 226
HIEBERT, E.H., 161
HILL, M., 133
HODGE, M.H., 70
HODGES, R.E., 281
HOGREBE, M.C., 68, 71
HOLLEY, C.D., 113
HOMEY, M., 211
HOUNSELL, D., 58
HUBERMAN, A.M., 91
HULL, G., 249
HUOT, B., 161
HYND, C.R., 259, 272, 273, 277

J

JACKSON, L.S., 170
JACOBS, J., 19, 20, 21, 26
JENKINS, J.G., 156

JENKINS, P., 77
JENSEN, E., 207, 210
JOHNS, J.L., 288
JOHNSON, L., 184
JOHNSTON, P., 26
JONES, R., 77, 133
JOYCE, M., 205

K

KAHN, J.V., 164
KAZEMEK, F., 271
KELLY, B.W., 115
KELLY, P.R., 170
KENNEAVY, J.L., 152
KING, J.R., 13, 71, 130
KINGSTON, A.J., 8
KINTSCH, W., 69, 70
KINZIE, M.C., 178
KIRBY, J., 21
KIRBY, K., 68, 69, 70
KIRKLAND, M.R., 134
KIRSCH, I.S., 13
KNUFER, N., 211
KONOPAK, J.P., 235, 240
KRAUS, C., 20, 21
KRUITHOF, A., 262
KRUMBOLTZ, J.D., 215

L

LANCASTER, M.B., 185
LANDOW, G.P., 210, 236
LARKIN, K.M., 23, 78
LAUER, J.M., 152
LEAVELL, A.G., 236, 237, 239
LEIRSBURG, P. VAN, 288
LEONARD, R., 170
LEY, T.C., 170
LINCOLN, Y., 298
LIOU, H.C., 177, 182

LIPSKY, S., 71, 130
LIPSON, M.Y., 19, 20, 26, 223, 232
LOCKE, E.Q., 24
LOCKHART, R.S., 61, 111, 112, 259
LONG, G.L., 127
LONGMAN, D., 197
LONGO, J.A., 149, 150, 151, 152
LOWE, N., 177
LUNSFORD, R.F., 151, 152

M

MACDONALD, L., 185
MANY, J., 273
MANZO, A.V., 26, 115, 215, 220, 260, 262
MARKMAN, E.M., 23, 262
MARKS, C., 259
MARSHALL, J.D., 161
MARTIN, C.E., 220
MARTIN, N., 96, 97
MÄRTON, F., 58, 59, 60, 61, 62
MATTHEWS, R., 207
MAXWELL, M., 14
MAYER, R.E., 238
MAZURKIEWICZ, A.J., 170, 171, 172, 173
MCCARTHY, S.A., 89
MCCLEARY, W., 89
MCCURDY, D.W., 91
MCDONALD, B.A., 127
MCGEE, L.M., 69
MCGINLEY, W., 89
MCGRAW, B., 130
MCISAAC, M., 211
MCLEOD, A., 96, 97
MCMILLAN, J., 13
MCNEIL, J., 259
MEALEY, D.L., 248

MEYER, B.J.F., 69, 70, 72
MEYER, C.A., 286, 287
MICKLER, M.J., 69
MIKULECKY, L., 118
MILES, M.B., 91
MOFFETT, C., 205
MOFFETT, J., 88, 94, 276
MONTAGUE, G., 152
MOORE, D.W., 118, 119, 151
MOORE, P.J., 19, 21
MORGAN, A., 60, 65
MULDOON, P., 276
MULLINS, C.J., 177
MURNAME, Y., 290, 291, 292
MURPHY, A.G., 118, 119
MURSELL, J.B., 7
MYERS, M., 20, 21, 22, 225

N

NAKADATE, N., 152
NAPOLI, A.R., 15
NEWEL, G., 273
NEWELL, G.E., 126
NICOLAUS, C., 77
NIE, N.H., 156
NIST, S.L., 68, 69, 70, 71, 235, 248, 287, 288

O

ODELL, L., 126, 260
O'FLAVAHAN, J.F., 89
O'HEAR, M.F., 149, 150, 151, 152
OKA, E., 19, 20, 26
OLLILA, L., 170
OLSHAVSKY, J.E., 225
ORLANDO, V.P., 23, 120, 248
ORNSTEIN, R., 207
OSMONT, P., 170
OSSON, J.R., 288

Ostertag, J., 69
Owings, R.A., 223, 226, 249

P

Padak, N., 271
Page, W.D., 126
Palincsar, A., 223, 226, 250
Palmatier, R.A., 215
Paris, S.G., 19, 20, 21, 22, 26,
   223, 225, 232
Pauk, W., 102, 105, 107
Paulson, L.F., 286, 287
Paulson, P.R., 286, 287
Pearson, P.D., 88, 133, 161, 249,
   250, 275
Pennsylvania State Assessment
   System, 164
Penrose, A.M., 249
Perfumo, P., 298
Perry, W.G., 71
Peterson, C., 184
Petrosky, A.R., 88, 89
Phelps, S.E., 281
Pherson, V.E., 149, 150, 151, 152
Platt, G.M., 184
Pobywajlo, M., 177
Popken, R.L., 149, 150, 151
Poulet, G., 32
Powers, S.M., 178
Pressey, L.C., 7
Price, C., 30, 36
Price, M., 273
Probst, R.E., 33, 273, 274
Pulliam, C., 23

R

Rachal, J.R., 170
Radebaugh, M., 271
Ramsey, R.N., 149, 150, 151

Raphael, T.E., 26, 89
Readence, J.E., 151, 235, 250
Reagan, S.B., 91
Reckase, M.D., 288
Reed, V., 170
Reis, R., 223
Rhodes, L.K., 89
Rickards, J.P., 68
Rinehart, S.D., 26
Robinson, F.P., 7, 9, 102, 105,
   106, 127, 215, 220, 225,
   240
Robinson, H.A., 7, 9
Robinson, R., 77
Robyak, J.E., 215
Rogers, B., 75
Rogers, T., 275
Rose, M., 249
Rosen, H., 96, 97
Rosenblatt, L.M., 95, 161, 272
Ross, G., 236, 250
Rothkopf, E.Z., 66
Rumelhart, D., 133, 134
Rye, J., 170, 173

S

Säljö, R., 60, 61, 62
Samuels, S.J., 71
Sanders, P.L., 126
Saunders, M.A., 134
Scales, A.M., 177, 184
Schaer, B.B., 170
Schallert, D.L., 118
Schatz, E.K., 239
Schatzberg-Smith, K., 161
Schellings, G.L., 134
Schenk, S.M., 62, 63, 65
Schmidt, P., 13
Schumm, J.S., 235, 236, 237, 239

SCHWARTZ, B.J., 127
SCOLL, J.A., 161
SEGAL, J.W., 60
SEGURA, D., 184
SERRA, J.K., 70, 239
SHANAHAN, T., 55, 89, 161
SHAPIRO, J., 170, 173
SHATTUCK, R., 15
SHELTON, T.S., 223, 226, 249
SHEPHERD, J.F., 197
SHERIDAN, D., 272, 275
SILVERMAN, S.L., 13, 15
SIMPSON, M.L., 235, 259, 287, 288
SINGER, H., 126, 130, 236
SMILEY, S.S., 25, 68, 225, 262
SMILKSTEIN, R., 207
SMITH, B., 273
SMITH, D.C., 23
SMITH, E.M., 26
SMITH, F.R., 118, 123
SMITH, H.K., 23
SMITH, S., 76, 216
SMITH-BURKE, M.T., 233
SOLDNER, L.B., 280, 281
SOTER, A., 89
SPANN, M., 201
SPEER, J.R., 262
SPILICH,, G.J., 249
SPIRES, H.A., 249, 250
SPIRO, R.J., 248, 275
SPORE, M.B., 15
SPRADLEY, J.P., 91
SQUIRE, J.R., 161
STAHL, N.A., 13, 273
STAHL, S.A., 26
STAUFFER, R.G., 127
STEENWYK, F.L., 126, 259
STEIN, B.S., 223, 226, 249
STEINBRENNER, K., 156

STEWARD, O., 23
STONE, D., 250
STRODE, S.L., 260
SUSZYNSKI, K., 273
SVENSON, L., 62
SWAFFORD, J., 248
SYLWESTER, R., 205

T

TAYLOR, B.M., 69, 71, 126, 133
TAYLOR, E., 60, 65
TAYLOR, K.K., 133
TEI, E., 23
THOMSON, D., 170
THORNDIKE, E.L., 19
TIERNEY, R., 71, 88, 89, 118, 161
TINKER, M.A., 8
TOWNSEND, M.A.R., 262
TREMBLEY, D., 215
TRIGGS, F.O., 7
TROYKA, L.Q., 161
TULLOCK, R.R., 170

V

VACCA, J.L., 275
VACCA, R.T., 130, 271, 275
VALENCIA, S., 290
VALERI-GOLD, M., 288
VAN BRUGGEN, J.V., 113
VAN DIJK, T.A., 69, 70, 137
VAN HOUT-WALTERS, B.H., 134
VAN LEIRSBURG, P., 288
VAN ROSSUM, E.J., 62, 63, 65
VISSER, P., 262
VOSS, J.F., 249
VYGOTSKY, L.S., 89, 250

W

WAGNER, B., 276
WALBERG, H., 13
WALLACE, W.P., 68
WALLER, T., 21, 23
WATSON, D., 77, 79
WEATHERALL, D., 77, 79
WEBB, A.J., 273
WEBER, R.M., 23
WEINGART, R., 273
WEINSTEIN, C., 66, 216, 235, 238
WELLMAN, H.M., 21, 223
WHIMBEY, A., 197
WHITE, W.G., 13
WILKINSON, I.A.G., 161
WILLEY, R.J., 275, 276
WILLIAMS, S., 127

WILLIAMSON, B.L., 177, 182
WILSON, J.D., 59, 67
WILSON, N., 275
WINCHOCK, J.M., 171, 173
WINOGRAD, P., 21, 26, 133
WISEMAN, D., 273
WITTROCK, M.C., 69, 126, 161, 259
WOLF, A.E., 118
WOOD, D., 250
WULFHORST, C., 287
WYATT, M., 13, 14, 277

Y–Z

YULE, G., 142
ZAHORIK, J., 212
ZHANG, J., 287, 288

Subject Index

A

ACADEMIC SUCCESS, 16, 62–63, 75, 86, 98, 191, 202
ACADEMIC SUPPORT PROGRAMS, 75
ACHIEVEMENT, 15, 23, 55, 59, 64, 79, 89, 117, 137, 173, 222, 269, 273–274, 286–288, 300, 303–304
ACTIVE PARTICIPANTS, 174
ACTIVE READERS, 10
ANALOGICAL STUDY GUIDES, 126–127, 129, 131
ANALYSIS, 6, 15, 29, 31, 35–36, 56, 77, 79, 81–82, 87, 92–93, 95, 100, 104, 108, 112, 129–130, 132, 134, 136, 138, 141–143, 152, 155, 157, 166, 173, 179, 192, 211, 235–236, 238, 247, 255, 259, 279, 296
ANNOTATING, 73, 76, 265, 269–270
APPLICATION, 66, 102, 118, 121, 124, 187, 205–206, 210, 216, 233, 283, 286, 294
ASSESSMENT, 3, 10, 13, 67, 71, 124, 130–131, 164, 168, 187–188, 233, 237, 285–295, 297–301
AT-RISK COLLEGE STUDENTS, 170–175, 258
ATTITUDES, 3, 35, 55, 57, 75–76, 78, 86, 170–176, 178, 183, 190, 193–196, 199, 215, 248, 258, 273, 280, 283
ATTITUDINAL RESPONSES, 33
ATWELL'S WRITER'S WORKSHOP, 96
AUDIENCE, 1, 95–98, 100, 279
AUTHENTIC TEACHING AND LEARNING, 89
AUTHORIAL RESPONSES, 30
AWARENESS, 19–23, 25–29, 73, 77–78, 85, 118, 124, 158, 162, 188–189, 191–194, 198, 216, 224–225, 231, 233–234, 236, 238, 249, 270–271, 278–281, 285, 294, 303

B–C

BURKE READING INTERVIEW, 79
CHECKING, 105, 118, 201, 221, 231
CLOZE TECHNIQUE, 23
COGNITION, 2, 28, 77, 80, 223, 234, 250, 253, 257–258
COGNITIVE PROCESSES, 26, 60, 74, 78, 111, 215

COLLABORATION, 48, 59, 89, 96, 210, 250, 253, 287, 292, 304
COLLEGE CREDIT, 8
COLLEGE READING PROGRAMS, 2–3, 5–6, 8–10, 75, 86, 247, 287
COMMUNICATIVE ARTS, 175
COMMUNITY OF LEARNERS, 90, 93, 98, 276, 278
COMPETENCE, 64, 75, 127, 215
COMPREHENSION, 6, 8–11, 16, 19–29, 56, 69, 73–82, 84–88, 90, 94,
    100, 112–113, 117, 124, 131–134, 142–144, 161, 188,
    190–194, 198, 201–202, 206, 213, 223, 226, 232, 234,
    238–239, 244–245, 249, 252, 257–260, 264, 269–270,
    272–273, 278–281, 289, 291, 295–296, 298, 302
CONCENTRATION AND SELF-DISCIPLINE, 190, 193, 195
CONTENT AREA, 14–16, 102–103, 110, 115, 125, 191, 193, 218, 222,
    229, 235, 247–248, 279–281, 283, 285
CONTENT FORMAT, 295
CONTENT-SENSITIVE PROCESS, 159
CONTENT VALIDITY, 58–59, 298
CRITICAL THINKING, 33, 89, 188, 254, 271, 289

D

DEEP APPROACH, 61–62, 64–66
DEGREES OF READING POWER (DRP) TEST, 289
DEVELOPMENTAL EDUCATORS, 13–15, 188, 280
DEVELOPMENTAL LITERACY, 286
DEVELOPMENTAL READING PROGRAMS, 85, 190
DEVELOPMENTAL STUDENTS, 14, 25, 88–89, 97, 164, 191, 195, 295, 297
DISCOURSE ANALYSIS, 143
DISCUSSION, 8, 34–35, 38, 48, 59, 79–80, 82, 85, 90, 94–95, 99, 107,
    110–111, 113, 119–120, 123, 130, 135, 158, 165, 167, 169,
    173, 178, 199, 202, 207, 210–212, 217, 221, 227, 231, 233,
    235, 238, 255, 274–277, 292–293, 297, 299, 302

E

EFFECTIVE READERS, 75, 77–78, 81, 86
ENCODING, 111–115, 213, 238–239, 269
ETHICAL PRINCIPLES OF PSYCHOLOGISTS AND CODE OF CONDUCT, 172, 176
EVALUATIVE TECHNIQUES, 75
EXAMINATIONS, 5, 10, 31, 56, 119–124, 137, 162, 165–166, 284
EXPLICIT INSTRUCTION, 25, 225, 231, 249–250, 253, 257

EXPRESSIVE LANGUAGE, 88
EYE MOVEMENTS, 8, 12

F–G

FRESHMAN COMPOSITION, 30–31, 33
GENDER, 170–171, 175–176
GLOBALIZATION, 15
GOALS, 1, 5–6, 8, 21, 55, 123, 131, 174, 188, 190–191, 193–195, 197, 199, 201, 203, 216–218, 224, 227, 231, 271, 287–289, 291, 299

H–I

HYPOTHESIS, 23, 111, 114, 170–171
INFERENCES, 24, 27, 71–72, 259
INSTRUMENTAL, 64, 94, 133, 216
INTENTION, 30, 60, 64, 83, 261, 267–268
INTERACTIVE AND CONSTRUCTIVE PROCESS, 288
INTERACTIVE STRATEGIES, 25
INTERPRETATION, 5, 24, 31, 62, 121, 124, 250, 272, 277
INTERVENTION, 21, 63, 91, 136, 142
INTERVIEWS, 21, 56, 59, 92–93, 96
INTRINSIC, 64–65, 77, 123–124, 267

J–L

JOURNALS, 90–92, 150, 163, 185, 190, 198, 275, 295, 302
KEY WORDS, 149, 155–159, 244
LEARNING, 1–3, 7, 14–17, 19–21, 26–27, 29, 31, 39, 42–46, 49, 51–53, 55–68, 73–76, 78, 83–90, 92–93, 95–98, 100–101, 109–110, 112–118, 123–127, 129–133, 137, 143, 159, 162–164, 168, 176, 184–185, 187–188, 191, 193, 195–197, 201–203, 205–207, 210, 212–216, 220, 222–226, 229, 231–235, 238–239, 242, 247–250, 257–258, 270–271, 273, 276, 278–295, 297, 299–304
LEARNING SITUATIONS, 64
LEARNING STRATEGIES, 19, 60, 66–67, 76, 86–87, 90, 117, 162, 168, 187, 222, 238, 247, 249
LEARNING-THINKING EFFICIENCY, 19
LEFT/RIGHT BRAIN, 33

LITERACY LEARNING, 89
LITERACY SKILLS, 13
LITERARY ANALYSIS, 31
LITERARY CRITICISM, 32
LITERARY GENRES, 174
LITERATURE, 7, 9–10, 30–32, 34–37, 47, 55, 58, 97, 151, 169–170, 178, 207, 210, 223, 240, 252, 256, 259–260, 262, 272–273, 275, 278–280

M

MACROPROPOSITIONS, 70–71
MAIN IDEA, 73, 76–77, 80, 142, 149–153, 155–160, 165, 239, 246, 267, 292
MAPPING, 113, 117, 248, 289, 296
MATURE READERS, 24, 75–80, 84, 118
MATURITY, 63, 75–76, 78, 86–87, 273
MAZURKIEWICZ MALE-FEMALE ATTITUDE ACTIVITY INVENTORY, 171–172, 175
MEANS-END APPROACH, 115
MEMORIZATION, 10, 64, 84
MICROPROPOSITIONS, 70–71
MISCUES, 77, 81, 87
MODELING, 230, 250–253, 276, 283
MONITORING, 19–21, 23–29, 78–79, 81, 87, 102, 118, 224, 229–230, 232, 234, 258, 270, 281, 289, 291
MOTIVATION, 22, 60, 64–67, 76, 85, 92, 98, 110, 131, 199, 207, 215, 258, 261, 267–268, 291, 299
MULTIPLE REGRESSION ANALYSIS, 152, 155, 157

N

NATIONAL ADULT LITERACY SURVEY, 13, 17
NATIONAL ASSESSMENT OF EDUCATIONAL PROGRESS, 13
NATIONAL CENTER FOR EDUCATION STATISTICS, 14
NELSON-DENNY READING TEST, 193, 197, 199–200
NOTETAKING, 222

O

ORAL LANGUAGE, 92, 94–95, 98–99, 161
ORAL READING, 23, 77, 81, 83, 87
OUTLINING, 76, 112–113, 117, 192, 289, 296

P

PARA FICTIONAL EXPERIENCES, 33

PEARSON'S *r* CORRELATION, 152

PERCEPTIONS, 35, 55–56, 58, 61, 88–89, 91, 93, 95, 97–98, 119–120, 122–123, 125, 170, 173–174, 176, 178, 204, 240, 248–250, 267

PERSONAL COUNSELING, 8, 10

PERSPECTIVE, 2, 6, 32, 56, 58, 60, 65–66, 96, 124, 131, 210, 218, 223, 247, 255, 267, 290, 300

PLANNING, 118, 142, 205, 222, 224

PORTFOLIO, 187–188, 286–295, 297–301

PRACTICING, 114, 207

PRACTITIONERS, 10, 13, 56–57, 66, 205, 303

PREDICTIONS, 88, 122, 275

PREWRITING ACTIVITIES, 91, 98

PROCESS ORIENTATION, 58

PROCESSING VARIABLES, 110–111

PROFICIENT READERS, 3, 21, 56, 75–82, 84–86, 248

PROFICIENT READING, 20, 75, 77, 83, 86. *See also* reading proficiency

PSYCHOLINGUISTIC, 75, 124

PUBLIC LAW, 7

PURPOSE FOR READING, 69, 207

Q–R

QUALITATIVE RESEARCH, 55

READABILITY, 57, 103, 105, 111, 117, 149–153, 155–160, 236, 247

READER SELECTED MISCUE, 77, 79–80, 87

READER-BASED CRITICISM, 30–33

READER RESPONSE, 32, 37, 188, 271–275, 277–279

READING AND LEARNING STRATEGIES, 19, 249

READING AND WRITING, 16, 37–39, 41, 43, 45, 47–49, 51–53, 55–56, 83, 88–101, 132, 161, 167–168, 176, 184–185, 188, 254, 258–259, 270, 273, 285, 303

READING BEHAVIOR, 27–28, 56, 73, 78, 86, 131–132, 176, 234, 247, 258, 269–270, 278

READING IMPROVEMENT, 7, 75, 151, 168, 202, 222, 283

READING INTERVIEW, BURKE, 79, 87

READING LOGS, 198, 279

READING MATURITY, 75–76, 78, 86

READING MISCUE INVENTORY, 77, 79–81, 87

READING PROFICIENCY, 13–14, 76. *See also* proficient reading

READING RATE, 8–9, 245

READING SPECIALISTS, 7, 10–11, 58, 60, 150

READING STRATEGIES, 20, 75–76, 78, 80, 82, 84–87, 102, 142, 207, 226, 234, 258

RECALL, 24, 42–43, 53, 71–74, 84, 112–114, 120–121, 124, 131, 133, 163, 165, 213, 240–241, 258–259, 273–274, 279

RECEPTION THEORY, 31

RECEPTIVE LANGUAGE, 88

RECITING, 45, 114, 219, 228

REFLECTION, 85, 195, 275, 280–281, 283, 285, 287–288, 291–292, 301

RELIABILITY, 135, 145, 149, 178, 297–298

REMEDIAL PROGRAMS, 7

REPETITION, 149, 151, 155–159, 244

RESPONSIBILITY ON THE LEARNER, 287

RETELL RESPONSE, 81

RETRIEVAL CUES, 111

RETROSPECTIVE MISCUE ANALYSIS, 77, 79, 81

RETROSPECTIVE TECHNIQUES, 78

REVISIONS, 88, 91

S

SCHEMA, 70–71, 88, 94–95, 131, 133–135, 192, 210–211, 249–252, 257, 270, 272

SCHEMATIC STRUCTURE, 69

SECONDARY TEACHERS, 118

SELF-AWARENESS, 19, 75

SELF-CONTROL, 19, 26, 225

SELF-DIAGNOSIS, 198

SELF-EVALUATION, 92–93, 287–288, 291–292

SELF-PERCEPTION, 80, 84–85

SELF-QUESTIONING, 25, 27, 56, 73, 126, 128–130, 188, 224, 227–231, 233, 258

SELF-REFLECTION, 286–287

SELF-REGULATORY MECHANISMS, 20

SELF-RESPONSIBILITY, 194–195

SEMANTIC STRUCTURE, 21

SENSORY PERCEPTION, 33

SEXIST ATTITUDES, 170–171, 173, 175–176
SILENT READING, 11, 77, 87, 176
SOCIAL AND CULTURAL EXPECTATIONS, 170
SOCIAL INTERACTIONS, 93, 250
SOCRATIC METHOD, 99
STANDARDIZED TESTS, 76, 85, 169, 287–288
STATISTICALLY SIGNIFICANT, 136, 155, 157
STEREOTYPES, 170, 176
STRATEGY VARIABLES, 21–22, 26
STRUCTURAL KNOWLEDGE, 69
STUDENT ACHIEVEMENT, 286
STUDENT RETENTION, 16
STUDENTS' ATTITUDES, 170, 194, 273
STUDY GUIDES, 56, 116, 126–131
STUDY STRATEGIES, 11, 27, 67, 69, 73, 78, 132, 188, 215–217, 219, 221, 234, 258–259, 296
STUDY TECHNIQUES, 72–73, 78, 86, 112–113, 116, 188
SUBTEXT, 33
SUMMARIZATION, 24–27, 73, 80, 131–134, 141–142, 228, 231–233, 262, 270
SURFACE APPROACH, 60–66
SURFACE LANGUAGE STRUCTURE, 81

T

TEACHERS' EXPECTATIONS AND PERCEPTIONS, 173
TEACHING COMPOSITION, 7
TECHNOLOGY, 15, 57, 145, 177, 303–304
TEST SCORES, 165
TEST TAKING, 91
TEXAS ACADEMIC SKILLS PROGRAM, 13
TEXT STRUCTURES, 69, 103
THINKING, 3, 19, 33, 48–49, 51, 56, 58, 67, 78, 83, 86, 88–89, 93–99, 101, 126, 132, 143, 163, 184, 187–188, 192, 194, 206, 211–212, 217–218, 250, 254, 256, 269, 271, 276, 278, 280–281, 288–289
TRANSACTIONAL THEORY OF READING, 168, 289
TUTORIAL PROGRAMS, 16

U

UNDERLINING, 68, 71–74, 84, 112
UNDERPREPARED, 5, 10, 13–15, 18, 48, 57, 89–90, 98, 168, 183, 271, 277, 304
UNDERSTANDING, 20, 22–24, 27–28, 31, 38, 48, 55–56, 59, 61–63, 65–67, 72, 76–77, 79–80, 82, 84–85, 87–88, 91, 106, 113, 118–119, 124, 137, 165, 210, 212–213, 219–225, 227–228, 230–233, 248, 255, 257–258, 269, 272–274, 278, 280–281, 285, 290, 299–300, 302–304

V

VARIABLES, 21–22, 26, 55, 68, 79, 110–111, 154, 156–157, 164
VOCABULARY DEVELOPMENT, 9–10, 90, 161, 270
VOCATIONAL CURRICULUM, 171

W–Z

WRITING AND LEARNING, 43, 45, 96, 303
WRITING EXERCISES, 161–167, 169
WRITING PROCESS, 91, 99–100, 168, 276, 282
WRITTEN ACADEMIC DISCOURSE, 158
WRITTEN AND ORAL LANGUAGE, 95, 131, 161
ZONE OF PROXIMAL DEVELOPMENT, 89, 250